The Curse of Money-Laundering

The Curse of Money-Laundering

Chander Mehra

GYAN

First Published, 2018

Published by

Gyan Publishing House
5, Ansari Road
Daryaganj, New Delhi-110002
Phone: 9811692060
E-mail: books@gyanbooks.com

Printed at: G. Print Process, Delhi.

Cataloging in Publication Data—DK
Courtesy: D.K. Agencies (P) Ltd. <docinfo@dkagencies.com>

Mehra, Chander, author.
The curse of money-laundering / Chander Mehra.
pages cm
ISBN 9788121214124

1. Money laundering. I. Title.

LCC HV6768.M44 2017 | DDC 364.168 23

Contents

Chapter - 1

The Missing Trillions

Money laundering is perhaps the most heinous crime, having roots in Grand Corruption in all spheres of perversions in human activity and economic sabotage of society with clear links to international terrorism.

Technically, it is the process whereby proceeds of crime are transformed into ostensibly legitimate money and other assets. However, in a number of legal and regulatory systems the term money laundering has become conflated with other forms of financial crime, and sometimes used more generally to include misuse of the financial system, including terrorism financing, tax evasion and evading of international sanctions. Most anti-money laundering laws openly conflate money laundering (which is concerned with *source* of funds) with terrorism financing (which is concerned with *destination* of funds) when regulating the financial system.

Money obtained from certain crimes, such as extortion, insider trading, drug trafficking, illegal gambling and tax evasion is "dirty". It needs to be cleaned to appear to have derived from non-criminal activities so that banks and other financial institutions will deal with it without suspicion. Originally, the term applied to real money but now money laundering applies to the proceeds of crime that are laundered using a variety of monetary instruments including securities, digital currencies such as bitcoin, credit cards, and traditional currency. Money can be laundered by many methods, which vary in complexity and sophistication.

Different countries may or may not treat tax evasion or payments in breach of international sanctions as money laundering. Some jurisdictions differentiate these for definition purposes, and others do not. Some jurisdictions define money laundering as obfuscating sources of money, either intentionally or by merely using financial systems or services that do not identify or track sources or destinations.

Other jurisdictions define money laundering to include money from activity that *would have been* a crime in that jurisdiction, even if it were legal where the actual conduct occurred. This broad brush of applying the term "money laundering" to merely incidental, extraterritorial, or simply privacy-seeking behaviours has led some to label it "financial thought-crime".

Many regulatory and governmental authorities issue estimates each year for the amount of money laundered, either worldwide or within their national economy. In 1996, the International Monetary Fund estimated that two to five per cent of the worldwide global economy involved laundered money. The Financial Action Task Force on Money Laundering (FATF), an intergovernmental body set up to combat money laundering.

It stated, "Overall, it is absolutely impossible to produce a reliable estimate of the amount of money laundered and therefore the FATF does not publish any figures in this regard." Academic commentators have likewise been unable to estimate the volume of money with any degree of assurance. Various estimates of the scale of global money laundering are repeated often enough to make some people regard them as factual—but no researcher has overcome the inherent difficulty of measuring an actively concealed practice.

Regardless of the difficulty in measurement, the amount of money laundered each year is in the billions (US dollars) and poses a significant policy concern for governments. As a result, governments and international bodies have undertaken efforts to deter, prevent, and apprehend money launderers. Financial institutions have likewise undertaken efforts to prevent and detect transactions involving dirty money, both as a result of government requirements and to avoid the reputational risk involved. Issues relating to money laundering have existed as long as there have been large scale criminal enterprises. Modern anti-money laundering laws have developed along with the modern War on Drugs.

In more recent times anti-money laundering legislation is seen as adjunct to the financial crime of terrorist financing in that both crimes usually involve the transmission of funds through the financial system (although money laundering relates to where the money has come *from*, and terrorist financing relating to where the money is going *to*).

Reverse money laundering is a process that disguises a legitimate source of funds that are to be used for illegal purposes. In an affidavit filed March 24, 2014 in United States District Court, Northern California, San Francisco

Division, FBI special agent Emmanuel V. Pascau alleged that several people associated with the Chee Kung Tong Organisation, and California State Senator Leland Yee, engaged in reverse money laundering activities.

Methods

Money laundering is commonly defined as occurring in three steps: "Placement", the first step involves introducing cash into the financial system by some means.

"Layering", the second involves carrying out complex financial transactions to camouflage the illegal source.

And finally, "Integration", the final step entails acquiring wealth generated from the transactions of the illicit funds.

Some of these steps may be omitted, depending on the circumstances; for example, non-cash proceeds that are already in the financial system would have no need for placement.

Money laundering takes several different forms, although most methods can be categorised into one of a few types. These include "bank methods, smurfing [also known as structuring], currency exchanges, and double-invoicing".

- **Structuring:** Often known as *smurfing*, this is a method of placement whereby cash is broken into smaller deposits of money, used to defeat suspicion of money laundering and to avoid anti-money laundering reporting requirements. A sub-component of this is to use smaller amounts of cash to purchase bearer instruments, such as money orders, and then ultimately deposit those, again in small amounts.
- **Bulk cash smuggling:** This involves physically smuggling cash to another jurisdiction and depositing it in a financial institution, such as an offshore bank, with greater bank secrecy or less rigorous money laundering enforcement.
- **Cash-intensive businesses:** In this method, a business typically involved in receiving cash uses its accounts to deposit both legitimate and criminally derived cash, claiming all of it as legitimate earnings. Service businesses are best suited to this method, as such businesses have no variable costs, and it is hard to detect discrepancies between revenues and costs. Examples are parking buildings, strip clubs, tanning beds, and casinos.
- **Trade-based laundering:** This involves under- or over-valuing invoices to disguise the movement of money.

- **Shell companies and trusts:** Trusts and shell companies disguise the true owner of money.

  Trusts and corporate vehicles, depending on the jurisdiction, need not disclose their true, beneficial, owner.

- **Round-tripping:** Here, money is deposited in a controlled foreign corporation offshore, preferably in a tax haven where minimal records are kept, and then shipped back as a foreign direct investment, exempt from taxation. A variant on this is to transfer money to a law firm or similar organisation as funds on account of fees, then to cancel the retainer and, when the money is remitted, represent the sums received from the lawyers as a legacy under a will or proceeds of litigation.
- **Bank capture:** In this case, money launderers or criminals buy a controlling interest in a bank, preferably in a jurisdiction with weak money laundering controls, and then move money through the bank without scrutiny.
- **Casinos:** In this method, an individual walks into a casino with cash and buys chips, plays for a while, and then cashes in the chips, taking payment in a check, or just getting a receipt, claiming it as gambling winnings.
- **Other gambling:** Money is spent on gambling, preferably on higher odds. The wins are shown if the source for money is asked for, while the losses are hidden.
- **Real estate:** Someone purchases real estate with illegal proceeds and then sells the property. To outsiders, the proceeds from the sale look like legitimate income.

  Alternatively, the price of the property is manipulated: the seller agrees to a contract that under-represents the value of the property, and receives criminal proceeds to make up the difference.

- **Black salaries:** A company may have unregistered employees without a written contract and pay them cash salaries. Dirty money might be used to pay them.
- **Tax amnesties:** For example, those that legalise unreported assets in tax havens and cash.
- **Fictional loans**
- A goal of money laundering is to be able to use the dirty money for private consumption. If unable to use it openly, the traditional

way to keep the dirty money near is hiding it as cash at home or other places. A more modern method is a credit card connected to a tax haven bank.

Enforcement

Anti-money laundering (AML) is a term mainly used in the financial and legal industries to describe the legal controls that require financial institutions and other regulated entities to prevent, detect, and report money laundering activities. Anti-money laundering guidelines came into prominence globally as a result of the formation of the Financial Action Task Force (FATF) and the promulgation of an international framework of anti-money laundering standards. These standards began to have more relevance in 2000 and 2001, after FATF began a process to publicly identify countries that were deficient in their anti-money laundering laws and international cooperation, a process colloquially known as "name and shame".

An effective AML programme requires a jurisdiction to have criminalised money laundering, given the relevant regulators and police the powers and tools to investigate; be able to share information with other countries as appropriate; and require financial institutions to identify their customers, establish risk-based controls, keep records, and report suspicious activities.

Criminalising money laundering

The elements of the crime of money laundering are set forth in the United Nations Convention Against Illicit Traffic in Narcotic Drugs and Psychotropic Substances and Convention against Transnational Organised Crime. It is defined as knowingly engaging in a financial transaction with the proceeds of a crime for the purpose of concealing or disguising the illicit origin of the property from governments.

Role of financial institutions

While banks operating in the same country generally have to follow the same AML laws and regulations, financial institutions all structure their AML efforts slightly different. Today, most financial institutions globally, and many non-financial institutions, are required to identify and report transactions of a suspicious nature to the financial intelligence unit in the respective country. For example, a bank must verify a customer's identity and, if necessary, monitor transactions for suspicious activity. This is often termed as "know your customer". This means knowing the identity of the customer and understanding the kinds of transactions in which the customer is likely to engage. By knowing one's customers, financial institutions can often identify unusual or suspicious behaviour, termed anomalies, which may be an indication of money laundering.

Bank employees, such as tellers and customer account representatives, are trained in anti-money laundering and are instructed to report activities that they deem suspicious. Additionally, anti-money laundering software filters customer data, classifies it according to level of suspicion, and inspects it for anomalies. Such anomalies include any sudden and substantial increase in funds, a large withdrawal, or moving money to a bank secrecy jurisdiction. Smaller transactions that meet certain criteria may also be flagged as suspicious. For example, structuring can lead to flagged transactions. The software also flags names on government "blacklists" and transactions that involve countries hostile to the host nation. Once the software has mined data and flagged suspect transactions, it alerts bank management, who must then determine whether to file a report with the government.

Value of enforcement costs and associated privacy concerns

The financial services industry has become more vocal about the rising costs of anti-money laundering regulation and the limited benefits that they claim it brings. One commentator wrote that "Without facts, anti-money laundering legislation has been driven on rhetoric, driving by ill-guided activism responding to the need to be "seen to be doing something" rather than by an objective understanding of its effects on predicate crime. The social panic approach is justified by the language used—we talk of the battle against terrorism or the war on drugs." *The Economist* magazine has become increasingly vocal in its criticism of such regulation, particularly with reference to countering terrorist financing, referring to it as a "costly failure", although it concedes that other efforts (like reducing identity and credit card fraud) may still be effective at combating money laundering.

There is no precise measurement of the costs of regulation balanced against the harms associated with money laundering, [and given the evaluation problems involved in assessing such an issue, it is unlikely that the effectiveness of terror finance and money laundering laws could be determined with any degree of accuracy. *The Economist* estimated the annual costs of anti-money laundering efforts in Europe and North America at US$5 billion in 2003, an increase from US$700 million in 2000. Government-linked economists have noted the significant negative effects of money laundering on economic development, including undermining domestic capital formation, depressing growth, and diverting capital away from development. Because of the intrinsic uncertainties of the amount of money laundered, changes in the amount of money laundered, and the cost of anti-money laundering systems, it is almost impossible to tell which anti-money laundering systems work and which are more or less cost effective.

Besides economic costs to implement anti-money-laundering laws improper attention to data-protection practices may entail disproportionate costs to individual privacy rights. In June 2011, the data-protection advisory committee to the European Union, issued a report on data protection issues related to the prevention of money laundering and terrorist financing, which identified numerous transgressions against the established legal framework on privacy and data protection. The report made recommendations how to address money laundering and terrorist financing in ways that safeguard personal privacy rights and data-protection laws. In the United States, groups such as the American Civil Liberties Union have expressed concern that money laundering rules require banks to report on their own customers, essentially conscripting private businesses "into agents of the surveillance state".

Many countries are obligated by various international instruments and standards, such as the 1988 United Nations Convention Against Illicit Traffic in Narcotic Drugs and Psychotropic Substances, the 2000 Convention against Transnational Organised Crime, the 2003 United Nations Convention against Corruption, and the recommendations of the 1989 Financial Action Task Force on Money Laundering to enact and enforce money laundering laws in an effort to stop narcotics trafficking, international organised crime, and corruption. Mexico, which has faced a significant increase in violent crime, established anti-money laundering controls in 2013 to curb the underlying crime issue.

Global Organisations working against money laundering

Formed in 1989 by the G7 countries, the FATF is an intergovernmental body whose purpose is to develop and promote an international response to combat money laundering. The FATF Secretariat is housed at the headquarters of the OECD in Paris. In October 2001, FATF expanded its mission to include combating the financing of terrorism. FATF is a policy-making body that brings together legal, financial, and law enforcement experts to achieve national legislation and regulatory AML and CFT reforms. As of 2014 its membership consists of 36 countries and territories and two regional organisations. FATF works in collaboration with a number of international bodies and organisations. These entities have observer status with FATF, which does not entitle them to vote, but permits them full participation in plenary sessions and working groups.

FATF has developed 40 recommendations on money laundering and nine special recommendations regarding terrorist financing. FATF assesses each member country against these recommendations in published reports. Countries seen as not being sufficiently compliant with such recommendations are subjected to financial sanctions.

FATF's three primary functions with regard to money laundering are:

1. Monitoring members' progress in implementing anti-money laundering measures.
2. Reviewing and reporting on laundering trends, techniques, and countermeasures.
3. Promoting the adoption and implementation of FATF anti-money laundering standards globally.

The FATF currently comprises 34 member jurisdictions and 2 regional organisations, representing most major financial centres in all parts of the globe:

- Argentina
- Australia
- Austria
- Belgium
- Brazil
- Canada
- China
- Denmark
- European Commission
- Finland
- France
- Germany
- Greece
- Gulf Cooperation Council
- Hong Kong
- Iceland
- India
- Ireland
- Italy
- Japan
- Luxembourg

- Mexico
- Netherlands
- New Zealand
- Norway
- Portugal
- Russia
- Singapore
- South Africa
- South Korea
- Spain
- Sweden
- Switzerland
- Turkey
- United Kingdom
- United States

The United Nations Office on Drugs and Crime maintains the *International Money Laundering Information Network*, a website that provides information and software for anti-money laundering data collection and analysis. The World Bank has a website that provides policy advice and best practices to governments and the private sector on anti-money laundering issues.

Laws and Enforcement by Region

Many jurisdictions adopt a list of specific predicate crimes for money laundering prosecutions, while others criminalise the proceeds of any serious crime.

Afghanistan

The Financial Transactions and Reports Analysis Centre of Afghanistan (FinTRACA) was established as a Financial Intelligence Unit (FIU) under the Anti Money Laundering and Proceeds of Crime Law passed by decree late in 2004. The main purpose of this law is to protect the integrity of the Afghan financial system and to gain compliance with international treaties and conventions. The Financial Intelligence Unit is a semi-independent body that is administratively housed within the Central Bank of Afghanistan (Da Afghanistan Bank). The main objective of FinTRACA is to deny the use of the Afghan financial system to those who obtained funds as the result of illegal activity, and to those who would use it to support terrorist activities.

To meet its objectives, the FinTRACA collects and analyses information from a variety of sources. These sources include entities with legal obligations to submit reports to the FinTRACA when a suspicious activity is detected, as well as reports of cash transactions above a threshold amount specified by regulation. Also, FinTRACA has access to all related Afghan government information and databases. When the analysis of this information supports the supposition of illegal use of the financial system, the FinTRACA works closely with law enforcement to investigate and prosecute the illegal activity. FinTRACA also cooperates internationally in support of its own analyses and investigations and to support the analyses and investigations of foreign counterparts, to the extent allowed by law. Other functions include training of those entities with legal obligations to report information, development of laws and regulations to support national-level AML objectives, and international and regional cooperation in the development of AML typologies and countermeasures.

Australia

AUSTRAC (Australian Transaction Reports and Analysis Centre) is Australia's anti-money laundering and counter-terrorism financing regulator and specialist financial intelligence unit.

The Anti-Money Laundering and Counter Terrorism Financing Act 2006 (Cth) (AMLCTF) is the principal legislative instrument, although there are also offence provisions introduced into the Crimes Act 1901 (Cth). Upon its introduction the AMLCTF was further amended by a second tranche of reforms to extend inter alia to other commercial contexts such as real estate agents, but those further reforms have since not been effectuated.

AUSTRAC works collaboratively with Australian industries and businesses in their compliance with anti-money laundering and counter-terrorism financing legislation.

Financial institutions in Australia are required to track significant cash transactions (greater than A$10,000.00 or equivalent in physical cash value) that can be used to finance terrorist activities in and outside Australia's borders and report them to AUSTRAC.

Bangladesh

In Bangladesh, this issue has been dealt with by the Prevention of Money Laundering Act, 2002 (Act No. VII of 2002). In terms of section 2, "Money Laundering means (a) Properties acquired or earned directly or indirectly through illegal means; (b) Illegal transfer, conversion, concealment of location or assistance in the above act of the properties acquired or earned directly or indirectly through legal or illegal means". In this Act, "properties" means movable or immovable properties of any nature and description.

To prevent these Illegal uses of money, the Bangladesh government has introduced the Money Laundering Prevention Act. The Act was last amended in the year 2009 and all the financial institutes are following this act. Till today there are 26 circulars issued by Bangladesh Bank under this act. To prevent money laundering, a banker must do the following:

- While opening a new account, the account opening form should be duly filled up by all the information of the customer.
- The KYC must be properly filled.
- The Transaction Profile (TP) is mandatory for a client to understand his/her transactions.

  If needed, the TP must be updated at the client's consent.
- All other necessary papers should be properly collected along with the National ID card.
- If any suspicious transaction is noticed, the Branch Anti Money Laundering Compliance Officer (BAMLCO) must be notified and accordingly the Suspicious Transaction Report (STR) must be filled out.
- The cash department should be aware of the transactions. It must be noted if suddenly a big amount of money is deposited in any account. Proper documents are required if any client does this type of transaction.
- Structuring, over/ under invoicing is another way to do money laundering. The foreign exchange department should look into this matter cautiously.
- If any account has a transaction over 10.00 lakh in a single day, it must be reported in a cash transaction report (CTR).
- All bank officials must go through all the 26 circulars and use them.

Canada

In 1991, the Proceeds of Crime (Money Laundering) Act was brought into force in Canada to give legal effect to the former FATF Forty Recommendations by establishing record keeping and client identification requirements in the financial sector to facilitate the investigation and prosecution of money laundering offences under the Criminal Code of Canada and the Controlled Drugs and Substances Act.

In 2000, the Proceeds of Crime (Money Laundering) Act was amended to expand the scope of its application and to establish a financial intelligence unit with national control over money laundering, namely FINTRAC.

In December 2001, the scope of the Proceeds of Crime (Money Laundering) Act was again expanded by amendments enacted under the Anti-Terrorism Act with the objective of deterring terrorist activity by cutting off sources and channels of funding used by terrorists in response to 9/11. The Proceeds of Crime (Money Laundering) Act was renamed the Proceeds of Crime (Money Laundering) and Terrorist Financing Act.

In December 2006, the Proceeds of Crime (Money Laundering) and Terrorist Financing Act was further amended, in part, in response to pressure from the FATF for Canada to tighten its money laundering and financing of terrorism legislation. The amendments expanded the client identification, record-keeping and reporting requirements for certain organisations and included new obligations to report attempted suspicious transactions and outgoing and incoming international electronic fund transfers, undertake risk assessments and implement written compliance procedures in respect of those risks.

The amendments also enabled greater money laundering and terrorist financing intelligence-sharing among enforcement agencies.

In Canada, casinos, money service businesses, notaries, accountants, banks, securities brokers, life insurance agencies, real estate salespeople and dealers in precious metals and stones are subject to the reporting and record keeping obligations under the Proceeds of Crime (Money Laundering) and Terrorist Financing Act.

European Union

The EU directive 2005/60/EC "on the prevention of the use of the financial system for the purpose of money laundering and terrorist financing" tries to prevent such crime by requiring banks, real estate agents and many more companies to investigate and report usage of cash in excess of €15,000. The earlier EU directives 91/308/EEC and 2001/97/EC also relate to money laundering. The European Union is currently negotiating a New 4th Anti-Money Laundering Directive that will change the nature of anti-money laundering compliance across the European Union. The current draft Directive has some laudable features and improvements over the previous Directive, not least the intention to move to a risk-based and evidence-based approach to identifying and managing money laundering and counter terrorist finance risks rather than a tick-box approach to compliance. However, the draft Directive is also causing concern from experts within the financial services and gambling industries due to its failure to co-ordinate cross-border issues for electronic businesses, the risk that it will be disproportionately burdensome and costly for European businesses, it will damage innovation in new business areas such as the regulated e-money and payment services sectors (e.g. prepaid cards, e-wallets and money remittance) and will perversely increase the use of cash where there are less controls and there is less monitoring information available to the relevant authorities and law enforcement agencies. The 4th Directive is currently going through the European Parliament and is intended to be finalised in 2014.

India

In 2002, Parliament of India passed an Act called the Prevention of Money Laundering Act, 2002. The main objectives of this Act are to prevent money-laundering as well as to provide for confiscation of property either derived from or involved in, money-laundering.

Section 12 (1) describes the obligations that banks, other financial institutions, and intermediaries have to

(a) Maintain records that detail the nature and value of transactions, whether such transactions comprise a single transaction or a series of connected transactions, and where these transactions take place within a month.

(b) Furnish information on transactions referred to in clause (a) to the Director within the time prescribed, including records of the identity of all its clients.

Section 12 (2) prescribes that the records referred to in sub-section (1) as mentioned above, must be maintained for ten years after the transactions finished. It is handled by the Indian Income Tax Department.

The provisions of the Act are frequently reviewed and various amendments have been passed from time to time.

The recent activity in money laundering in India is through political parties, corporate companies and the shares market. It is investigated by the Enforcement Directorate and Indian Income Tax Department.

Bank accountants must record all transactions over ₹ 10 Lakhs. Bank accountants must maintain this records for 10 years. Banks also must make cash transaction reports (CTRs) and suspicious transaction reports over ₹ 10 Lakhs within 7 days of doubt. They must submit the report to the enforcement directorate and income tax department.

United Kingdom

Money laundering and terrorist funding legislation in the UK is governed by four Acts of primary legislation:-

- Terrorism Act 2000
- Anti-terrorism, Crime and Security Act 2001
- Proceeds of Crime Act 2002
- Serious Organised Crime and Police Act 2005
- Money Laundering Regulations 2007

Money Laundering Regulations are designed to protect the UK financial system. If a business is covered by these regulations then controls are put in place to prevent it being used for money laundering.

The Proceeds of Crime Act 2002 contains the primary UK anti-money laundering legislation, including provisions requiring businesses within the "regulated sector" (banking, investment, money transmission, certain professions, etc.) to report to the authorities suspicions of money laundering by customers or others.

Money laundering is broadly defined in the UK. In effect any handling or involvement with any proceeds of any crime (or monies or assets representing the proceeds of crime) can be a money laundering offence. An offender's possession of the proceeds of his own crime falls within the UK definition of money laundering. The definition also covers activities within the traditional definition of money laundering, as a process that conceals or disguises the proceeds of crime to make them appear legitimate.

Unlike certain other jurisdictions (notably the US and much of Europe), UK money laundering offences are not limited to the proceeds of serious crimes, nor are there any monetary limits. Financial transactions need no money laundering design or purpose for UK laws to consider them a money laundering offence. A money laundering offence under UK legislation need not even involve money, since the money laundering legislation covers assets of any description. In consequence, any person who commits an acquisitive crime (i.e., one that produces some benefit in the form of money or an asset of any description) in the UK inevitably also commits a money laundering offence under UK legislation.

This applies also to a person who, by criminal conduct, evades a liability (such as a taxation liability)—which lawyers call "obtaining a pecuniary advantage"—as he is deemed thereby to obtain a sum of money equal in value to the liability evaded.

The principal money laundering offences carry a maximum penalty of 14 years imprisonment.

Secondary regulation is provided by the Money Laundering Regulations 2003, which was replaced by the Money Laundering Regulations 2007. They are directly based on the EU directives 91/308/EEC, 2001/97/EC and 2005/60/EC.

One consequence of the Act is that solicitors, accountants, tax advisers, and insolvency practitioners who suspect (as a consequence of information received in the course of their work) that their clients (or others) have engaged in tax evasion or other criminal conduct that produced a benefit, now must report their suspicions to the authorities (since these entail suspicions of money laundering). In most circumstances it would be an offence, "tipping-off", for the reporter to inform the subject of his report that a report has been made. These provisions do not however require disclosure to the authorities of information received by certain professionals in privileged circumstances or where the information is subject to legal professional privilege. Others that are subject to these regulations include financial institutions, credit institutions, estate agents (which includes chartered surveyors), trust and company service providers, high value dealers (who accept cash equivalent to £ 15,000 or more for goods sold), and casinos.

Professional guidance (which is submitted to and approved by the UK Treasury) is provided by industry groups including the Joint Money Laundering Steering Group, the Law Society and the Consultative Committee of Accountancy Bodies (CCAB). However there is no obligation on banking institutions to routinely report monetary deposits or transfers above a specified value. Instead reports must be made of all suspicious deposits or transfers, irrespective of their value.

The reporting obligations include reporting suspicious gains from conduct in other countries that would be criminal if it took place in the UK Exceptions were later added for certain activities legal where they took place, such as bullfighting in Spain.

More than 200,000 reports of suspected money laundering are submitted annually to authorities in the UK (there were 240,582 reports in the year ended 30 September 2010. This was an increase from the 228,834 reports submitted in the previous year). Most of these reports are submitted by banks and similar financial institutions (there were 186,897 reports from the banking sector in the year ended 30 September 2010).

Although 5,108 different organisations submitted suspicious activity reports to the authorities in the year ended 30 September 2010 just four organisations submitted approximately half of all reports, and the top 20 reporting organisations accounted for three-quarters of all reports.

The offence of failing to report a suspicion of money laundering by another person carries a maximum penalty of five years imprisonment.

Bureaux de change

All UK *Bureaux de change* are registered with Her Majesty's Revenue and Customs, which issues a trading licence for each location. Bureaux de change and money transmitters, such as Western Union outlets, in the UK fall within the "regulated sector" and are required to comply with the Money Laundering Regulations 200. Checks can be carried out by HMRC on all Money Service Businesses.

United States

The approach in the United States to stop money laundering is usually broken into two areas: preventive (regulatory) measures and criminal measures.

Preventive

In an attempt to prevent dirty money from entering the U.S. financial system in the first place, the United States Congress passed a series of laws, starting in 1970, collectively known as the Bank Secrecy Act (BSA). These laws, contained in sections 5311 through 5332 of Title 31 of the United States Code, require financial institutions, which under the current definition include a broad array of entities, including banks, credit card companies, life insurers, money service businesses and broker-dealers in securities, to report certain transactions to the United States Department of the Treasury. Cash transactions in excess of US$10,000 must be reported on a currency transaction report (CTR), identifying the individual making the transaction as well as the source of the cash. The U.S. is one of the few countries in the world to require reporting of all cash transactions over a certain limit, although certain businesses can be exempt from the requirement. [*citation needed*] Additionally, financial institutions must report transaction on a Suspicious Activity Report (SAR) that they deem "suspicious", defined as a knowing or suspecting that the funds come from illegal activity or disguise funds from illegal activity, that it is structured to evade BSA requirements or appears to serve no known business or apparent lawful purpose; or that the institution is being used to facilitate criminal activity. Attempts by customers to circumvent the BSA, generally by structuring cash deposits to amounts lower than US$10,000 by breaking them up and depositing them on different days or at different locations also violates the law.

The financial database created by these reports is administered by the U.S.'s Financial Intelligence Unit (FIU), called the Financial Crimes Enforcement Network (FinCEN), located in Vienna, Virginia. The reports are made available to U.S. criminal investigators, as well as other FIU's around the globe, and FinCEN conducts computer assisted analyses of these reports to determine trends and refer investigations

The BSA requires financial institutions to engage in customer due diligence, which is sometimes known in the parlance as know your customer. This includes obtaining satisfactory identification to give assurance that the account is in the customer's true name, and having an understanding of the expected nature and source of the money that flows through the customer's accounts. Other classes of customers, such as those with private banking accounts and those of foreign government officials, are subjected to enhanced due diligence because the law deems that those types of accounts are a higher risk for money laundering. All accounts are subject to ongoing monitoring, in which internal bank software scrutinises transactions and flags for manual inspection those that fall outside certain parameters. If a manual inspection reveals that the transaction is suspicious, the institution should file a Suspicious Activity Report.

The regulators of the industries involved are responsible to ensure that the financial institutions comply with the BSA. For example, the Federal Reserve and the Office of the Comptroller of the Currency regularly inspect banks, and may impose civil fines or refer matters for criminal prosecution for non-compliance. A number of banks have been fined and prosecuted for failure to comply with the BSA. Most famously, Riggs Bank, in Washington D.C., was prosecuted and functionally driven out of business as a result of its failure to apply proper money laundering controls, particularly as it related to foreign political figures.

In addition to the BSA, the U.S. imposes controls on the movement of currency across its borders, requiring individuals to report the transportation of cash in excess of US$10,000 on a form called Report of International Transportation of Currency or Monetary Instruments (known as a CMIR). Likewise, businesses, such as automobile dealerships, that receive cash in excess of US$10,000 must file a Form 8300 with the Internal Revenue Service, identifying the source of the cash.

On 1 September 2010, the Financial Crimes Enforcement Network issued an advisory on "informal value transfer systems."

Criminal sanctions

Money laundering has been criminalised in the United States since the Money Laundering Control Act of 1986. The law, contained at section 1956 of Title 18 of the United States Code, prohibits individuals from engaging in a financial transaction with proceeds that were generated from certain specific crimes, known as "specified unlawful activities" (SUAs). The law requires that an individual specifically intend in making the transaction to conceal the source, ownership or control of the funds. There is no minimum threshold of money, and no requirement that the transaction succeeded in actually disguising the money. A "financial transaction" has been broadly defined, and need not involve a financial institution, or even a business. Merely passing money from one person to another, with the intent to disguise the source, ownership, location or control of the money, has been deemed a financial transaction under the law. The possession of money without either a financial transaction or an intent to conceal is not a crime in the United States. Besides money laundering, the law contained in section 1957 of Title 18 of the United States Code, prohibits spending more than US$10,000 derived from an SUA, regardless of whether the individual wishes to disguise it. It carries a lesser penalty than money laundering, and unlike the money laundering statute, requires that the money pass through a financial institution. According to the records compiled by the United States Sentencing Commission, in 2009, the United States Department of Justice typically convicted a little over 81,000 people; of this, approximately 800 are convicted of money laundering as the primary or most serious charge. The Anti-Drug Abuse Act of 1988 expanded the definition of financial institution to include businesses such as car dealers and real estate closing personnel and required them to file reports on large currency transaction. It required verification of identity of those who purchase monetary instruments over $3,000. The Annunzio-Wylie Anti-Money Laundering Act of 1992 strengthened sanctions for BSA violations, required so called "Suspicious Activity Reports" and eliminated previously used "Criminal Referral Forms", required verification and record keeping for wire transfers and established the Bank Secrecy Act Advisory Group (BSAAG). The Money Laundering Suppression Act from 1994 required banking agencies to review and enhance training, develop anti-money laundering examination procedures, review and enhance procedures for referring cases to law enforcement agencies, streamlined the Currency transaction report exemption process, required each Money services business (MSB) to be registered by an owner or controlling person, required every MSB to maintain a list of businesses authorised to act as agents in connection with the financial services offered by the MSB, made operating an unregistered MSB a federal crime, and recommended that states adopt uniform laws applicable to MSBs. The Money Laundering and Financial Crimes Strategy Act of 1998 required banking agencies to develop anti-money laundering training for examiners, required the Department of the Treasury and other agencies to develop a "National Money Laundering Strategy", created the "High Intensity Money Laundering and Related Financial Crime Area" (HIFCA) Task Forces to concentrate law enforcement efforts at the federal, state and local levels in zones where money laundering is prevalent. HIFCA zones may be defined geographically or can be created to address money laundering in an industry sector, a financial institution, or group of financial institutions. The Intelligence Reform and Terrorism Prevention Act of 2004 amended the Bank Secrecy Act to require the Secretary of the Treasury to prescribe regulations requiring certain financial institutions to report cross-border electronic transmittals of funds, if the Secretary determines that reporting is "reasonably necessary" in "anti-money laundering/combatting financing of terrorists (Anti-Money Laundering/Combating the Financing of Terrorism AML/CFT)".

Electronic money

In theory, electronic money should provide as easy a method of transferring value without revealing identity as untracked banknotes, especially wire transfers involving anonymity-protecting numbered bank accounts. In practice, however, the record-keeping capabilities of Internet service providers and other network resource maintainers tend to frustrate that intuition. While some cryptocurrencies under recent development have aimed to provide for more possibility of transaction anonymity for various reasons, the degree to which they succeed—and, in consequence, the degree to which they offer benefits for money laundering efforts—is controversial.

In 2013, Jean-Loup Richet, a research fellow at ESSEC ISIS, surveyed a new techniques that cybercriminals were using in a report written for the United Nations Office on Drugs and Crime A common approach was to use a digital currency exchanger service which converted dollars into a digital currency called Liberty Reserve and could be sent and received anonymously. The receiver could convert the Liberty Reserve currency back into cash for a small fee. In May 2013, the US authorities shut down Liberty Reserve charging its founder and various others with money laundering. Another increasingly common way of laundering money is to use online gaming. In a growing number of online games such as Second Life or World of Warcraft, it is possible to convert money into virtual goods, services or virtual cash that can later be converted back into money.

Notable Cases

1998 investigation, United States Senate, Contribution Laundering/ Third-Party Transfers. Includes investigation of Gandhi Memorial International Foundation.

- **Bank of Credit and Commerce International:** Unknown amount, estimated in billions, of criminal proceeds, including drug trafficking money, laundered during the mid-1980s.
- **Bank of New York:** US$7 billion of Russian capital flight laundered through accounts controlled by bank executives, late 1990s.
- **Ferdinand Marcos:** Unknown amount, estimated at US$10 billion of government assets laundered through banks and financial institutions in the United States, Liechtenstein, Austria, Panama, Netherlands Antilles, Cayman Islands, Vanuatu, Hong Kong, Singapore, Monaco, the Bahamas, the Vatican and Switzerland.
- **In December 2012, HSBC:** Paid a record $1.9 Billion fines for money-laundering hundreds of millions of dollars for drug traffickers, terrorists and sanctioned governments such as Iran. The money-laundering occurred throughout the 2000s.
- In May 2013, Liberty Reserve was seized by United States federal authorities for laundering $6 billion.
- **Institute for the Works of Religion:** Italian authorities investigated suspected money laundering transactions amounting to US$218 million made by the IOR to several Italian banks.
- **Nauru:** US$70 billion of Russian capital flight laundered through unregulated Nauru offshore shell banks, late 1990s.
- **Sani Abacha:** US$2–5 billion of government assets laundered through banks in the UK, Luxembourg, Jersey (Channel Islands), and Switzerland, by the president of Nigeria.
- **Standard Chartered:** Paid $330 million in fines for money-laundering hundreds of billions of dollars for Iran. The money-laundering took place in the 2000s and occurred for "nearly a decade to hide 60,000 transactions worth $250 billion".

Chapter - 2

Safe and Tax-free Havens

A safe and **tax haven** is a state, country or territory where certain taxes are levied at a low rate or not at all. Individuals or corporations find it attractive to establish shell subsidiaries or move themselves to areas with reduced or nil taxation levels relative to typical international taxation. This creates tax competition among governments. Different jurisdictions tend to be havens for different types of taxes, and for different categories of people or companies.

Sovereign or self-governing states under international law have theoretically unlimited powers to enact tax laws affecting their territories, unless limited by previous international treaties. There are several definitions of tax havens. According to *The Economist*, London: "What ... identifies an area as a tax haven is the existence of a composite tax structure established deliberately to take advantage of, and exploit, a worldwide demand for opportunities to engage in tax avoidance." This definition would still exclude a number of jurisdictions traditionally thought of as tax havens. Similarly, others have suggested that any country which modifies its tax laws to attract foreign capital could be considered a tax haven.

According to other definitions, the central feature of a haven is that its laws and other measures can be used to evade or avoid the tax laws or regulations of other jurisdictions. In its December 2008 report on the use of tax havens by American corporations, the U.S. Government Accountability Office was unable to find a satisfactory definition of a tax haven but regarded the following characteristics as indicative of it: nil or nominal taxes; lack of effective exchange of tax information with foreign tax authorities; lack of transparency in the operation of legislative, legal or administrative provisions; no requirement for a substantive local presence; and self-promotion as an offshore financial centre.

A 2012 report from the Tax Justice Network estimated that between $21 trillion and $32 trillion is sheltered from taxes in unreported tax havens worldwide. If such wealth earns 3 per cent annually and such capital gains were taxed at 30 per cent, it would generate between $190 billion and $280 billion in tax revenues, more than any other tax shelter. If such hidden offshore assets are considered, many countries with governments nominally in debt are shown to be net creditor nations. However, despite being widely quoted, the methodology used in the calculations has been questioned, and the tax policy director of the Chartered Institute of Taxation also expressed skepticism over the accuracy of the figures. A study of 60 large US companies found that they deposited $166 billion in offshore accounts during 2012, sheltering over 40 per cent of their profits from U.S. taxes.

The Organisation for Economic Co-operation and Development (OECD) identifies three key factors in considering whether a jurisdiction is a tax haven:

Nil or only nominal taxes. Tax havens impose nil or only nominal taxes (generally or in special circumstances) and offer themselves, or are perceived to offer themselves, as a place to be used by non-residents to escape high taxes in their country of residence.

Protection of personal financial information. Tax havens typically have laws or administrative practices under which businesses and individuals can benefit from strict rules and other protections against scrutiny by foreign tax authorities. This prevents the transmittance of information about taxpayers who are benefiting from the low tax jurisdiction.

Lack of transparency. A lack of transparency in the operation of the legislative, legal or administrative provisions is another factor used to identify tax havens. The OECD is concerned that laws should be applied openly and consistently, and that information needed by foreign tax authorities to determine a taxpayer's situation is available. Lack of transparency in one country can make it difficult, if not impossible, for other tax authorities to apply their laws effectively. 'Secret rulings', negotiated tax rates, or other practices that fail to apply the law openly and consistently are examples of a lack of transparency. Limited regulatory supervision or a government's lack of legal access to financial records are contributing factors.

However, the OECD found that its definition caught certain aspects of its members' tax systems (some countries have low or zero taxes and ring fencing for certain favoured groups). Its later work has therefore focused on the single aspect of information exchange. This is generally thought to be an inadequate definition of a tax haven, but is politically expedient, because it includes the small tax havens (with little power in the international political arena) but exempts the powerful countries with tax haven aspects such as the USA and UK.

In deciding whether or not a jurisdiction is a tax haven, the first factor to look at is whether there are no or nominal taxes. If this is the case, the other two factors–whether or not there is an exchange of information and transparency–must be analysed. Having no or nominal taxes is not sufficient, by itself, to characterise a jurisdiction as a tax haven. The OECD recognises that every jurisdiction has a right to determine whether to impose direct taxes and, if so, to determine the appropriate tax rate.

Classification

Corporations, in order to achieve effective tax avoidance, use multiple types of tax havens. Three types of tax haven form a *Dutch Sandwich*:

1. *Primary tax havens:* The location where financial capital winds up. Subsidiary shell companies there have obtained rights to collect profits from corporate intellectual property (IP) by transfers from their parent.
2. *Semi-tax havens:* Locations that produce goods for sale primarily outside of their territorial boundaries and have flexible regulations to encourage job growth, such as free trade zones, territorial-only taxation, and similar inducements.
3. *Conduit tax havens:* Locations where income from sales, primarily made outside their boundaries, is collected, and then distributed. Semi-tax havens are reimbursed for actual product costs, perhaps with a commodity markup. The remaining profits are transferred to the primary tax haven, because it holds rights to profits due to the corporate IP. By matching outflow to income they do not retain capital and their role, while crucial, remains invisible.

Large multinational corporations may have dozens of such tax haven entities interacting with each other. Each haven can claim that it does not satisfy definitions that attempt to place all tax havens into a single class. Even increased transparency does not change the effectiveness of corporate tax avoidance.

Capital held offshore

While incomplete, and with the limitations discussed below, the available statistics nonetheless indicate that offshore banking is a very sizable activity. The OECD estimated in 2007 that capital held offshore amounted to between $5 trillion and $7 trillion, making up approximately 6–8 per cent of total global investments under management. The Tax Justice Network (an anti-tax haven pressure group) estimated more recently in 2012 that capital held offshore amounted to between $21 trillion and $32 trillion (between 24-32 per cent of total global investments).

In 2000, the International Monetary Fund calculated based on Bank for International Settlements data that for selected offshore financial centres, on-balance sheet cross-border assets held in offshore financial centres reached a level of $4.6 trillion at the end of June 1999 (about 50 per cent of total cross-border assets). Of that $4.6 trillion, $0.9 trillion was held in the Caribbean, $1 trillion in Asia, and most of the remaining $2.7 trillion accounted for by the major International Finance Centres (IFCs), namely London, the U.S. IBFs, and the Japanese offshore market. The U.S. Department of Treasury estimated that in 2011 the Caribbean Banking Centres, which include Bahamas, Bermuda, Cayman Islands, Netherlands Antilles and Panama, held almost $2 trillion dollars in United States debt. Of this, approximately US$1.4 trillion is estimated to be held in the Cayman Islands alone.

The *Wall Street Journal* in a study of 60 large U.S. companies found that they deposited US$ 166 billion in offshore accounts in 2012, sheltering over 40 per cent of their profits from U.S. taxes. Similarly, Desai, Foley and Hines in the *Journal of Public Economics* found that: "in 1999, 59 per cent of U.S. firms with significant foreign operations had affiliates in tax haven countries", although they did not define "significant" for this purpose. In 2009, the Government Accountability Office (GAO) reported that 83 of the 100 largest U.S. publicly traded corporations and 63 of the 100 largest contractors for the U.S. federal government were maintaining subsidiaries in countries generally considered havens for avoiding taxes. The GAO did not review the companies' transactions to independently verify that the subsidiaries helped the companies reduce their tax burden, but said only that historically the purpose of such subsidiaries is to cut tax costs.

James Henry, former chief economist at consultants McKinsey and Company, in his report for the Tax Justice Network gives an indication of the amount of money that is sheltered by wealthy individuals in tax havens. The report estimated conservatively that a fortune of $21 trillion is stashed away in off-shore accounts with $9.8 trillion alone by the top tier—less than 100,000 people—who each own financial assets of $30 million or more. The report's author indicated that this hidden money results in a "huge" lost tax revenue—a "black hole" in the economy—and many countries would become creditors instead of being debtors if the money of their tax evaders would be taxed.

Lost tax revenue

The Tax Justice Network estimated that global tax revenue lost in 2012 to tax havens is between USD $190 billion and $255 billion per year, assuming a 3 per cent capital gains rate, a 30 per cent capital gains tax rate, and $21 trillion to $32 trillion hidden in tax havens worldwide. If such hidden offshore assets are considered, many countries with governments nominally in debt are shown to be net creditor nations. However, the tax policy director of the Chartered Institute of Taxation expressed skepticism over the accuracy of the figures. If true, those sums would amount to approximately five to eight times the total amount of currency presently in circulation in the world. Daniel J. Mitchell of the Cato Institute says that the report also assumes, when considering notional lost tax revenue, that 100 per cent money deposited offshore is evading payment of tax.

In October 2009, research commissioned from Deloitte for the Foot Review of British Offshore Financial Centres (London is a tax haven for much of Europe, Asia, and South America, it should be noted) said that much less tax had been lost to tax havens than previously had been thought. The report indicated "We estimate the total UK corporation tax potentially lost to avoidance activities to be up to £2 billion per annum, although it could be much lower." An earlier report by the U.K. Trades Union Congress, concluded that tax avoidance by the 50 largest companies in the FTSE 100 was depriving the UK Treasury of approximately £11.8 billion. The report also stressed that British Crown Dependencies make a "significant contribution to the liquidity of the UK market". In the second quarter of 2009, they provided net funds to banks in the UK totalling $323 billion (£195 billion), of which $218 billion came from Jersey, $74 billion from Guernsey and $40 billion from the Isle of Man.

The Tax Justice Network reports that this system is "basically designed and operated" by a group of highly paid specialists from the world's largest private banks (led by UBS, Credit Suisse, and Goldman Sachs), law offices, and accounting firms and tolerated by international organisations such as Bank for International Settlements, the International Monetary Fund, the World Bank, the OECD, and the G20. The amount of money hidden away has significantly increased since 2005, sharpening the divide between the super-rich and the rest of the world.

The U.S. National Bureau of Economic Research has suggested that roughly 15 per cent of the countries in the world are tax havens, that these countries tend to be small and affluent, and that better governed and regulated countries are more likely to become tax havens, and are more likely to be successful if they become tax havens.

- Switzerland
- Luxembourg—primarily a conduit tax haven.

Other sovereign countries that have such low tax rates and lax regulation that they can be considered semi-tax havens are:

- Ireland
- Netherlands—primarily a conduit tax haven.

Non-sovereign jurisdictions commonly labelled as tax havens include:

- Jersey
- Isle of Man
- British Overseas Territory
    - Bermuda
    - British Virgin Islands
    - Cayman Islands
- Delaware, United States Puerto Rico (United States)

Some tax havens including some of the ones listed above do charge income tax as well as other taxes such as capital gains tax, inheritance tax, and so forth. Criteria distinguishing a taxpayer from a non-taxpayer can include citizenship and residency and source of income. For example, in the United States foreign nonresidents are not charged various taxes, including income tax on interest on U.S. bank deposits by income tax; since the Clinton administration the IRS has proposed collecting information on these depositors to share with their home countries as a regulation; these regulations were eventually finalised in April 2012.

In September 2013, British Prime Minister David Cameron said "I do not think it is fair any longer to refer to any of the Overseas Territories or Crown Dependencies as tax havens. They have taken action to make sure that they have fair and open tax systems. It is very important that our focus should now shift to those territories and countries that really are tax havens." Mr Cameron's comments were interpreted as a direct reference to Jersey, Guernsey, Isle of Man, the British Virgin Islands and the Cayman Islands, and followed a period of negotiations with those (and other) British territories during which those jurisdictions had made a number of concessions relating to tax transparency and sharing of information. Anti-tax haven pressure groups immediately accused the Prime Minister of taking leave of his senses, and commenting sarcastically "It was Cameron's father's tax haven activities that are repotted [sic] to have paid for his Eton education. Was it ever realistic to think he'd change his spots?".

Former tax havens

- Beirut, Lebanon formerly had a reputation as the only tax haven in the Middle East. However, this changed after the Intra Bank crash and the subsequent political and military deterioration of Lebanon dissuaded foreign use of the country as a tax haven.
- Liberia had a prosperous ship registration industry. The series of violent and bloody civil wars in the 1990s and early 2000s severely damaged confidence in the jurisdiction. The fact that the ship registration business still continues is partly a testament to its early success, and partly a testament to moving the national shipping registry to New York, United States.
- Tangier had a brief but colourful existence as a tax haven in the period between the end of effective control by the Spanish in 1945 until it was formally reunited with Morocco in 1956.
- A number of Pacific based tax havens have reduced their effectiveness to operate as tax havens in response to OECD demands for better regulation and transparency in the late 1990s. Vanuatu's Financial Services commissioner announced in May 2008 that his country would reform its laws so as to cease being a tax haven. "We've been associated with this stigma for a long time and we now aim to get away from being a tax haven.
- As of March 2013, major Cyprus banks have sustained severe damage from Greek bond defaults and (at least temporarily) closed their doors in an attempt to stem a flight of capital from the island. Depositors are expected to incur heavy losses.

Methodology

At the risk of gross oversimplification, it can be said that the advantages of tax havens are viewed in the following four principal contexts.

Personal residency

Since the early twentieth century, wealthy individuals from high-tax jurisdictions have sought to relocate themselves in low-tax jurisdictions. In most countries in the world, residence is the primary basis of taxation – see

Tax residence. In some cases the low-tax jurisdictions levy no, or only very low, income tax. But almost no tax haven assesses any kind of capital gains tax, or inheritance tax. Individuals who are unable to return to a higher-tax country in which they used to reside for more than a few days a year are sometimes referred to as tax exiles.

Corporate residency

Corporate persons, in contrast to *natural persons,* can own subsidiary corporations in many countries. That allows them to take advantage of the variety of laws, regulations, and conventions in multiple countries, without overtly engaging in any questionable activities. Only in extreme cases will they move their formal corporate headquarters.

Asset holding

Asset holding involves utilising an offshore trust or offshore company, or a trust owning a company. The company or trust will be formed in one tax haven, and will usually be administered and resident in another. The function is to hold assets, which may consist of a portfolio of investments under management, trading companies or groups, physical assets such as real estate or valuable chattels. The essence of such arrangements is that by changing the ownership of the assets into an entity which is not tax resident in the high-tax jurisdiction, they cease to be taxable in that jurisdiction. Often the mechanism is employed to avoid a specific tax. For example, a wealthy testator could transfer his house into an offshore company; he can then settle the shares of the company on trust (with himself being a trustee with another trustee, whilst holding the beneficial life estate) for himself for life, and then to his daughter. On his death, the shares will automatically vest in the daughter, who thereby acquires the house, without the house having to go through probate and being assessed with inheritance tax. (Most countries assess inheritance tax, and all other taxes, on real estate within their jurisdiction, regardless of the nationality of the owner, so this would not work with a house in most countries. It is more likely to be done with intangible assets.)

Trading and other business activity

Many businesses which do not require a specific geographical location or extensive labour are set up in tax havens, to minimise tax exposure. Perhaps the best illustration of this is the number of reinsurance companies which have migrated to Bermuda over the years. Other examples include internet based services and group finance companies. In the 1970s and 1980s, corporate groups were known to form offshore entities for the purposes of "reinvoicing". These reinvoicing companies simply made a margin without performing any economic function, but as the margin arose in a tax free jurisdiction, it allowed the group to "skim" profits from the high-tax jurisdiction. Most sophisticated tax codes now prevent transfer pricing schemes of this nature.

Financial intermediaries

Much of the economic activity in tax havens today consists of professional financial services such as mutual funds, banking, life insurance and pensions. Generally the funds are deposited with the intermediary in the low-tax jurisdiction, and the intermediary then on-lends or invests the money (often back into a high-tax jurisdiction). Although such systems do not normally avoid tax in the principal customer's jurisdiction, it enables financial service providers to provide multi-jurisdictional products without adding an additional layer of taxation. This has proved particularly successful in the area of offshore funds. This type of methodology has been used by Google and came to light in the year 2010 when it was reported that Google uses techniques called the "Double Irish" and "Dutch Sandwich" to reduce its corporate income tax to 2.4 per cent, by funnelling its corporate income through Ireland and from there to a shell in the Netherlands where it can be transferred to Bermuda, which has no corporate income tax. The search engine is using Ireland as a conduit for revenues that end up being costed to another country where its intellectual property (the brand and technology such as Google's algorithms) is registered. In Google's case this country is Bermuda. In the year 2009, the internet giant made a gross profit of €5.5bn, but reported an operating profit of €45m after "administrative expenses" of €5.467bn were stripped out. In classic economic analysis, if a company was spending 99.4 per cent of gross profits on administrative expenses, then the company would be considered to operating very inefficiently. Administrative expenses largely refer to royalties (or a licence fee) Google pays it Bermuda HQ for the right to operate. Google has uncovered a highly efficient tax structure across six territories that meant Google paid just 2.4 per cent tax on operations outside the US.

Anonymity and bearer shares

Bearer shares allow for anonymous ownership, and thus have been criticised for facilitating money laundering and tax evasion; these shares are also available in some OECD countries, such as in the U.S. state of Wyoming. :7 In 2010, a study in which the researcher attempted to set-up anonymous corporations found that 13 of the 17 attempts were successful in OECD countries such as the United States and the United Kingdom while 4 of 28 attempts were successful in countries typically labeled tax havens. In 2011, an OECD peer review recommended that the United Kingdom improve its bearer share laws.

The *Guardian* wrote that there are 28 persons as directors for 21,500 companies.

Money and exchange control

Most tax havens have a double monetary control system which distinguish residents from non-resident as well as foreign currency from the domestic one. In general, residents are subject to monetary controls but not non-residents. A company, belonging to a non-resident, when trading overseas is seen as non-resident in terms of exchange control. It is possible for a foreigner to create a company in a tax haven to trade internationally; the company's operations will not be subject to exchange controls as long as it uses foreign currency to trade outside the tax haven. Tax havens usually have currency easily convertible or linked to an easily convertible currency. Most are convertible to US dollars, euro or to pounds sterling.

Incentives for nations to become tax havens

There are several reasons for a nation to become a tax haven. Some nations may find they do not need to charge as much as some industrialised countries in order for them to be earning sufficient income for their annual budgets. Some may offer a lower tax rate to larger corporations, in exchange for the companies locating a division of their parent company in the host country and employing some of the local population. Other domiciles find this is a way to encourage conglomerates from industrialised nations to transfer needed skills to the local population. Still yet, some countries simply find it costly to compete in many other sectors with industrialised nations and have found a low tax rate mixed with a little self-promotion can go a long way to attracting foreign companies.

Many industrialised countries claim that tax havens act unfairly by reducing tax revenue which would otherwise be theirs. Various pressure groups also claim that money launderers also use tax havens extensively, although extensive financial and know your customer regulations in tax havens can actually make money laundering more difficult than in large onshore financial centres with significantly higher volumes of transactions, such as New York City or London. In 2000, the Financial Action Task Force published what came to be known as the " FATF Blacklist" of countries which were perceived to be uncooperative in relation to money laundering; although several tax havens have appeared on the list from time to time (including key jurisdictions such as the Cayman Islands, Bahamas and Liechtenstein), no offshore jurisdictions appear on the list at this time.

Regulation measures

To avoid tax competition, many high tax jurisdictions have enacted legislation to counter the tax sheltering potential of tax havens. Generally, such legislation tends to operate in one of five ways:

1. Attributing the income and gains of the company or trust in the tax haven to a taxpayer in the high-tax jurisdiction on an arising basis. Controlled Foreign Corporation legislation is an example of this.
2. Transfer pricing rules, standardisation of which has been greatly helped by the promulgation of OECD guidelines.
3. Restrictions on deductibility, or imposition of a withholding tax when payments are made to offshore recipients.
4. Taxation of receipts from the entity in the tax haven, sometimes enhanced by notional interest to reflect the element of deferred payment. The EU withholding tax is probably the best example of this.
5. Exit charges, or taxing of unrealised capital gains when an individual, trust or company emigrates.

However, many jurisdictions employ blunter rules. For example, in France securities regulations are such that it is not possible to have a public bond issue through a company incorporated in a tax haven.

Also becoming increasingly popular is "forced disclosure" of tax mitigation schemes. Broadly, these involve the revenue authorities compelling tax advisors to reveal details of the scheme, so that the loopholes can be closed during the following tax year, usually by one of the five methods indicated above. Although not specifically aimed at tax havens, given that so many tax mitigation schemes involve the use of offshore structures, the effect is much the same.

Anti-avoidance came to prominence in 2010/2011 as nongovernmental organisations and politicians in the leading economies looked for ways of reducing tax avoidance, which plays a role in forcing unpopular cuts to social and military programmes. The International Financial Centres Forum (IFC Forum) has asked for a balanced debate on the issue of tax avoidance and an understanding of the role that the tax neutrality of small international financial centres plays in the global economy.

Modern developments

U.S. Legislation

Foreign Account Tax Compliance Act

The Foreign Account Tax Compliance Act (FATCA) was passed by the US Congress to stop the outflow of money from the country into tax haven bank accounts. With the strong backing of the Obama Administration, Congress drafted the FATCA legislation and added it into the Hiring Incentives to Restore Employment Act (HIRE) signed into law by President Obama in March 2010.

FATCA requires foreign financial institutions (FFI) of broad scope–banks, stock brokers, hedge funds, pension funds, insurance companies, trusts–to report directly to the Internal Revenue Service (IRS) all clients who are U.S. persons. Starting January 2014, FATCA requires FFIs to provide annual reports to the IRS on the name and address of each U.S. client, as well as the largest account balance in the year and total debits and credits of any account owned by a U.S. person. If an institution does not comply, the U.S. will impose a 30 per cent withholding tax on all its transactions concerning U.S. securities, including the proceeds of sale of securities.

In addition, FATCA requires any foreign company not listed on a stock exchange or any foreign partnership which has 10 per cent U.S. ownership to report to the IRS the names and tax identification number (TIN) of any U.S. owner. FATCA also requires U.S. citizens and green card holders who have foreign financial assets in excess of $50,000 to complete a new Form 8938 to be filed with the 1040 tax return, starting with fiscal year 2010. The delay is indicative of a controversy over the feasibility of implementing the legislation as evidenced in this paper from the Peterson Institute for International Economics.

An unintended consequence of FATCA and its cost of compliance for non-US banks is that some non-US banks are refusing to serve American investors. Concerns have also been expressed that, because FATCA operates by imposing withholding taxes on U.S. investments, this will drive foreign financial institutions (particularly hedge funds) away from investing in the U.S. and thereby reduce liquidity and capital inflows into the US.

Bank data leak 2013

Details of thousands of owners of offshore companies were published in April 2013 in a joint collaboration between *The Guardian* and the International Consortium of Investigative Journalists. The data was later published on a publicly accessible website in an attempt to "crowd-source" the data. The publication of the list appeared to be timed to coincide with the 2013 G8 summit chaired by British Prime Minister David Cameron which emphasised tax evasion and transparency.

Liechtenstein banking scandal

Main article: 2008 Liechtenstein tax affair

Germany announced in February 2008 that it had paid €4.2 million to Heinrich Kieber, a former data archivist of LGT Treuhand, a Liechtenstein bank, for a list of 1,250 customers of the bank and their accounts' details. Investigations and arrests followed relating to charges of illegal tax evasion. The German authorities shared the data with U.S. tax authorities, but the British government paid a further £100,000 for the same data. Other governments, notably Denmark and Sweden, refused to pay for the information regarding it as stolen property. The Liechtenstein authorities subsequently accused the German authorities of espionage.

However, regardless of whether unlawful tax evasion was being engaged in, the incident has fuelled the perception among European governments and the press that tax havens provide facilities shrouded in secrecy designed to facilitate unlawful tax evasion, rather than legitimate tax planning and legal tax mitigation schemes. This in turn has led to a call for "crackdowns" on tax havens. Whether the calls for such a crackdown are mere posturing or lead to more definitive activity by mainstream economies to restrict access to tax havens is yet to be seen. No definitive announcements or proposals have yet been made by the European Union or governments of the member states.

German legislation

Peer Steinbrück, the former German finance minister, announced in January 2009 a plan to amend fiscal laws. New regulations would disallow that payments to companies in certain countries that shield money from disclosure rules to be declared as operational expenses. The effect of this would make banking in such states unattractive and expensive.

U.K. Foot report

In November 2009, Sir Michael Foot, a former Bank of England official and Bahamas bank inspector, delivered a report on the British Crown Dependencies and Overseas Territories for HM Treasury. The report indicated that while many of the territories "had a good story to tell", others needed to improve their abilities to detect and prevent financial crime. The report also stressed the view that narrow tax bases presented long-term strategic risks and that the economies should seek to diversify and broaden their tax bases. It indicated that tax revenue lost by the UK government appeared to be much smaller than had previously been estimated (see above under Lost tax revenue), and also stressed the importance of the liquidity provided by the territories to the United Kingdom. The Crown Dependencies and Overseas Territories broadly welcomed the report. However, the pressure group Tax Justice Network, unhappy with the findings, commented that "[a] weak man, born to be an apologist, has delivered a weak report."

G20 tax haven blacklist

At the London G20 summit on 2 April 2009, G20 countries agreed to define a blacklist for tax havens, to be segmented according to a four-tier system, based on compliance with an "internationally agreed tax standard." The list as per April 2 of 2009 can be viewed on the OECD website. The four tiers were:

1. Those that have substantially implemented the standard (includes most countries but China still excludes Hong Kong and Macau).
2. Tax havens that have committed to–but not yet fully implemented–the standard (includes Montserrat, Nauru, Niue, Panama, and Vanuatu).
3. Financial centres that have committed to–but not yet fully implemented–the standard (includes Guatemala, Costa Rica and Uruguay).
4. Those that have not committed to the standard (an empty category).

Those countries in the bottom tier were initially classified as being 'non-cooperative tax havens'. Uruguay was initially classified as being uncooperative. However, upon appeal the OECD stated that it did meet tax transparency rules and thus moved it up. The Philippines took steps to remove itself from the blacklist and Malaysian Prime Minister Najib Razak had suggested earlier that Malaysia should not be in the bottom tier. On April 7, 2009, the OECD, through its chief Angel Gurria, announced that Costa Rica, Malaysia, the Philippines and Uruguay have been removed from the blacklist after they had made "a full commitment to exchange information to the OECD standards." Despite calls from the former French President Nicolas Sarkozy for Hong Kong and Macau to be included on the list separately from China, they are as yet not included independently, although it is expected that they will be added at a later date.

Government response to the crackdown has been broadly supportive, although not universal. Luxembourg Prime Minister Jean-Claude Juncker has criticised the list, stating that it has "no credibility", for failing to include various states of the USA which provide incorporation infrastructure which are indistinguishable from the aspects of pure tax havens to which the G20 object. As of 2012, 89 countries have implemented reforms sufficient to be listed on the OECD's white list. According to Transparency International half of the least corrupted countries were tax havens.

Criticism

Tax havens have been criticised because they often result in the accumulation of idle cash which is expensive and inefficient for companies to repatriate. The tax shelter benefits result in a tax incidence disadvantaging the poor. Many tax havens are thought to have connections to fraud, money laundering and terrorism. While investigations of illegal tax haven abuse have been ongoing, there have been few convictions. Lobbying pertaining to tax havens and associated transfer pricing has also been criticised.

Some politicians, such as magistrate Eva Joly, have begun to stand up against the use of tax havens by large companies. She describes the act of avoiding tax as a threat to democracy. Accountants 'opinions on the propriety of tax havens have been evolving as have the opinions of their corporate users, governments, and politicians, although their use by Fortune 500 companies and others remains widespread. Reform proposals centreing on the Big Four accountancy firms have been advanced. Some governments appear to be using computer spyware to scrutinise some corporations' finances.

History

The use of differing tax laws between two or more countries to try to mitigate tax liability is probably as old as taxation itself. In Ancient Greece, some of the Greek Islands were used as depositories by the sea traders of the era to place their foreign goods to thus avoid the two-per cent tax imposed by the city-state of Athens on imported goods. It is sometimes suggested that the practice first reached prominence through the avoidance of the Cinque Ports and later the staple ports in the twelfth and fourteenth centuries respectively. In 1721, American colonies traded from Latin America to avoid British taxes.

Various countries claim to be the oldest tax haven in the world. For example, the Channel Islands claim their tax independence dating as far back as Norman Conquest, while the Isle of Man claims to trace its fiscal independence to even earlier times. Nonetheless, the modern concept of a tax haven is generally accepted to have emerged at an uncertain point in the immediate aftermath of World War I. Bermuda sometimes optimistically claims to have been the first tax haven based upon the creation of the first offshore companies legislation in 1935 by the newly created law firm of Conyers Dill and Pearman. However, the Bermudian claim is debatable when compared against the enactment of a Trust Law by Liechtenstein in 1926 to attract offshore capital.

Most economic commentators suggest that the first "true" tax haven was Switzerland, followed closely by Liechtenstein. Swiss banks had long been a *capital haven* for people fleeing social upheaval in Russia, Germany, South America and elsewhere. However, in the early part of the twentieth century, in the years immediately following World War I, many European governments raised taxes sharply to help pay for reconstruction efforts following the devastation of World War I. By and large, Switzerland, having remained neutral during the Great War, avoided these additional infrastructure costs and was consequently able to maintain a low level of taxes. As a result, there was a considerable influx of capital into the country for tax related reasons. It is difficult, nonetheless, to pinpoint a single event or precise date which clearly identifies the emergence of the modern tax haven.

The use of modern tax havens has gone through several phases of development subsequent to the interwar period. From the 1920s to the 1950s, tax havens were usually referenced as the avoidance of personal taxation. The terminology was often used with reference to countries to which a person could retire and mitigate their post-retirement tax position. However, from the 1950s onwards, there was significant growth in the use of tax havens by corporate groups to mitigate their global tax burden. This strategy generally relied upon there being a double taxation treaty between a large jurisdiction with a high tax burden (that the company would otherwise be subject to), and a smaller jurisdiction with a low tax burden. Thus, corporations, by structuring the group ownership through the smaller jurisdiction, could take advantage of the double taxation treaty, thereby paying taxes at the much lower rate. Although some of these double tax treaties survive, in the 1970s, most major countries began repealing their double taxation treaties with micro-states to prevent corporate tax leakage in this manner.

In the early to mid-1980s, most tax havens changed the focus of their legislation to create corporate vehicles which were "ring-fenced" and exempt from local taxation (although they usually could not trade locally either). These vehicles were usually called "exempt companies" or "international business corporations". However, in the late 1990s and early 2000s, the OECD began a series of initiatives, details of which need to be investigated.

Chapter - 3

Filthy Drug Money

Illegal drug trade generates much of the black money generated for laundering in safe havens. There is a global black market dedicated to the cultivation, manufacturing, distribution and sale of drugs that are subject to drug prohibition laws. Most jurisdictions prohibit trade, except under license, of many types of drugs through the use of drug prohibition laws.

A UN report said, "the global drug trade generated an estimated US $321.6 billion in 2003." With a world GDP of US$36 trillion in the same year, the illegal drug trade may be estimated as nearly one per cent of total global trade.

History of opium in China

Chinese edicts against opium smoking were made in 1729, 1796 and 1800. Addictive drugs were prohibited in the west in the late nineteenth and early twentieth centuries. China retaliated by enforcing the ban on imports of opium that led to the First Opium War (1839–1842) between Britain and the Qing dynasty in China. Chinese authorities had banned opium, but the United Kingdom forced China to allow British merchants to trade opium with the general population. Smoking opium had become common in the nineteenth century, and British merchants increased their trade with the Chinese. Trading in opium was lucrative. As a result of this illegal trade, by 1838 the number of Chinese opium addicts had grown to between four and twelve million.The Second Opium War broke out in 1856, with the British this time joined by the French. After the two Opium Wars, the British Crown, via the treaties of Nanking and Tianjin respectively, took large sums of money from the Chinese government through this illegal trade, which were referred to as "reparations".

In 1868, as the result of the increased use of opium, the UK restricted the sale of opium in Britain by implementing the 1868 Pharmacy Act. In the United States, control remained a state responsibility until the introduction of the Harrison Act in 1914, following the passing of the International Opium Convention in 1912.

Between 1920 and 1933, alcohol was banned in the United States. This law was considered to have been very difficult to enforce and resulted in the growth of vast criminal organisations, including the modern American Mafia.

Since drugs traded on the black market can provide a secretive source of money, they have long been used by organisations such as the U.S. Central Intelligence Agency to fund covert operations and proxy wars. CIA involvement in heroin trafficking began with the French Connection in Marseille and continued with anti-Communist operations in Southeast Asia. In the early 1980s, the CIA used cocaine as a medium to launder money in Central America (allegedly as part of the Iran–Contra affair).

The Australian Crime Commission's illicit drug data report for 2011–2012 was released in western Sydney on 20 May 2013 and revealed that the seizures cause by illegal substances in Australia during the reporting period were the largest in a decade due to record interceptions of amphetamines, cocaine and steroids.

The beginning of the twenty-first century saw drug use go up in North America and Europe, with particularly increased demand for marijuana and cocaine. As a result, international organised crime syndicates such as the Sinaloa Cartel and 'Ndrangheta have increased cooperation among each other in order to facilitate trans-Atlantic drug trafficking. Another illicit drug with increased demand in Europe is hashish, which is generally smuggled from Morocco to Spain, from where it is later exported to its final market (mostly France and Western Europe).

The UN Commission on Narcotic Drugs (CND), the principal drug policymaking body at the United Nations, held its annual meeting in Vienna, Austria, in mid-March 2014 following a period of historic drug policy reforms throughout the world, such as the decision of the Uruguay government to become the first national jurisdiction in the world to legalise cannabis. The International Drug Policy Consortium stated in the lead-up to the meeting: "The meeting itself is likely to feature standoffs between reform-oriented countries and governments that favour failed criminal justice models, which have resulted in mass incarceration and rampant human rights abuses such as the death penalty for non-violent drug offences." The support of drug policy reform by Joanne Csete, deputy director of the

Open Society Global Drug Policy Programme, was also published in the Consortium's media release: "There will be no shortage of governments that seek to bury their heads in the sand and pretend these drug policy reforms aren't happening. But try as they might, the movement for drug law reform is unstoppable."

Legal penalties

Drug smuggling carries severe penalties in many countries. Sentencing may include lengthy periods of incarceration, flogging and even the death penalty (in Singapore, Malaysia, etc.). In December 2005, Van Tuong Nguyen, a 25 years old Australian drug smuggler, was hanged in Singapore after being convicted in March 2004. In 2010, two people were sentenced to death in Malaysia for trafficking 1 kilogram of cannabis into the country.

Drug trafficking is widely regarded as the most serious of drug offenses around the world. However, sentencing often depends on the type of drug (and its classification in the country into which it is being trafficked), the quantity trafficked, where the drugs are sold and how they are distributed. If the drugs are sold to underage people, then the penalties for trafficking may be harsher than in other circumstances.

Effects of illegal drug trade on societies

The countries of drug production and drug transit are some of the worst affected by the drug trade though countries receiving the illegally-imported substances are also adversely affected by problems stemming from drug trade. For example, Ecuador has absorbed up to 300,000 refugees from Colombia who are running from guerrillas, paramilitaries and drug lords. While some applied for asylum, others are still illegal. The drugs that pass from Colombia through Ecuador to other parts of South America create economic and social problems.

Honduras, through which an estimated 79 per cent of cocaine passes on its way to the United States, has the highest murder rate in the world.

Violent crime

In many countries worldwide, the illegal drug trade is thought to be directly linked to violent crimes such as murder. This is especially true in developing countries, such as Honduras, but is also an issue for many developed countries worldwide.

In the late 1990s in the United States the Federal Bureau of Investigation estimated that five per cent of murders were drug-related.

After a crackdown by U.S. and Mexican authorities in the first decade of the twenty-first century as part of tightened border security in the wake of the September 11 attacks, border violence inside Mexico surged. The Mexican government estimates that 90 per cent of the killings are drug-related.

A report by the UK government's drug strategy unit that was subsequently leaked to the press, stated that due to the expensive price of highly addictive drugs heroin and cocaine, that drug use was responsible for the great majority of crime, including 85 per cent for shoplifting, 70-80 per cent of burglaries and 54 per cent of robberies. "The cost of crime committed to support illegal cocaine and heroin habits amounts to £16 billion a year in the UK" (*Note:* this is more than the entire annual UK Home Office budget).

Illegal cocaine trade via West Africa

Cocaine produced in Colombia and Bolivia has been increasingly shipped via West Africa (especially in Cape Verde, Mali, Benin, Togo, Nigeria, Cameroon, Guinea-Bissau, and Ghana. The money is often laundered in countries such as Nigeria, Ghana and Senegal.

Cargo planes are now also used as a method of transport from the production countries to West-Africa. Before this, the cocaine was only shipped to the USA. Because the market became saturated there, illicit drug traders decided to increase shipping to Europe. When these new drug routes were uncovered by the authorities, West Africa was chosen as a stop-over. In 2005, the first major cocaine shipment was intercepted by the police. In 2007, 30 per cent of all cocaine shipped to the UK was estimated to come from West Africa. In 2009, 50 per cent of all cocaine shipped to the UK was estimated to come from West Africa.

Drug mules, fishing boats, container ships, and submarines have been used to transship illegal drugs from West Africa to Europe.

Especially in Guinea-Bissau, the drugs have been traded with the help of political leaders such as former presidents, the son of dictator Lansana Conté, and chiefs of staff of the army.

According to the Africa Economic Institute, the value of illicit drug smuggling in Guinea-Bissau is almost twice the value of the country's GDP. Policemen are often bribed. A policeman's normal monthly wage of € 75 is less than two per cent of the value of one kilogram of cocaine (€ 7000).

The money can also be laundered using real estate. A house is built using illegal funds, and when the house is sold, legal money is earned.

When drugs are sent over land, through the Sahara, the drug traders have been increasingly forced to cooperate with terrorist organisations, such as Al Qaida in Islamic Maghreb.

Main drug trafficking route in Asia

A large amount of drugs are smuggled into Europe from Asia. The main source of these drugs is Afghanistan. Farmers in Afghanistan produce drugs which are smuggled into the West and central Asia. Iran is a main route for smugglers. The Border Police Chief of Iran says his country "is a strong barrier against the trafficking of illegal drugs to Caucasus, especially the Republic of Azerbaijan."

US$207 million and additional amounts in other currencies were confiscated from Mexican Zhenli Ye Gon in 2007.

Hashish seized in Operation Albatross, a joint operation of Afghan officials, NATO and the DEA.

Statistics about profits from the drug trade are largely unknown due to its illicit nature. In its 1997 World Drugs Report the UNODC estimated the value of the market at US$400 billion, ranking drugs alongside arms and oil among the world's largest traded goods. An online report published by the UK Home Office in 2007 estimated the illicit drug market in the UK at £4–6.6 billion a year.

In December 2009 United Nations Office on Drugs and Crime Executive Director Antonio Maria Costa claimed illegal drug money saved the banking industry from collapse. He claimed he had seen evidence that the proceeds of organised crime were "the only liquid investment capital" available to some banks on the brink of collapse during 2008. He said that a majority of the US$352bn (£216bn) of drugs profits was absorbed into the economic system as a result. "In many instances, the money from drugs was the only liquid investment capital. In the second half of 2008, liquidity was the banking system's main problem and hence liquid capital became an important factor...Inter-bank loans were funded by money that originated from the drugs trade and other illegal activities... There were signs that some banks were rescued that way". Costa declined to identify countries or banks that may have received any drug money, saying that would be inappropriate because his office is supposed to address the problem, not apportion blame.

Drug Cartels in the Western Hemisphere

Background

There are several arguments on whether or not free trade has a correlation to an increased activity in the illicit drug trade. Currently, the structure and operation of the illicit drug industry is described mainly in terms of an international division of labour. Free trade can open new markets to domestic producers who would otherwise resort to exporting illicit drugs. Additionally, extensive free trade among states increases cross-border drug enforcement and coordination between law enforcement agencies in different countries. However, free trade also increases the sheer volume of legal cross-border trade and provides cover for drug smuggling by providing ample opportunity to conceal illicit cargo in licit trade. While international free trade continues to expand the volume of legal trade, the ability to detect and interdict drug trafficking is severely diminished. Towards the late 1990s, the top ten seaports in the world processed 33.6 million containers. Free trade has fostered integration of financial markets and has provided drug traffickers with more opportunities to launder money and invest in other activities. This strengthens the drug industry while weakening the efforts of law enforcement to monitor the flow of drug money into the legitimate economy. Cooperation expands the power of cartels to distant markets and strengthens their abilities to evade detection by local law enforcement. Additionally, criminal organisations work together to coordinate money-laundering activities by having separate organisations handle specific stages of the laundering process. One organisation structures the process through which financial transactions will be laundered, while another criminal group provides the "dirty" money to be cleaned. By fostering expansion of trade and global transportation networks, free trade encourages cooperation and formation of alliances among criminal organisations across different countries.

Drug trade in Latin America emerged in the early 1930s. It saw significant growth in the Andean countries, including Peru, Bolivia, Chile, Ecuador, Colombia and Argentina. The underground market in the early half of the twentieth century mainly had ties to Europe. After World War II, the Andean countries saw an expansion of trade, specifically with cocaine.

The United States

Background

The effects of the illegal drug trade in the United States can be seen in a range of political, economic and social aspects. Increasing drug related violence can be tied to the racial tension that arose during the late twentieth century along with the political upheaval prevalent throughout the 1960s and 70's. The second half of the twentieth century was a period when increased wealth, concurrent increased discretionary spending, increased the demand for illicit drugs in certain areas of the United States.

Political impact

A numerically large generation, the baby boomers, came of age in the 1960s. Their social tendency to confront the law on specific issues, including illegal drugs, overwhelmed the understaffed judicial system. The federal government attempted to enforce the law, but with meager affect.

Marijuana was a popular drug seen through the Latin American trade route in the 1960s. Cocaine became a major drug product in the later decades. Much of the cocaine is smuggled from Colombia and Mexico via Jamaica. This led to several administrations combating the popularity of these drugs. Due to the influence of this development on the U.S. economy, the Reagan Administration began "certifying" countries for their attempts at controlling drug trafficking. This allowed the U.S. to intervene in activities related to illegal drug transport in Latin America. Continuing into the 1980s, the United States instated stricter policy pertaining to drug transit through sea and as a result, there was an influx in drug-trafficking across the Mexican–U.S. border. This increased the drug cartel activity in Mexico. By the early 1990s, so much as 50 per cent of the cocaine available on the United States market originated from Mexico, and by the 2000s, over 90 per cent of the cocaine in the United States was imported from Mexico. In Colombia, however, there was a fall of the major drug cartels in the mid-1990s. Visible shifts occurred in the drug market in the United States. Between the years 1996 and 2000, U.S. consumption of cocaine had dropped by 11 per cent.

In 2008, the United States government initiated another programme, known as The Merida Initiative, to help combat drug trafficking in Mexico. This programme increased U.S. security assistance to $1.4 billion over several years, which helped supply Mexican forces with "high-end equipment from helicopters to surveillance technology" However, despite U.S. aid, Mexican "narco-gangs" continue to outnumber and outgun the Mexican Army, allowing for the continued activities of drug cartels across the U.S.-Mexican border.

Social impacts

Although narcotics are illegal in the U.S., they have become integrated into the nation's culture and are seen as a recreational activity by sections of the population. Illicit drugs are considered to be a commodity with strong demand, as they are typically sold at a high value. This high price is caused by a combination of factors that include the potential legal ramifications that exist for suppliers of illicit drugs and their high demand. (limited supply can be caused by a range of factors). Despite the constant effort by politicians to win the war on drugs, the U.S. is still the world's largest importer of illegal drugs.

Throughout the twentieth century, narcotics other than cocaine also crossed the Mexican border, meeting the U.S. demand for alcohol during 1920's Prohibition, opiates in the 1940s, marijuana in the 1960s, and heroin in the 1970s." Most of the U.S. imports of drugs come from Mexican drug cartels. In the United States, around 195 cities have been infiltrated by drug trafficking that originated in Mexico. An estimated $10 billion of the Mexican drug cartel's profits come from the United States, not only supplying the Mexican drug cartels with the profit necessary for survival, but also furthering Americans' economic dependence on drugs As the drug industry expands in the U.S., a greater population of the public are beginning to rely on the drug industry for their source of income.

Demographics

With a large wave of immigrants in the 1960s and onwards, the United States saw an increased heterogeneity in its public. In the 1980s and 1990s, drug related homicide was at a record high. This increase in drug violence became increasingly tied to these ethnic minorities. Though the rate of violence varied tremendously among cities in America, it was a common anxiety in communities across urban America. An example of this could be seen in Miami, a city with a host of ethnic enclaves. Between 1985 and 1995, the homicide rate in Miami was one of the highest in the nation and rated four times the national homicide average. This crime was correlated with regions with low employment and was not entirely dependent on ethnicity. The baby boomer generation also felt the effects of the drug trade in their increased drug use from the 1960s to 1980's. Along with substance abuse, criminal involvement, suicide and murder were also on the rise during this time. Due to the large size of the baby boomers, commercial marijuana use was on the rise. This increased the supply and demand for marijuana during this time period.

Mexico

In Mexico, desperate teens everywhere are struggling for even the smallest increments of money. Some teens will go as far as to accept $300 to take illegal narcotics over the US border to recipients. Drug dealers claim that, because the children are minors, they will have no problem in the event that they are caught.

Political influences

Corruption in Mexico has contributed to the domination of Mexican cartels in the illicit drug trade. Since the beginning of the twentieth century, Mexico's political environment allowed the growth of drug-related activity. The loose regulation over the transportation of illegal drugs and the failure to prosecute known drug traffickers and gangs increased the growth of the drug industry. Toleration of drug trafficking has undermined the authority of the Mexican government and has decreased the power of law enforcement officers in regulation over such activities. These policies of tolerance fostered the growing power of drug cartels in the Mexican economy and have made drug traders wealthy. Many states in Mexico lack policies that establish stability in governance. There also is a lack of local stability, as mayors cannot be re-elected. This requires electing a new mayor each term. Drug gangs have manipulated this, ensuing a vacuum in local leadership to their own advantage.

In 1929, The PRI (The Institutional Revolutionary Party) was formed to resolve the chaos resulting from the Mexican Revolution. Over time, this party gained political influence and had a major impact on Mexico's social and economic policies. The PRI created ties with various groups as a power play in order to gain influence, and as a result stirred corruption in the government. One such power play was an alliance with drug traffickers. This political corruption obscured justice, making it difficult to identify violence when it related to drugs. By the 1940s, the tie between the drug cartels and the PRI had solidified. This arrangement created immunity for the leaders of the drug cartels and allowed drug trafficking to grow under the protection of the government officials. During the 1990s, the PRI lost some elections to the new PAN (National Action Party). Chaos again emerged as elected government in Mexico arrived a turning point. As the PAN party took control, drug cartel leaders took advantage of the ensuing confusion and used their existing influence to further gain power. Instead of negotiating with the central government as was done with the PRI party intact, drug cartels utilised new ways to distribute their supply and continued operating through force and intimidation. As Mexico became more democratised, the corruption fell from a centralised power to the local authorities. Cartels began to bribe local authorities, thus eliminating the structure and rules placed by the government, giving cartels more freedom. As a response, Mexico saw an increase in violence caused by drug trafficking.

The massive amounts of corruption cartels created resulted in distrust of government by the Mexican public. This distrust became more prominent after the collapse of the PRI party. In response, the presidents of Mexico, in the late twentieth century and early twenty-first century, implemented several different programmes relating to law enforcement and regulation. In 1993, President Salinas created the National Institute for the Combat of Drugs in Mexico. From 1995–1998, President Zedillo established policies regarding increased punishment of organised crime, allowing "telephonic interception, protected witnessed, covert agents and seizures of goods", and increasing the quality of law enforcement at the federal level. From 2001–2005, President Vicente Fox created the Federal Agency of Investigation (comparable to the FBI of the United States. These policies resulted in the arrests of major drug-trafficking bosses Miguel Angel Felix Gallardo of the Sinaloa Cartel in 1989, Joaquín Guzmán Loera of the Sinaloa Cartel in 1993, Héctor Luis Palma Salazar in 1995, Juan Garcia Abrego of the Gulf Cartel in 1996, Ismael Higuera Guerreroand Jesus Labra of the Tijuana Cartel, Adan Amezcua of the Colima Cartel, Benjamin Arellano Felix of the Tijuana Cartel in 2002 and Osiel Cardenas of the Gulf Cartel in 2003.

Mexico's Economy

Over the past few decades drug cartels have become integrated into Mexico's economy. Approximately 500 cities are directly engaged in drug trafficking and nearly 450,000 people are employed by drug cartels. Additionally, 3.2 million people's livelihood is dependent on the drug cartels. Between local and international sales, such as to Europe and the United States, drug cartels in Mexico see a $25–30 billion yearly profit. Drug cartels are fundamental in local economics. A percentage of the profits seen from these most cartels trade are invested in the local community. Such profits contribute to the education and healthcare of the community. While these cartels bring violence and hazard into communities, they create jobs and provide income for its many members.

Culture of Drug Cartels

Major cartels saw growth due to a prominent set culture of Mexican society that created the means for drug capital. One of the sites of origin for drug trafficking within Mexico, was the state of Michoacán. In the past, Michoacán was mainly an agricultural society. This provided an initial growth of trade. Industrialisation of rural areas of Mexico allowed facilitated a greater distribution of drugs, expanding the drug market into different provinces. Once towns became industrialised, cartels started to form and expand. The proliferation of drug cartel culture largely stemmed from the ranchero culture seen in Michoacán. Ranchero culture values the individual as opposed to the society as a whole This culture fostered the drug culture of valuing the family that is formed within the cartel. This ideal allowed for greater organisation within the cartels. Gangs play a major role in the activity of drug cartels. Two such gangs (the MS-13 and Deiciocho) are notorious for their contributions and influence over drug trafficking throughout Latin America. MS-13 has controlled much of the activity in the drug trade spanning from Mexico to Panama. Female involvement is present in the Mexican drug culture. Although females are not treated as equals to males, they typically hold more power than their culture allows and acquire some independence. The increase in power has attracted females from higher social classes. Financial gain has also prompted women to become involved in the illegal drug market. Many women in the lower levels of major drug cartels belong to a low economic class. Drug trafficking offers women an accessible way to earn income. Females from all social classes have become involved in the trade due to outside pressure from their social and economic environment.

Colombia

Political Ties

It was common for smugglers, specifically in Colombia, to import liquor, alcohol, cigarettes and textiles, while exporting cocaine. Personnel with knowledge of the terrain were able to supply the local market while also exporting a large amount of product. The established trade that began in the 1960s involved Peru, Bolivia, Colombia and Cuba. Peasant farmers produced coca paste in Peru and Bolivia, while Colombian smugglers would process the coca paste into cocaine in Colombia and trafficked product through Cuba. This trade route led to established ties between Cuban and Colombian organised crime. From Cuba, cocaine would be transported to Miami, Florida, and Union City, New Jersey. Quantities of the drug were then smuggled throughout the US. The international drug trade created political ties between the involved countries, encouraging the governments of the countries involved to collaborate and instate common policies to eradicate drug cartels. Cuba stopped being a centre for transport of cocaine following the establishment of a communist government in 1959. As a result Miami and Union City became the sole locations for trafficking. The relations between Cuban and Colombian organised crime remained strong until the 1970s, when Colombian cartels began to vie for power. In the 1980s and 1990s, Colombia emerged as a key contributor of the drug trade industry in the Western Hemisphere. While the smuggling of drugs such as marijuana, poppy, opium and heroin became more ubiquitous during this time period, the activity of cocaine cartels drove the development of the Latin American drug trade. The trade emerged as a multinational effort as supplies (i.e. coca plant substances) were imported from countries such as Bolivia and Peru, were refined in Colombian cocaine labs and smuggled through Colombia, and were exported to countries such as the U.S.

Colombia's Economy

Colombia has had a significant role in the illegal drug trade in Latin America. While active in the drug trade since the 1930s, Colombia's role in the drug trade did not truly become dominant until the 1970s. When Mexico eradicated marijuana plantations, demand stayed the same. Colombia met much of the demand by growing more marijuana. Grown in the strategic northeast region of Colombia, marijuana soon became the leading cash crop in Colombia. This success was short-lived however due to anti-marijuana campaigns that were enforced by the US military throughout the Caribbean. Instead, drug traffickers in Colombia continued their focus on the exportation of cocaine. Having been an export of Colombia since the early 1950s, cocaine remained popular for a host of reasons. Colombia's location facilitated its transportation from South America, into Central America, and then to its destination of North America. This continued into the 1990s where Colombia remained the chief exporter of cocaine. The business of drug trafficking can be seen in several stages in Colombia towards the latter half of the twentieth century. Colombia served as the dominant force in the distribution and sale of cocaine by the 1980s. As drug producers gained more power, they became more centralised and organised into what became drug cartels. Cartels controlled the major aspects of each stage in the traffic of their product. Their organisation allowed cocaine to be distributed in great amounts throughout the United States. By the late 1980s, intra-industry strife arose within the cartels. This stage was marked by increased violence as different cartels fought for control of export markets. Despite this strife, this power struggle led to then having multiple producers of coca leaf farms. This in turn caused an improvement in quality control and reduction of police interdiction in the distribution of cocaine. This also led to cartels attempting to repatriate their earnings which would eventually make up 5.5 per cent of Colombia's GDP. This drive to repatriate earnings led to the pressure of legitimising their wealth. This caused an increase in violence throughout Colombia.

Throughout the 1980s, estimates of illegal drug value in Colombia ranged from \$2 billion to \$4 billion. This made up about 7-10 per cent of the \$36 billion estimated GNP of Colombia during this decade. In the 1990s, the estimates of the illegal drug value remained roughly within the same range (~\$2.5 billion). As the Colombian GNP rose throughout the 90's (\$68.5 billion in 1994 and \$96.3 billion in 1997), the illegal drug value began to comprise a decreasing fraction of the national economy. By the early 1990s, though Colombia led in the exportation of cocaine, it found increasing confrontations within its state. These confrontations were primarily between cartels and government institutions. This led to a decrease in the drug trade's contribution to the GDP of Colombia, dropping from 5.5 per cent to 2.6 per cent. Though a contributor of wealth, the distribution of cocaine has had negative effects on the socio-political situation of Colombia and has weakened its economy as well.

Social Impacts

By the 1980s, Colombian cartels became the dominant cocaine distributors in the US. This led to the spread of increased violence throughout both Latin America and Miami. In the 1980s, two major drug cartels emerged in Colombia: the Medellin and Cali groups. Throughout the 90's however, several factors led to the decline of these major cartels and to the rise of smaller Colombian cartels. The U.S. demand for cocaine dropped while Colombian production rose, pressuring traffickers to find new drugs and markets. In this time period, there was an increase in activity of Caribbean cartels that led to the rise of an alternate route of smuggling through Mexico. This led to the increased collaboration between major Colombian and Mexican drug traffickers. Such drastic changes in the execution of drug trade in Colombia paired with the political instabilities and rise of drug wars in Medellin and Cali, gave way for the rise of the smaller Colombian drug trafficking organisations (and the rise of heroin trade). As the drug trade's influence over the economy increased, drug lords and their networks grew in their power and influence in society. The occurrences in drug-related violence increased during this time period as drug lords fought to maintain their control in the economy. Typically a drug cartel had support networks that consisted of a number of individuals. These people individuals ranged from those directly involved in the trade (such as suppliers, chemists, transporters, smugglers, etc.) as well as those involved indirectly in the trade (such as politicians, bankers, police, etc.). As these smaller Colombian drug cartels grew in prevalence, several notable aspects of the Colombian society gave way for further development of the Colombian drug industry. For example, until the late 1980s, the long-term effects of the drug industry were not realised by much of society. Additionally, there was a lack of regulation in prisons where captured traffickers were sent. These prisons were under-regulated, under-funded, and under-staffed, which allowed for the formation of prison gangs, for the smuggling of arms/weapons/etc., for feasible escapes, and even for captured drug lords to continue running their businesses from prison.

Trade in Specific Drugs

Cannabis

While the recreational use of (and consequently the distribution of) cannabis is illegal in most countries throughout the world, it is available by prescription or recommendation in many places, including Canada and some US states, with Washington state and Colorado being the two first states to legalise marijuana for recreational use, although importation and distribution is prohibited at the federal level. Beginning in 2014, Uruguay will be the first country to legalise cultivation, sale, and consumption of cannabis for recreational use for adult residents.

Cannabis use is tolerated in some areas, most notably the Netherlands which has legalised the possession and licensed sale (but not cultivation) of the drug. Many nations have decriminalised the possession of small amounts of marijuana. Due to the hardy nature of the cannabis plant, marijuana is grown all across the world and is today the world's most popular illegal drug with the highest level of availability. Cannabis is grown legally in many countries for industrial, non-drug use (known as hemp) as well. Cannabis-hemp may also be planted for other non-drug domestic purposes, such as seasoning that occurs in Aceh.

The demand for cannabis around the world, coupled with the drug's relative ease of cultivation, makes the illicit cannabis trade one of the primary ways in which organised criminal groups finance many of their activities. In Mexico, for example, the illicit trafficking of cannabis is thought to constitute the majority of many of the cartels' earnings, and thus the main way in which they (the cartels) finance many other illegal activities ranging from the purchase of other illegal drugs for trafficking and weapons that are ultimately used to commit murders (causing a burgeoning in the homicide rates of many areas of the world, but particularly Latin America).

Alcohol

Alcohol, in the context of alcoholic beverages rather than denatured alcohol, is illegal in a number of countries, such as Saudi Arabia, and this has resulted in a thriving illegal trade in alcohol being commonplace. The manufacture, sale, transportation, importation and exportation of alcoholic beverage were illegal in the United States during the time known as prohibition in the 1920s and early 1930s.

Heroin

Up until around 2004 the majority of the world's heroin was produced in an area known as the Golden Triangle (Southeast Asia). However, by 2007, 93 per cent of the opiates on the world market originated in Afghanistan. This amounted to an export value of about US$64 billion, with a quarter being earned by opium farmers and the rest going to district officials, insurgents, warlords and drug traffickers. Another significant area where poppy fields are grown for the manufacture of heroin is Mexico.

According to the United States Drug Enforcement Administration, the price of heroin is typically valued 8 to 10 times that of cocaine on American streets, making it a high-profit substance for smugglers and dealers. In Europe, (except the transit countries Portugal and the Netherlands), for example, a purported gram of street heroin, usually consisting of 700–800 mg of a light to dark brown powder containing 5-10 per cent heroin base, costs between 30 and 70 euros, making the effective value per gram of pure heroin between 300 and 700 euros. Heroin is generally a preferred target for smuggling and distribution over unrefined opium due to the cost-effectiveness and increased efficacy of heroin.

Because of the high cost per volume, heroin is easily smuggled. A US quarter-sized (2.5 cm) cylindrical vial can contain hundreds of doses. From the 1930s to the early 1970s, the so-called French Connection supplied the majority of US demand. Allegedly, during the Vietnam War, drug lords such as Ike Atkinson used to smuggle hundreds of kilos of heroin to the U.S. in coffins of dead American soldiers (see Cadaver Connection). Since that time it has become more difficult for drugs to be imported into the United States than it had been in previous decades, but that does not stop the heroin smugglers from getting their product onto U.S. soil. Purity levels vary greatly by region with, for the most part, Northeastern cities having the most pure heroin in the United States.

Penalties for smuggling heroin and/or morphine are often harsh in most countries. Some countries will readily hand down a death sentence (e.g. Singapore) or life in prison for the illegal smuggling of heroin or morphine, which are both, internationally, Schedule I drugs under the Single Convention on Narcotic Drugs.

Methamphetamine

Methamphetamine is another popular drug among distributors. Three common street names are "crystal meth", "meth", and "ice". According to the Community Epidemiology Work Group, the numbers of clandestine methamphetamine laboratory incidents reported to the National Clandestine Laboratory Database decreased from 1999 to 2009. During this same period, methamphetamine lab incidents increased in mid-western States (Illinois, Michigan, Missouri, and Ohio), and in Pennsylvania. In 2004, more lab incidents were reported in Missouri (2,788) and Illinois (1,058) than in California (764). In 2003, methamphetamine lab incidents reached new highs in Georgia (250), Minnesota (309), and Texas (677). There were only seven methamphetamine lab incidents reported in Hawaii in 2004, though nearly 59 per cent of substance abuse treatment admissions (excluding alcohol) were for primary methamphetamine abuse during the first six months of 2004. As of 2007, Missouri leads the United States in clandestine lab seizures, with 1,268 incidents reported. Often canine units are used for detecting rolling meth labs which can be concealed on large vehicles, or transported on something as small as a motorcycle. These labs are more difficult to detect than stationary ones, and can often be obscured with the legal cargo on big trucks.

Methamphetamine is sometimes used in an injectable form, placing users and their partners at risk for transmission of HIV and hepatitis C. "Meth" can also be inhaled, most commonly vaporised on aluminum foil, or through a test tube or light bulb fashioned into a pipe. This method is reported to give "an unnatural high" and a "brief intense rush".

In South Africa methamphetamine is called "tik" or "tik-tik". Children as young as eight are abusing the substance, smoking it in crude glass vials made from light bulbs. Since methamphetamine is easy to produce, the substance is manufactured locally in staggering quantities.

The government of North Korea currently operates methamphetamine production facilities. There, the drug is used as medicine since no others are available; it also is smuggled across its border with China. The Australian Crime Commission's illicit drug data report for 2011–2012 stated that the average strength of crystal methamphetamine doubled in most Australian jurisdictions within a 12-month period and the majority of domestic laboratory closures involved small "addict-based" operations.

Temazepam

Temazepam, a strong hypnotic benzodiazepine, is illicitly manufactured in clandestine laboratories (called *jellie labs*) to supply the increasingly high demand for the hypnotic drug internationally. Many clandestine temazepam labs are in Eastern Europe. The labs manufacture temazepam by chemically altering diazepam, oxazepam or lorazepam. Clandestine "jellie labs" have been identified and shutdown in Russia, Ukraine, Czech Republic, Latvia and Belarus.

In the United Kingdom, temazepam is the most widely-abused legal prescription drug. It is also the most commonly abused benzodiazepine in Finland, Ireland, the Netherlands, Poland, Czech Republic, Hungary, India, Russia, People's Republic of China, New Zealand, Australia and some parts of Southeast Asia.

In Sweden, it has been banned due to a problem with drug abuse issues and a high rate of death caused by temazepam alone relative to other drugs of its group.

Chapter - 4

Money-Laundering Capital Ruled by Britain B

Cayman Islands: Safest Money-laundering haven

Mind-boggling trillions! Stolen from the people who are today's faces of hunger, the masses deprived by those who possess dirt.

Audacious advertisement

Not too long ago, I read in a popular international news magazine the most audacious advertisement openly assuring ruthless economic saboteurs that they could "move money silently into your offshore account".

Here's how the advertisement went:

Secret Banking

- Learn how you and your money can achieve total anonymity and safety.
- How to move money silently into your offshore account.
- How to avoid reporting requirements.
- The world's best banking haven. How to obtain an anonymous corporate credit card.

FOR FREE INFORMATION PLEASE WRITE OR FAX TO...

Godman Chandraswami

The best banking havens? Surely not Switzerland or Liechenstein any longer. Panama and Channel Islands or some of the playground islands where the notorious godman Chandraswami was sent by his political cronies as a super-sleuth to try and dig up evidence of dollars stashed away by their rivals.

"I have brought back an atom bomb," boasted Chandraswami on his return. But the bomb never exploded.

Avoid reporting

So, don't hesitate! We will tell you how to avoid reporting requirements is a claim few can dispute. And we will give you tips on how to obtain an anonymous corporate credit card, said the ad in the popular publication.

Ultimate in credit cards

It is the ultimate in credit cards, the Gold of Golds, and it will not only ensure your cash reserves in secret accounts but even use that money to buy things with, including those young suicide **Soldiers of Allah** and their bloodlust in the name of Jihad.

Spies, Revolts

Secret bank accounts cater to the nefarious activities of those engaged in clandestine pursuits such as payments to spies, engineering, revolts in unfriendly countries and financing terrorism. In the main, they are meant for crooks, drug-peddlers, smugglers, arms merchants and even owners of financial institutions.

A hypothetical situation?

However, there are occasions when perfectly law-abiding citizens find it necessary to make use of the facilities provided by the system. Here is one hypothetical problem, not really a problem but a matter of serious thought: A stridently independent and ethical journalist may be caught up in the rising tide of intolerance and rage, does he or doesn't he have simple reason to try and take advantage of this offer to be let into the secret banking?

Crusade?

Of course, he is, you might say. But the catch here is that an honest journalist is unlikely to have enough money, not even sufficient to get drunk! Nevertheless, he retains the courage to investigate the secrets of secret banking; that is, if his media baron employer will let him have access to legitimate funds to carry on with his crusade!

British Overseas Territory: Safest haven for terrorists and saboteurs

Cayman Islands are a British Overseas Territory, situated south of Cuba and Northwest of Jamaica,

Queen Elizabeth II is the monarch.

In other words, Britain, a member of the United Nations Security Council, is directly responsible for providing the safest wealth cache to the most nefarious members of the global community, including terrorists and politico-economic saboteurs.

Chapter - 5

Transparency International

Transparency International (TI) is a non-governmental organisation that monitors and publicises corporate and political corruption in international development. Originally founded in Germany in May 1993 as a not-for-profit organisation, Transparency International is now an international non-governmental organisation. It publishes an annual Global Corruption Barometer and Corruption Perceptions Index, a comparative listing of corruption worldwide. The headquarters are located in Berlin, Germany.

The organisation defines corruption as the abuse of entrusted power for private gain which eventually hurts everyone who depends on the integrity of people in a position of authority.

Candidly, Transparency International appears to have been lless than transparent in its voluminous reports and its corruption perception. Transparency International consists of chapters–locally established, independent organisations–that address corruption in their respective countries. From small bribes to large-scale looting, corruption differs from country to country. As chapters are staffed with local experts they are ideally placed to determine the priorities and approaches best suited to tackling corruption in their countries. This work ranges from visiting rural communities to provide free legal support to advising their government on policy reform. Corruption does not stop at national borders. The chapters play a crucial role in shaping its collective work and realising its regional and global goals, such as Strategy 2015. Transparency International's multi-country research and advocacy initiatives are driven by the chapters.

In 2013, Transparency International published the Government Defence Anti-corruption Index with which corruption in the defence sector of

82 countries was measured. Some governments expressed criticism towards the methodology of the report. Mark Pyman defended the report in an interview and stressed the importance of transparency in the military sector. The plan is to publish the index every two years.

Transparency International's headquarters in Berlin (5th floor).

Transparency International was founded in May 1993, with the participation of Peter Eigen, a former regional director for the World Bank. Other founding board members included Hansjörg Elshorst, Joe Githongo, Fritz Heimann, Michael Hershman, Kamal Hossain, Dolores L. Español, George Moody Stuart, Jerry Parfitt, Jeremy Pope and Frank Vogl.

In 1995, Transparency International developed the Corruption Perceptions Index (CPI). The CPI ranked nations on the prevalence of corruption within each country, based upon surveys of business people. The CPI was subsequently published annually. It was criticised for poor methodology and unfair treatment of developing nations, while also being praised for highlighting corruption and embarrassing governments.

In 1999, Transparency International began publishing the Bribe Payers Index (BPI) which ranked nations according to the prevalence that a country's multinational corporations would offer bribes.

Organisation

Transparency International consists of over 100 locally established, independent national chapters as well as an international secretariat in Berlin, Germany. Each chapter tackles corruption in their respective country, constructing methods relevant to their national context in order to bring about change. The secretariat provides support and cooperation among chapters, as well as collaborating with these chapters in order to approach corruption on a global and regional scale.

Role

Transparency International claims that:

"Transparency International is the global civil society organisation leading the fight against corruption. It brings people together in a powerful worldwide coalition to end the devastating impact of corruption on men, women and children around the world. TI's mission is to create change towards a world free of corruption."

Since 1995, Transparency International has issued an annual Corruption Perceptions Index (CPI); it also publishes a Global Corruption Report, a Global Corruption Barometer and a Bribe Payers Index.

Transparency International does not undertake investigations on single cases of corruption or expose individual cases. It develops tools for fighting corruption and works with other civil society organisations, companies and governments to implement them.

Transparency International's biggest success has been to put the topic of corruption on the world's agenda. International Institutions such as the World Bank and the International Monetary Fund now view corruption as one of the main obstacles for development, whereas prior to the 1990s this topic was not broadly discussed. Transparency International furthermore played a vital role in the introduction of the United Nations Convention against Corruption and the OECD Anti-Bribery Convention.

Corruption Perceptions Index

The Corruption Perceptions Index (CPI) ranks countries and territories based on how corrupt their public sector is perceived to be. It is a composite index–a combination of polls–drawing on corruption-related data collected by a variety of reputable institutions. The CPI reflects the views of observers from around the world.

The Corruption Perceptions Index has received criticisms over the years. The main one stems from the difficulty in measuring corruption, which by definition happens behind the scenes. The Corruption Perceptions Index therefore needs to rely on third-party survey which have been criticised as potentially unreliable. Data can vary widely depending on the public perception of a country, the completeness of the surveys and the methodology used. The second issue is that data cannot be compared from year to year because Transparency International uses different methodologies and samples every year. This makes it difficult to evaluate the result of new policies. The Corruption Perceptions Index authors replied to these criticisms by reminding that the Corruption Perceptions Index is meant to measure *perception* and not "reality". They argue that "perceptions matter in their own right, since...firms and individuals take actions based on perceptions".

Chapter - 6

Eight Dictators Still in Power

Muammar Gaddafi and Kim Jong Il may have passed, but the Human Rights Watch still has their eye on plenty of power hungry madmen. Here are a handful of those lunatics that you should know, posted on Dec. 19, 2011, at 10:57 a.m.

1. Isaias Afewerki, President of Eritrea

Age: 65

Assumed office: 4/27/91

Afewerki has not set up any formal constitution to protect the rights of his people, and yet two-thirds of his nation is reportedly malnourished. Every male at 18 must enter military service for an indefinite period of time, unless they prefer to be imprisoned or killed. According to one

WikiLeaks cable, the U.S. ambassador called the Eritrea dictator "unhinged, cruel, and defiant."

2. Bashar al-Assad, President of Syria

Age: 46

Assumed office: 6/20/2000

Assad succeeded his father Hafez's 29-year reign with 97 percent of the nation's vote but without publicly disclosing voter statistics. His security forces continue to arrest citizens without warrants and torture them under a "no freedom, no rights" policy. He is responsible for approximately 3,000 civilian lives since the recent Arab Spring demonstrations have begun on Syrian ground.

3. Omar al-Bashir, President of Sudan

Age: 67

Assumed office: 10/16/93

Bashir has an outstanding arrest warrant from the International Criminal Court for war crimes in Darfur and killing up to 400,000 civilians to date. It is also said that Sudan hosted pre-9/11 training grounds for Osama bin Laden to train members of al-Qaeda. Bashir's security officials continue to arrest, sexually abuse, and torture demonstrators active in the Arab Spring protests.

4. Meles Zanawi Asres, Prime Minister of Ethiopia

Age: 56
Assumed office: 8/23/95

The Ethiopian P.M. is responsible for losing tens of thousands of civilian lives through what is often thought of as a pointless conflict with the state of Eritrea. He also had his forces massacre 193 civilians who protested during his disputed 2005 reelection.

5. Islam Karimov, President of Uzbekistan

Age: 73
Assumed office: 3/24/90

Uzbekistan's torture has been described by the United Nations as "systematic." In 2005, Karimov's regime shot several hundred civilians on site who were protesting the arrests of 23 local businessmen. That very day, the government issued a statement that 9 people were killed and 34 sustained injuries during a "clash." Reporters Without Borders characterises Karimov as one of the world's "Predators of Press Freedom, breaking his own records for repression and paranoia."

6. Teodoro Obiang Nguema Mbasogo, President of Equatorial Guinea

Age: 69
Assumed office: 8/3/79

Nguema staged a coup to take over Equatorial Guinea, a.k.a. "the Auschwitz of Africa," from his very own uncle Francisco Macias Nguema. Since, Nguema has maintained a reputation as a murdering and a cannibalizing his own people for 30-plus years as he reels in billions of dollars from oil exports.

7. Robert Mugabe, President of Zimbabwe

Age: 87

Assumed office: 12/31/87

Mugabe continues his 24-year reign through means of election rigging, media control, and the threat of starvation. Barry Bearak, a "New York Times" journalist who had been imprisoned in the state's capital in 2008, reported that "power had flourished through methodical cruelty, including the murder of thousands of people… as he and cronies then acquired lavish mansions and enormous bank accounts."

8. Yoweri Museveni, President of Uganda

Age: 71

Assumed office: 1/26/86

In 2005, the International Criminal Court oversaw a case accusing Uganda of invading Congo and massacring its civilians. Museveni has roundly defended his actions as a means to keep peace, but, according to Human Rights Watch, "the Ugandan police Rapid Response Unit frequently operates outside the law, carrying out torture, extortion, and in some cases, extrajudicial killings."

Via cbsnews.com

This post was created by a user and has not been vetted or endorsed by BuzzFeed's editorial staff. BuzzFeed Community is a place where anyone can post awesome lists and creations.

Chapter - 7

Terrorism Financing

Terrorism financing came into limelight in the United States after the terrorist attacks in the United States on the 11th September in 2001. The US Government passed the USA PATRIOT Act to, among other reasons, attempt thwarting the financing of terrorism (CFT) and anti-money laundering (AML) making sure these were given some sort of adequate focus by US financial institutions. The Act also had extraterritorial impact and non-US banks having correspondent banking accounts or doing business with US banks had to upgrade their AML/CFT processes. The Patriot Act has generated a great deal of controversy in the United States since its enactment.

Initially the focus of CFT efforts was on non-profit organisations, unregistered money services businessess (MSBs) (including so called underground banking or 'Hawalas') and the criminalisation of the act itself. The Financial Action Task Force on Money Laundering (FATF) made nine special recommendations for CFT (first eight then a year later added a ninth). These nine recommendations have become the global standard for CFT and their effectiveness is assessed almost always in conjunction with AML.

The FATF Blacklist mechanism was used to coerce countries to bring about changes.

- 3 Bank processes
- 4 Germany
- 5 See also
- 6 References

Money laundering

Often linked in legislation and regulation, terrorism financing and money laundering are conceptual opposites. Money laundering is the process where cash raised from criminal activities is made to look legitimate for re-integration into the financial system, whereas terrorism financing cares little about the source of the funds, but it is what the funds are to be used for that defines its scope.

An in-depth study of the symbiotic relationship between organised crime and terrorist organisations detected within the United States of America and other areas of the world referred to as crime-terror nexus points has been published in the forensic literature. The Perri, Lichtenwald and MacKenzie article emphasises the importance of multi-agency working groups and the tools that can be used to identify, infiltrate, and dismantle organisations operating along the crime-terror nexus points.

Terrorists use low value but high volume fraud activity to fund their operations. Paramilitary groups in Northern Ireland are using legitimate businesses such as hotels, pubs and taxi operators to launder money and fund political activities. Even beyond Ireland, terrorists are buying out/controlling front-end businesses especially cash-intensive businesses including in some cases money services businesses to move monies. Bulk cash smuggling and placement through cash-intensive businesses is one typology. They are now also moving monies through the new online payment systems. They also use trade linked schemes to launder monies. Nonetheless, the older systems have not given way. Terrorists also continue to move monies through MSBs/ Hawalas, and through international ATM transactions. Charities also continue to be used in countries where controls are not so stringent.

Suspicious activity

Operation Green Quest, a US multi-agency task force established in October 2001 with the official purpose of countering terrorism financing considers the following patterns of activity as indicators of the collection and movement of funds that could be associated with terrorism financing:

- Account transactions that are inconsistent with past deposits or withdrawals such as cash, cheques, wire transfers, etc.
- Transactions involving a high volume of incoming or outgoing wire transfers, with no logical or apparent purpose that come

from, go to, or transit through locations of concern, that is sanctioned countries, non-cooperative nations and sympathiser nations.

- Unexplainable clearing or negotiation of third party cheques and their deposits in foreign bank accounts.
- Structuring at multiple branches or the same branch with multiple activities.
- Corporate layering, transfers between bank accounts of related entities or charities for no apparent reasons.
- Wire transfers by charitable organisations to companies located in countries known to be bank or tax havens.
- Lack of apparent fund raising activity, for example, a lack of small cheques or typical donations associated with charitable bank deposits.
- Using multiple accounts to collect funds that are then transferred to the same foreign beneficiaries.
- Transactions with no logical economic purpose, that is, no link between the activity of the organisation and other parties involved in the transaction.
- Overlapping corporate officers, bank signatories, or other identifiable similarities associated with addresses, references and financial activities.
- Cash debiting schemes in which deposits in the US correlate directly with ATM withdrawals in countries of concern. Reverse transactions of this nature are also suspicious.
- Issuing cheques, money orders or other financial instruments, often numbered sequentially, to the same person or business, or to a person or business whose name is spelled similarly.

It would be difficult to determine by such activity alone whether the particular act was related to terrorism or to organised crime. For this reason, these activities must be examined in context with other factors in order to determine a terrorism financing connection. Simple transactions can be found to be suspect and money laundering derived from terrorism will typically involve instances in which simple operations had been performed (retail foreign exchange operations, international transfer of funds) revealing links with other countries including FATF blacklisted countries. Some of the customers may have police records, particularly for trafficking in narcotics and weapons and may be linked with foreign terrorist groups.

The funds may have moved through a state sponsor of terrorism or a country where there is a terrorism problem. A link with a Politically Exposed Person (PEP) may ultimately link up to a terrorism financing transaction. A charity may be a link in the transaction. Accounts (especially student) that only receive periodic deposits withdrawn via ATM over two months and are dormant at other periods could indicate that they are becoming active to prepare for an attack.

The Operation Green Quest raids led to the convictions of two people, including Abdurahman Alamoudi, who worked for the SAAR Foundation. Alamoudi admitted that he planned with Libyan Authorities to assassinate the Saudi ruler and was sentenced to 23 years in jail.

Bank Processes

In addition to normal AML controls, banks must focus on the CFT angle, using knowledge derived from the extensive databank of case studies now available. Banks must focus on not just name matching with sanctions databases but also with other know your customer (KYC) high-risk databases of good third party vendors. They must use technologies like link analysis to establish second and third level links that identify transactions as potentially suspicious from a CFT perspective. Focus on preventing identity theft is an integral part of any CFT programme. Detection rules designed to capture the suspicious activity list given above, should be evaluated. Controls out of the transaction monitoring process, for example, account openings by groups of individuals, are also important to watch for. Any bank that is used for terrorism financing will suffer tremendous reputational damage and also a real business impact in terms of share price and expensive fines. To safeguard against this, financial institutions purchase anti-money laundering software from companies such as Lexis Nexis and C6 along with databases of high risk individuals and organisations developed by companies such as WorldCompliance and C6.

Chapter - 8

Interpol

The **International Criminal Police Organisation,** or **INTERPOL**, is an intergovernmental organisation facilitating international police cooperation. It was established as the International Criminal Police Commission (ICPC) in 1923 and adopted its telegraphic address as its common name in 1956.

Interpol has an annual budget of around €70 million most of which is provided through annual contributions by its membership of 190 countries. The organisation's headquarters is in Lyon, France. It is the second largest intergovernmental organisation after the United Nations by member states. In 2012, the Interpol General Secretariat employed a staff of 703 representing 98 member countries. Its current Secretary-General is Ronald Noble, a former United States Under Secretary of the Treasury for Enforcement. Succeeding Khoo Boon Hui, its current President is Deputy Central Director of the French Judicial Police Mireille Balestrazzi.

To keep Interpol as politically neutral as possible, its constitution forbids it, at least in theory, from undertaking interventions or activities of a political, military, religious, or racial nature. Its work focuses primarily on public safety, terrorism, crimes against humanity, environmental crime, genocide, war crimes, organised crime, piracy, illicit traffic in works of art, illicit drug production, drug trafficking, weapons smuggling, human trafficking, money laundering, child pornography, white-collar crime, computer crime, intellectual property crime and corruption.

History

In the first part of the twentieth century, several efforts were taken to formalise international police cooperation, but they initially failed.

Among these efforts were the First International Criminal Police Congress in Monaco in 1914 and the International Police Conference in New York in 1922. The Monaco Congress failed because it was organised by legal experts and political officials, not by police professionals, while the New York Conference failed to attract international attention.

In 1923, a new initiative was taken at the International Criminal Police Congress in Vienna where the International Criminal Police Commission (ICPC) was successfully founded as the direct forerunner of Interpol. Founding members included police officials from Russia, Austria, Germany, Belgium, Poland, China, Egypt, France, Greece, Hungary, Italy, the Netherlands, Romania, Sweden, Switzerland and Yugoslavia. The United States did not join Interpol until 1938, although a US police officer unofficially attended the 1923 congress. The United Kingdom joined in 1928.

Following the *Anschluss* (Germany's annexation of Austria) in 1938, the organisation fell under the control of Nazi Germany, and the Commission's headquarters were eventually moved to Berlin in 1942. From 1938 to 1945, the presidents of Interpol included Otto Steinhäusl, Reinhard Heydrich, Arthur Nebe, and Ernst Kaltenbrunner. All were generals in the SS, and Kaltenbrunner was the highest ranking SS officer executed after the Nuremberg Trials.

After the end of World War II in 1945, the organisation was revived as the International Criminal Police Organisation by officials from Belgium, France, Scandinavia and the United Kingdom. Its new headquarters were established in Saint-Cloud, a suburb of Paris. They remained there until 1989, when they were moved to their present location in Lyon.

Until the 1980s Interpol did not intervene in the prosecution of Nazi war criminals in accordance with Article 3 of its Constitution forbidding intervention in "political" matters.

In July 2010, former Interpol President Jackie Selebi was found guilty of corruption by the South African High Court in Johannesburg for accepting bribes worth €156,000 from a drug trafficker. After being charged in January 2008, Selebi resigned as president of Interpol and was put on extended leave as National Police Commissioner of South Africa. He was replaced by Arturo Herrera Verdugo, the National Commissioner of Investigations Police of Chile and former vice president for the American Zone, who remained acting president until October 2008 and the appointment of Khoo Boon Hui.

On 8 November 2012, the 81st INTERPOL General Assembly closed with the election of Deputy Central Director of the French Judicial Police

Mireille Balestrazzi as the new president of the organisation. She is Interpol's first female president.

Constitution

The role of Interpol is defined by the general provisions of its constitution.

Article 2 states that its role is:

1. To ensure and promote the widest possible mutual assistance between all criminal police authorities within the limits of the laws existing in the different countries and in the spirit of the Universal Declaration of Human Rights.
2. To establish and develop all institutions likely to contribute effectively to the prevention and suppression of ordinary law crimes.

Article 3 states:

It is strictly forbidden for the Organisation to undertake any intervention or activities of a political, military, religious or racial character.

Methodology

Interpol differs from most law-enforcement agencies—agents do not make arrests themselves, and there is no single Interpol jail where criminals are taken. The agency functions as an administrative liaison between the law-enforcement agencies of the member countries, providing communications and database assistance. This is vital when fighting international crime because language, cultural and bureaucratic differences can make it difficult for officers of different nations to work together. For example, if ICE and FBI special agents track a terrorist to Italy, they may not know whom to contact in the Polizia di Stato, if the Carabinieri have jurisdiction over some aspect of the case, or who in the Italian government must be notified of the ICE/FBI's involvement. ICE and FBI can contact the Interpol National Central Bureau in Italy, which acts as a liaison between the United States and Italian law-enforcement agencies.

Interpol's databases help law enforcement see the big picture of international crime. While other agencies have their own extensive crime databases, the information rarely extends beyond one nation's borders. Interpol can track criminals and crime trends around the world. They maintain collections of fingerprints and face photos, lists of wanted persons, DNA samples and travel documents. Their lost and stolen travel document database alone contains more than 12 million records. They also analyse all these data and release information on crime trends to the member countries.

A secure worldwide communications network allows Interpol agents and member countries to contact each other at any time. Known as I-24/7, the network offers constant access to Interpol's databases. While the National Central Bureaus are the primary access sites to the network, some member countries have expanded it to key areas such as airports and border access points. Member countries can also access each other's criminal databases via the I-24/7 system. Interpol issued more than 12,000 notices in 2012 of which 8,136 were Red Notices compared to 3,131 in 2007 and 1,212 in 2002.

In the event of an international disaster, terrorist attack or assassination, Interpol can send an Incident Response Team (IRTs). IRTs can offer a range of expertise and database access to assist with victim identification, suspect identification and the dissemination of information to other nations' law enforcement agencies. In addition, at the request of local authorities, they can act as a central command and logistics operation to coordinate other law enforcement agencies involved in a case. Such teams were deployed 10 times in 2012. Interpol began issuing its own travel documents in 2009 with hopes that member states would remove visa requirements for individuals travelling for Interpol business, thereby improving response times.

Finances

In 2012, Interpol's operating income was €70 million, of which 74 per cent was statutory contributions by member countries and 21 per cent came from externally funded projects, private foundations and commercial enterprises. From 2004 to 2010 Interpol's external auditors was the French Court of Audit. In November 2010 the Court of Audit was replaced by the Office of the Auditor General of Norway for a three-year term with an option for a further three years.

Controversy

Despite its political neutral stance, some have criticised the agency for its role in arrests that critics contend were politically motivated. An example involved journalist Hamza Kashgari, who in February 2012 fled his home country of Saudi Arabia to avoid prosecution for apostasy, and was subsequently arrested in Malaysia. The Royal Malaysian Police initially asserted that they had arrested Kashgari because they had received an Interpol Red Notice request to do so. However, Interpol stated that no such notice had been issued, and the Malaysian police retracted their claim.

In 2013, Interpol was criticised over its multi-million dollar deals with such private-sector bodies as FIFA, Philip Morris, and the pharmaceutical industry.

Chapter - 9

Prevention of Money-Laundering Act, 2002

The Prevention of Money Laundering Act, 2002	
An Act to prevent money-laundering and to provide for confiscation of property derived from, or involved in, money-laundering and for matters connected therewith or incidental thereto.	
Citation	Act No.15 of 2003
Enacted by	Parliament of India
Date enacted	17 January 2003
Date assented to	17 January 2003
Date commenced	1 July 2005
Amendments	
The Prevention of Money Laundering (Amendment) Act, 2005, The Prevention of Money Laundering (Amendment) Act, 2009	

Prevention of Money Laundering Act, 2002 is an Act of the Parliament of India enacted to prevent money-laundering and to provide for confiscation of property derived from money-laundering.

Objectives

The main objectives of this act are to prevent money-laundering as well as to provide for confiscation of property either derived from or involved in, money-laundering.

Key definitions

- **Attachment** : Prohibition of transfer, conversion, disposition or movement of property by an appropriate legal order.
- **Proceeds of crime:** Any property derived or obtained, directly or indirectly, by any person as a result of criminal activity relating to a scheduled offence.
- **Money-laundering:** Attempting to indulge or assist other person or actually involved in any activity connected with the proceeds of crime and projecting it as untainted property.

Salient features

Punishment for Money-Laundering

The Act prescribes that any person found guilty of money-laundering shall be punishable with rigorous imprisonment from three years to seven years. He could also be liable to fine of up to 500,000 (US$8,100). However, vide amendment of PMLA, 2002 in 2012, the upper ceiling on the quantum of fine has been done away with.

Powers of Attachment of Tainted Property

Appropriate authorities, appointed by the Govt. of India, can *provisionally* attach property believed to be "proceeds of crime" for 180 days. Such an order is required to be confirmed by an independent *Adjudicating Authority*.

Adjudicating Authority

The Adjudicating Authority is the authority appointed by the central government. It decides whether any of the property attached or seized is involved in money laundering.

Appellate Tribunal

An Appellate Tribunal is the body appointed by Govt of India. It is given the power to hear appeals against the orders of the Adjudicating Authority and any other authority under the Act. Orders of the tribunal can be appealed in appropriate High Court (for that jurisdiction) and finally to the Supreme Court.

Special Court under Section 43 of Prevention of Money Laundering Act, 2002 (PMLA) says that the Central Government, in consultation with the Chief Justice of the High Court, shall, for trial of offence punishable under Section 4, by notification, designate one or more Courts of Session as Special Court or Special Courts for such area or areas or for such case or class or group of cases as may be specified in the notification.

Burden of Proof

A person, who is accused of having committed the offence of money laundering, has to prove that alleged proceeds of crime are in fact lawful property.

Money Laundering Control Act of 1986

Main article: Money Laundering Control Act of 1986

This is an Act of the United States Congress that made money laundering a Federal crime. It for the first time in the United States criminalised money laundering.

Patriot Act

This is an Act of the United States Congress. The act, as a response to the terrorist attacks of 11 September, significantly reduced restrictions in law enforcement agencies' gathering of intelligence within the United States; expanded the Secretary of the Treasury's authority to regulate financial transactions, particularly those involving foreign individuals and entities; and broadened the discretion of law enforcement and immigration authorities in detaining and deporting immigrants suspected of terrorism-related acts. The act also expanded the definition of terrorism to include domestic terrorism, thus enlarging the number of activities to which the USA Patriot Act's expanded law.

Chapter - 10

Cayman Islands, Israel and Russia

Mind-boggling trillions! Stolen from the people who are today's faces of hunger, the masses deprived by those who possess dirt. The total amount currently stands at $20 trillion, India's share being $2 trillion.

The world's leading industrial nations named the 15 nations and territories as "potential" havens for ill-gotten wealth.

Apart from the countries and territories named are: the Bahamas, the Cayman Islands, the Cook Islands, Domiica, Lebanon, Leichetensein, the Marshall Islands, Naura, Niui, Panama, St. Kitts and Nevis, St. Vincent and Grenadines.

There is no mention of Switzerland.

Audacious advertisement

Not too long ago, I read in a popular international news magazine the most audacious advertisement openly assuring ruthless economic saboteurs that they could "move money silently into your offshore account".

Here's how the advertisement went:

Secret Banking

- Learn how you and your money can achieve total anonymity and safety.
- How to move money silently into your offshore account.
- How to avoid reporting requirements.
- The world's best banking haven. How to obtain an anonymous corporate credit card.

For Free Information Please Write or Fax To....

Godman Chandraswami

The best banking havens? Surely not Switzerland or Liechenstein any longer. Panama and Channel Islands or some of the playground islands where the notorious godman Chandraswami was sent by his political cronies as a super-sleuth to try and dig up evidence of dollars stashed away by their rivals.

"I have brought back an atom bomb," boasted Chandraswami on his return. But the bomb never exploded.

Avoid reporting

So, don't hesitate! We will tell you how to avoid reporting requirements is a claim few can dispute. And we will give you tips on how to obtain an anonymous corporate credit card, said the ad in the popular publication.

Ultimate in credit cards

It is the ultimate in credit cards, the Gold of Golds, and it will not only ensure your cash reserves in secret accounts but even use that money to buy things with, including those young suicide Soldiers of Allah and their bloodlust in the name of Jihad.

Spies, revolts

Secret bank accounts cater to the nefarious activities of those engaged in clandestine pursuits such as payments to spies, engineering, revolts in unfriendly countries and financing terrorism.

In the main, they are meant for crooks, drug-peddlers, smugglers, arms merchants and even owners of financial institutions.

A hypothetical situation?

However, there are occasions when perfectly law-abiding citizens find it necessary to make use of the facilities provided by the system. Here is one hypothetical problem, not really a problem but a matter of serious thought: A stridently independent and ethical journalist may be caught up in the rising tide of intolerance and rage, does he or doesn't he have simple reason to try and take advantage of this offer to be let into the secret banking?

Crusade?

Of course, he is, you might say. But the catch here is that an honest journalist is unlikely to have enough money, not even sufficient to get drunk! Nevertheless, he retains the courage to investigate the secrets of secret banking; that is, if his media baron employer will let him have access to legitimate funds to carry on with his crusade!

British Overseas Territory: Safest haven for terrorists and saboteurs

Cayman Islands are a British Overseas Territory, situated south of Cuba and Northwest of Jamaica,

Queen Elizabeth II is the monarch.

In other words, Britain, a member of the United Nations Security Council, is directly responsible for providing the safest wealth cache to the most nefarious members of the global community, including terrorists and politico-economic saboteurs.

Cayman Islands, the capital of human greed.

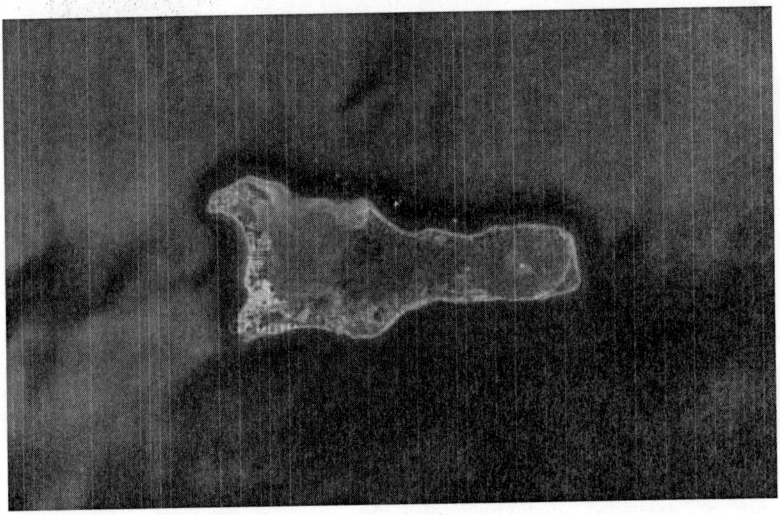

Chapter - 11

Expel Safe Havens from UN and their Clients from Civil Society

Last night, I woke with a start. We Indians are deriving some sort of pleasure with the poll cacophony all around us, not realising that more than $2 trillion worth of our sweat and blood is being dry-cleaned or whatever in one or more of the 15 so-far identified money-laundering places.

What is a trillion, in numbers? How many zeroes after 1? Eighteen! Would you believe it, which means 1,000 times one billion!. Or one million millions make one trillion.

And what is India's Gross National Product (GNP: $1,841. Question: How many times of our GNP has been looted? And when did the looting start? Long ago, I am sure.

Much research will have to go into that. But in 1972, delivering her keynote address at the launching of the United Nations Environment Programme (UNEP) in Stockholm, Mrs Indira Gandhi said: "Poverty is the biggest pollutant."

Wild ovation!

In 1982, in Nairobi, at the tenth anniversary of UNEP, she said the same thing. No ovation. Grim silence, I was there.

In the evening at the India House reception, I moved gingerly towards her to confront her, but stopped as I found Madam was in some argument with her daughter-in-law Menaka Gandhi, but continued all the same and they started smiling, "Do you really man, Madam, about poverty's linkage with the environment?"

She grimaced, but only momentarily and asked in her charimng smile: "Did you get my gift, Mehra?"

I nodded at her hint of bribe for a good story. In fact, I file no story and allowed the agencies to do so.

Of course, she was wrong, as she perhaps knew all along. Poverty-creators, the money-launderers, are the worst pollutant in every field, in peace and war, in games and in celebrations, in buying and selling.

Available indices of corruption are general and do not distinguish between high-level corruption such as a Defense Minister receiving kickbacks in exchange for purchase of armaments and low-level graft paid to a junior civil servant for expediting a driver's license.

Transparency is a legitimate concern of democracy. The people have the right to know how decisions that affect them are arrived at, by whom and under what circumstances; how public resources are administered, by whom and why.

Nor do they distinguish between well-organised greasing of wheels and chaotic corruption. In well-organised graft entrepreneurs know the person or group they need to bribe and how much to offer them, and are confident that they will obtain the necessary permits for their corporations.

It has also been argued that well-organised corruption is less harmful because, under such a system, a corrupt bureaucrat will take a clearly-defined share of a firm's profits, which gives him an interest in the success of the firm.

In contrast, under chaotic corruption, entrepreneurs may need to bribe several officials, but with no guarantee that they will not face further demands for bribes or that the permits they seek will actually be delivered. In addition, if multiple agents request bribes from the same entrepreneur without coordinating bribe themselves, they are likely to make excessive demands with the result that entrepreneurial activity comes to a halt.

While chaotic corruption seems to be more harmful than well-organised corruption, there is currently little data available to test the theory.

Many countries and institutions have paid increasing attention to the problem of corruption, and the debate on policy options is an on-going process. In deciding how to allocate funds some lending institutions and donor states have begun to give more attention to borrower countries' actions to curb corruption.

Member-states of the Otganisation of Economic Cooperation and Development (OECD - the rich nations' club) have acted to criminalise the bribery of foreigm public officials. The International Monetary Fund (IMF) and the World Bank insist on countries that they should liberalise their economies, for example, by eliminating trade restrictions, terminate off-budget operations and ensure transparency.

One of the most difficult policy issues is how to prevent corruption from distorting government expenditure. A possible approach that has been suggested is to have an international institution monitor the overall composition of government expenditure, as a service to citizens of a country which receives financial assistance and the lenders such as the World Bank and so on.

Transparency is a guarantee of good governance because maladministration shuns the light and prefers obscurity. The promotion of good governance involves a determined campaign against corruption at all levels.

Chapter - 12

India World's Richest Nation, Corruption Indices Show

India's Gross National Product is just under $1,500 billion. Peanuts! Against the GNP the figure for black money was $1.96 trillion in 2012, according to Transparency International.

It must now be above $2.5 trillion, given the tax-free high interest rates money-laundering havens provide.

The GNP of the United States is $16,188 billion for the current year. But no figures are available about US and British black money. After all, Israel, a safe haven would not be in mood to give secrets about the American Jews who reportedly control the US economy, largely that is.

On a similar token, it would be hard to find British figures because the capital of safe havens, Cayman Islands, is a British Overseas Territory, How can be find the truth? Little chance. World Bank, ING, Transparency *et. al.,* provide more than they hide.

So, in the absence of clear statistics, India is ranked 94th corrupt in the world, with war-like Sudan and Somalia with GNPs no more than $300.

Mind-boggling trillions! Stolen from the people who are today's faces of hunger, the masses deprived by those who possess dirt money and stash them at places not even known to them on their atlases. How did it all begun: Simple advertisements!

Audacious advertisement

Not too long ago, I read in a popular international news magazine the most audacious advertisement openly assuring ruthless economic saboteurs that they could "move money silently into your offshore account".

Here's how the advertisement went:

Secret Banking

- **Learn how you and your money can achieve total anonymity and safety.**
- **How to move money silently into your offshore account.**
- **How to avoid reporting requirements.**
- **The world's best banking haven. How to obtain an anonymous corporate credit card.**

For Free Information Please Write or Fax To....

Godman Chandraswami

The best banking havens? Surely not Switzerland or Liechenstein any longer. Panama and Channel Islans or some of the playground islands where the notorious godman Chandraswami was sent by his political cronies as a super-sleuth to try and dig up evidence of dollars stashed away by their rivals.

"I have brought back an atom bomb," boasted Chandraswami on his return. But the bomb never exploded.

Avoid Reporting

So, don't hesitate! We will tell you how to avoid reporting requirements is a claim few can dispute. And we will give you tips on how to obtain an anonymous corporate credit card, said the ad in the popular publication.

Ultimate in credit cards

It is the ultimate in credit cards, the Gold of Golds, and it will not only ensure your cash reserves in secret accounts but even use that money to buy things with, including those young suicide **Soldiers of Allah** and their bloodlust in the name of Jihad.

Spies, revolts

Secret bank accounts cater to the nefarious activities of those engaged in clandestine pursuits such as payments to spies, engineering, revolts in unfriendly countries and financing terrorism. In the main, they are meant for crooks, drug-peddlers, smugglers, arms merchants and even owners of financial institutions.

A hypothetical situation?

However, there are occasions when perfectly law-abiding citizens find it necessary to make use of the facilities provided by the system. Here is one hypothetical problem, not really a problem but a matter of serious thought: A stridently independent and ethical journalist may be caught up in the rising tide of intolerance and rage, does he or doesn't he have simple reason to try and take advantage of this offer to be let into the secret banking?

Crusade?

Of course, he is, you might say. But the catch here is that an honest journalist is unlikely to have enough money, not even sufficient to get drunk! Nevertheless, he retains the courage to investigate the secrets of secret banking; that is, if his media baron employer will let him have access to legitimate funds to carry on with his crusade!

British Overseas Territory: Safest haven for terrorists and saboteurs

Cayman Islands are a British Overseas Territory, situated south of Cuba and Northwest of Jamaica,

Queen Elizabeth II is the monarch.

In other words, Britain, a member of the United Nations Security Council, is directing responsible for providing the safest wealth cache to the most nefarious members of the global community, including terrorists and politico-economic saboteurs.

The black economies have moved on since the days of those ads. Internet, smart phones, internet banking.

The world has moved much beyond. The cyber space is magical and there are now "Reality Phones" through which such transactions are done without the risk of being.

Let us wake up the Cyber Hurricane!

Chapter - 13

Financial Action Task Force on Money Laundering

The **Financial Action Task Force on Money Laundering** (FATF) was established by the G-8 Summit that was held in Paris in 1989. Recognising the threat posed to the banking system and to financial institutions, the G-8 Heads of State or Government and President of the European Commission convened the Task Force from the G-8 member States, the European Commission and eight other countries.

The Task Force was given the responsibility of examining money laundering techniques and trends, reviewing the action which had already been taken at a national or international level, and setting out the measures that still needed to be taken to combat money laundering. In April 1990, less than one year after its creation, the FATF issued a report containing a set of Forty Recommendations, which provide a comprehensive plan of action needed to fight against money laundering.

In 2001, the development of standards in the fight against terrorism financing was added to the mission of the FATF. In October 2001, the FATF issued the Eight Special Recommendations to deal with the issue of terrorism financing. The continued evolution of money laundering techniques led the FATF to revise the FATF standards comprehensively in June 2003. In October 2004, the FATF published a Ninth Special Recommendations, further strengthening the agreed international standards for combating money laundering and terrorism financing-the 40+9 Recommendations. During 1991 and 1992, the FATF expanded its membership from the original 16 to 28 members. In 2000, the FATF expanded to 31 members, in 2003 to 33 members, in 2007 it expanded to 34 members, in 2009 to 35 members, and in 2010 to its current 36 members.

The FATF Forty Recommendations and Special Recommendations on Terrorism Financing.

The primary policies issued by the FATF are the Forty Recommendations on money laundering and the Nine Special Recommendations (SR) on Terrorism Financing (TF).

Together, the Forty Recommendation and Special Recommendations on Terrorism Financing set the international standard for anti-money laundering measures and combating the financing of terrorism and terrorist acts. They set out the principles for action and allow countries a measure of flexibility in implementing these principles according to their particular circumstances and constitutional frameworks. Both sets of FATF Recommendations are intended to be implemented at the national level through legislation and other legally binding measures.

The FATF issued the Forty Recommendations in 1990 and completely revised them in 1996 and 2003. The current (2003) Forty Recommendations require states, among other things, to:

- Implement relevant international conventions.
- Criminalise money laundering and enable authorities to confiscate the proceeds of money laundering.
- Implement customer due diligence (e.g., identity verification), record keeping and suspicious transaction reporting requirements for financial institutions and designated non-financial businesses and professions.
- Establish a financial intelligence unit to receive and disseminate suspicious transaction reports, and
- Cooperate internationally in investigating and prosecuting money laundering.

The FATF issued eighth Special Recommendations on Terrorism Financing in October 2001, following the September 11 terrorist attacks in the United States. The FATF issued a ninth Special Recommendation on Terrorism Financing in October 2004.

Since 9/11 the FATF has expanded its efforts to combat terrorist financing. FATF created eight additional "Special Recommendations" on terrorist financing in October 2001. Among the measures, "Special Recommendation VIII" (SR VIII) was targeted specifically at nonprofit organisations. This was followed by the International Best Practices Combating the Abuse of Non-Profit Organisations in 2002, released one month before the U.S. Department of Treasury's Anti-Terrorist Financing

Guidelines, and the Interpretive Note for SR VIII in 2006. In February 2008, the FATF published a report on terrorist financing typologies "to provide a contemporary snapshot of the ways in which terrorists raise, move and use funds", but it misrepresents the nonprofit sector as "compromised or complicit" with terrorist activities. The 2009 Handbook for Countries and Assessors outlines criteria for evaluating whether FATF standards are achieved in participating countries.

In February 2012, the FATF codified its recommendations and Interpretive Notes into one document that maintains SR VIII (renamed "Recommendation 8"), and also includes new rules on weapons of mass destruction, corruption and wire transfers ("Recommendation 16").

Non-cooperative countries or territories

Main article: FATF Blacklist

In addition to FATF's "Forty plus Nine" Recommendations, in 2000 FATF issued a list of "Non-Cooperative Countries or Territories" (NCCTs), commonly called the FATF Blacklist. This was a list of 15 jurisdictions that, for one reason or another, FATF members believed were uncooperative with other jurisdictions in international efforts against money laundering (and, later, terrorism financing). Typically, this lack of cooperation manifested itself as an unwillingness or inability (frequently, a legal inability) to provide foreign law enforcement officials with information relating to bank account and brokerage records, and customer identification and beneficial owner information relating to such bank and brokerage accounts, shell company, and other financial vehicles commonly used in money laundering. The FATF NCCT list is now defunct as the countries on it have made significant improvements in standards and cooperation.

The effect of the FATF Blacklist has been significant, and arguably has proven more important in international efforts against money laundering than has the FATF Recommendations. While, under international law, the FATF Blacklist carried with it no formal sanction, in reality, a jurisdiction placed on the FATF Blacklist often found itself under intense financial pressure.

Members

The FATF membership is currently made up of thirty-four member jurisdictions and two regional organisations. The FATF also works in close co-operation with a number of international and regional bodies involved in combating money laundering and terrorism financing. Associate members:

- The Asia/Pacific Group on Money Laundering (APG).
- Caribbean Financial Action Task Force (CFATF).
- The Council of Europe Select Committee of Experts on the Evaluation of Anti-Money Landering Measures (MONEYVAL) (formerly PC-R-EV).
- The Financial Action Task Force on Money Laundering in South America (GAFISUD).
- Middle East and North Africa Financial Action Task Force (MENAFATF).
- Eurasian Group (EAG).
- Eastern and Southern Africa Anti-Money Laundering Group (ESAAMLG).
- Intergovernmental Action Group against Money-Laundering in West Africa (GIABA).

Chapter - 14

Shredder of Human Rights

Hari Nath Rai was relentlessly pursuing his scoop of the century about false prophets and spurious secularists and to expose the proclivities and propensities of phony Jihad declared by over-hungry fanatics with covert support of seekers of minority votes. He was also an assiduous critic of the country's self idolising dictator Mandira Patel. This often landed him in detention.

Ironically, he was also petrified of pain inflicted to chasten him for criticizing the malpractices of the extra-constitutional emergency regime for its tyranny, corruption, opaqueness and flawed administration. But that did not deter him from pursuing the truth about the mindless carnage culture of perverted Jihad and soul-stifling brutality of the intoxication of power. It was the age of conspiratorial leadership, selfstyled peace-makers secretly hobnobbing with militants inebriated by lust, greed, covetousness and hatred against all those who did not fall in their multifarious traps. The ruthless Muslim and Hindu leaders were brainwashing the masses and playing snakes and ladders, snakes for the people and ladders for themselves.

"From the mixer-grinder of bigotry into the pressure cooker of political chicanery," Hari mocked while being grilled about the identity of the man who tried to assassinate the Pope during his explosive live face-to-face about fanatics of all faiths with the young chief editor of *Verdict Today*, the newspaper which prided itself on being free, fair, fearless, forthright and first.

"Who was the assailant?" grunted the chief of Research and Analysis Wing (RAW), Major Dial Singh, a cloak-and-dagger hireling of the shredder of human rights, Prime Minister Mandira Patel.

"I didn't see the hit man," Hari winced as the interrogator stamped on his toes with spiked boots; "How could I? I heard the report of a gun and pushed away the Pope with lightning speed. The bullet hit me instead, if you remember."

"Smart guy. Reflex action. Your ribcage! I've heard all that, dude. Who was the assassin? Speak up, bum, before I send you to the assembly line!"

Hari shuddered. He had enough experience of "the assembly line" to write a treatise on methods of torture routinely practiced by the sadist sycophants of the lullaby-voiced widow catapulted into the seat of Absolute Power by selfseeking knaves. Hari enjoyed stepping on the toes of militants and megalomaniacs. This time, he was at the receiving end from both presumptuous Islamic supremacists and minions of a populist leader who thrived on sloganeering and doubledealing with vote-bank leaders of all creeds.

"Who tried to assassinate the Pope?" repeated the green-eyed bully, the indefatigable chief of RAW, a close friend of a son of Mrs. Patel, the puppeteer. Hari was currently checking out on a rumor that a granddaughter of the Iraqi dictator Saddam Hussein was living in his private farmhouse outside the city.

"Not me, major, I swear," he laughed; "I was interviewing the Pontiff when I heard the report of a gun from behind, swirled around while simultaneously pushing the Pope away on the spur of the moment, the bullet hitting me in the ribcage."

"Incredible! And that was that, was it?" Singh grunted, reminding Hari of the sound of a faulty mixer-grinder.

"Reflex action," he said truthfully; "I don't know what happened after that as I passed out instantly and woke up in hospital."

"Did you see the hit man?" the cop asked.

"No. The shot was fired from the wings behind me. I suggest that you watch the TV replay of the interview to make sure," he said.

"Wise guy!" Singh sniggered; "How much have you been paid?"

"For what?"

"For concealing the culprit's identity!" the inquisitor boomed.

Hari laughed: "And for shooting myself by mistake?"

"You were there," Singh said, urging him to "quietly disclose the identity of the assailant, make the PM happy and forgive you for your unreasonable opposition to the great woman's authority. And help me wrap up the world's most sensitive case."

Hari shrugged: “I am not in the business of pleasing conscience-stranglers and harbingers of doom.”

“You are a bloody defiant snob, Hari. I hate you, buddy. Just make an admission about your links with Jihad,” he screamed; “I am being real nice to you, dude. You were talking to the Pope when this happened and you must have seen the hit man. Who was he? Tell me now before I take you to my favourite interrogation den and turn you over to the professional pain-inflictors you would never get accustomed to.”

Hari raised both hands in mockery: “All right. The Dalai Lama was also around. Why don’t you get him in.”

Highly-strung Mrs. Patel’s thick-skinned sycophant was livid. He had the reputation of never getting tired of causing agony to tight-lipped naïve idealists like Hari in her putrefying prisons designed for freedom-loving activists committed to fair play and the rule of law. Even so, the officer handed him over to routine third degree specialists who worked on his toes and lower back. “Take him to the pedicure unit,” thundered the inquisitionist.

But they gave up after two days when they were ordered to release him forthwith because New York-based Global Media Freedom Forum was “raising hell and threatening to launch a campaign to cut off all development assistance to India because of the government’s lackadaisical investigations into the attack on the Pope as well as outrageous mishandling of issues relating to governance and civil liberties”.

A full day in hospital and two in detention left Hari extremely debilitated and exhausted. But he didn’t go home and headed straight for the place where he often ended up whenever he was feeling low: Ivory Tower Lane. He made no secret of his personal dislike and professional abhorrence of “the lady who wanted to be both feared and loved like the goddess Durga while she was masquerading in Durga’s rampaging homicidal form”, Hari had written in his column on the day she assumed office in a *coup de grace* six months earlier.

Ever since that first pinprick, the politician who practiced politics without morals was at daggers drawn with the naïve idealist. She had enrolled many opportunists as her allies, among them his own managing director Karan M. Iyer, the saccharin-tongued son-in-law of the Parsi president of the holding company, Jal Wadia. The secretly adversarial MD described the chief editor as “the workaholic wine-guzzling womanizer!”

But the shrewd *Fortune 500* tycoon had full faith in Hari’s ability to turn obstacles into opportunities. Wadia’s success was largely attributed to meticulous picking of his teams in his multi-faceted business empire.

Hari was handpicked by him after he had the audacity to criticize Wadia Airways for its atrocious airline safety standards and poor in-flight hospitality in an article in *The Chronicle*, of which he was deputy editor at the time.

Wadia needed somebody like Hari to bring back *Verdict Today's* lost glory with his disarming charm, unflinching dynamism, fear-free result-orientation and team spirit. The tycoon sized him up thus to snub his son-in-law: "Unlike your gallivanting ways, son, there is no time for dalliance for the youngest editor in the country. Hari is playfully flirtatious, and cathartically flippant; unobtrusively intense, deceptively perceptive, and persistently intrusive…in other words, the ideal journalist hated by those who have something to hide."

Hari had no real interest in women and wealth though he was painted by gossip columnists as a flamboyant playboy. He loved work. And liquor was a necessary evil; he was unable to sleep well since childhood for reasons he was loathe to share with anyone. His detractors dismissed him as a schizophrenic upstart posing as a result-oriented idealist pampered by the feudal Zoroastrian tycoon and members of his family, including charming Roshan, slippery Karan's straight wife, and her brother Rustom.

Right now, Hari was in agony, having been released a short while earlier, nauseated by the acrid odour of rotting democratic values. He stepped out of a cab outside a pharmacy in Ivory Tower Heights, a building which in his view was possibly linked to Jihad, the Muslim holy war, the century's biggest scoop he was chasing and often getting into trouble with both the perpetrators and double-dealing oligarchs who failed to fulfill their solemn promise of curbing the scourge of fanaticism.

He hobbled into the pharmacy and was greeted by a distinguished-looking man smoking a hookah-shaped pipe:

"You look like a crushed carrot, Mr. Rai. What can we do for you?" The vibes Hari received inside the pharmacy made him feel strangely uneasy.

"That's a new one. How do you know me?" he winced, taking off one of his shoes; "Please fix my big toe." The man examined his toes and summoned a young man, who gave him an injection and dressed the crushed big toe without saying a word, mechanically, zombie-like. "Do you know me, sir?" he repeated feeling somewhat uneasy.

"Of course. Who doesn't after the attack on the Pope? Who shot the Pope? Did you see the hit man?" the man asked. Hari shrugged as he thought he felt a tremor anxiety in the man's deep voice.

"No, I couldn't see the hit man," Hari chuckled for no apparent reason, suddenly feeling light-hearted; "The Dalai Lama had the opportunity, but not the motive. But the Archbishop of Canterbury had both! Are you also a religious leader, sir?"

"I am Khalifa Hasham Ali," he said and gave him some pills. "Sit down and relax. You will be happy again in five minutes," he said condescendingly, sitting down next to Hari, who felt inexplicably repulsed by the man's proximity. "I am chairman of Ivory Tower Holdings."

Hari was examining the bandage on his toe, mutilated by the innovative interrogators forcing him to divulge the identity of the person who had taken a pot shot at the Pontiff as well as the names of his sources quoted in his column, *Below the Belt*, predicting indiscriminate attacks on Hindu temples and Christian churches in the near future.

Hari straightened and looked closely at Ali. Very fair, pointed nose, sparse rust-colour hair, the pipe. Opaque eyes. Handsome in a rugged sort of way. Around forty. Deep persuasive voice and acne-hardened cheeks. There was something indefinably revolting about him, like his sneer showing that he was drawing pleasure out of Hari's pain. Hari closed his eyes again, listening to the throbbing pain ebb out through the tips of his toes. The happy pills did their job in less than three minutes.

Presently, he felt a furtive movement near him and heard a whisper: "The device is placed inside the church, sir." He opened his eyes and saw a lad rush out of the pharmacy.

Hari thanked Ali, got up and limped cautiously towards the exit, crashing head-on into David John Crawford, Reuters South Asia bureau chief. They embraced, like long lost friends, throwing choicest Punjabi swear words at each other. David deliberately addressed him as *Harry* with emphasis because he hated any attempt to defile the pristine sanctity of his Hindu name with a Western affliction.

"The name is *not* Harry," he retorted, irritated by David's mock attempt; "Hari, as in hurry! How's your obscenely sexy mulatto wife?"

David laughed: " But she's not a Negro-Caucasian Mix, but half-Hindu-Muslim. She has left me, so I'm celebrating. Come to my bottle party this evening. Where have you been?"

"In the cooler! Those guys sure are inventive agony dispensers."

"What was it this time?"

"They pickled my toes."

"What for?"

"For shooting the Pope!"

"Can you pull a trigger?" David laughed; "Who was the hit man?"

"The Archbishop of Canterbury!"

"Seriously, why were you picked up this time? Was it your *Below the Belt* about Jihad, Sharia and rule of law?"

"Partly. They pulled the nail out of the dermis with a whitehot wrench and punctured my spine with a blunt spike."

"So you are truly spineless now," David laughed; "Why don't you go home, dude. You look terrible? Did you see the assassin?"

"My God, no! I need to go to a decent washroom in this city which has no cleanliness culture. And I need a drink! There's a swanky place on the top floor, Seventh Heaven. Excellent restrooms, the best, probably replicas of those in paradise."

"Expensive?"

"Don't worry, thanks to my bourgeoisie expense account," Hari grinned: "I have a gut feeling that this building is the current hub of Islamic Jihad. Something diabolical is being planned somewhere inside this elephant-shaped polyhedron. Perhaps the biggest story of the century!" he said.

David said: "Tell me more about it."

"We are up against two horrendous evils, Islamic Jihad on the one hand and a spurious secularist's tyranny on the other. We take on both simultaneously!" Hari said with such intensity that David was taken aback.

"You must be mad! We are mediocre wordsmiths, dude, not warriors," David snorted.

"Jihad being waged by a handful of Muslim fanatics is lunacy of the kind which will plunge the world into chaos and human beings will cease to be human whereas tyranny is the madness of one human being or a small coterie of oligarchs turning into a cannibalistic feast for packs of hungry wolves. We are up against two different but gargantuan breeds of terrorists which are dehumanising the civilised world which must not be allowed to take root," Hari said.

"Please explain, Mr. Crusader," David sneered.

"Islamic Jihad is one of the two scoops of the century I am working on," Hari said, lighting a cigarette, taking a neurotic puff, and crushing the lit end with his fingers; "Needless to say that Islam is a great faith which believes that the holy war or Jihad is conducted within, to purify oneself, kind of introspection as an exercise in self-improvement."

'And the second, Hari?" David asked

"The second? Yeah! State terrorism! Bad governance becoming the rule worldwide rather than the exception!"

Finally, Hari and David agreed to pursue the Jihad story together, subject to an official endorsement, in writing, by David's reticent headquarters in London snowed under by Vatican's complaints about the Anglican church's alleged conspiracy to denigrate the Holy See.

Hari said: "Jihad, the ill-conceived version of the holy war, aims to bifurcate the world into the to-be-affluent Faithful and their targeted non-Muslim Infidels, reversing the present world politico-economic and religious order in one horrendous swoop against Christianity and Hinduism as a first step.

Ivory Tower Heights is a major centre in planning and executing the systematic use of terror as a means of coercion and religious domination of the world. Globalisation of martyrdom. Three days ago, an attempt was made to kill the head of the Catholic Church, one of the most vibrant faiths."

"I know. I was present at the conference and filed comprehensive reports on the Pontiff's keynote address, his provocative face-to-face with you and my interviews with the Archbishop of Canterbury and the Dalai Lama. They said nothing about Jihad," David said.

Hari added: "There have been at least 1,270 terror attacks in the world since the recent ascendancy of Al-Qaeda, whose philosophy rejects national boundaries. This outfit, with national caucuses, is creating an elite global Muslim leadership to interact with Muslims around the world to revive the Caliphate, a much larger version of the Ottoman Caliphate which collapsed around 1924 because of economic stagnation in the original heart of militant Islam—the Arab world."

David's troubled mind seemed somewhere else.

But Hari continued: "The United States, Britain and some other European countries were blamed for the demise of the Ottoman Empire. The Arab population then totalled 260 million. The Ottoman trade networks were disrupted with the creation of new nation-states and the Middle East's diverse and growing economy was disrupted. For example, exports of even tiny Finland, a nation of merely five million, exceeded those of the entire Muslim world."

He added: "It was around that time that the Shia Ismaili leader, His Highness the Aga Khan, planted the seed of the idea of Pakistan in the mind of a brilliant young Indian barrister named Mohammed Ali Jinnah, who was later to become the founder of a new truncated state in

South Asia, East Pakistan at one end and West Pakistan separated by some two thousand miles of independent India. It's a long story, Pakistan rising from the ashes of the Ottoman Empire in a divide-and-conquer retribution for the woes of the Muslim world attributed to the scheming Anglo-American military-industrial-ethno-religious complex. Now, using Islamabad, Peshawar and Lahore as primary launching pads, Islamic Jihad is getting ready to attack its enemies—the US, Britain, Israel and Hindu India, Christians, Jews, Buddhists and Hindus everywhere. Plunder and pillage. Murder and mayhem. Death and destruction. *Dozakh* to *Kafirs* and *Jannat* to *Mujahids*."

David, however, seemed too preoccupied to pay close attention to the long narrative about Jihad. Hari shook his head: "What's your problem, David? I feel like narrating a tale about an impending cloudburst to a computer-generated deaf-mute apparition."

Finally, David spoke: "I'm in trouble over this Jihad leukemia, Harry! The attack on the Pope! Have you forgotten it in the haze of tranquilizers you habitually consume with Scotch?"

"I was there, remember, interviewing the Pontiff just after the Dalai Lama's address? And the bullet went right through my ribcage!" Hari said, peeved; "That gunshot became the catalyst of my personal holy war against Islamic Jihad. I am looking for the hit man. My gut feeling says the beast's lair is somewhere right here!"

"London is after me to make a final identification of the hit man because the Vatican continues to claim that the Anglican Church was involved in the abortive attempt on the Pope's life," David lamented.

"Can we discuss this tomorrow, I'm quite beat-up and need to get my spark back, if you don't mind?" Hari said and David agreed, adding that he wanted to stay on at the bar for a few minutes to check on any probable lead on Jihad.

Suddenly, David shot up from his chair and pointed to the large TV screen: "Look! That church. I was at the service there last Sunday. It's exploding! The Church of Holy Redemption near Rashtrapati Bhavan, the Presidential Palace."

"God! That lad in the pharmacy must have whispered about this church; stone by stone, there lies the debris of the nineteenth century colonial structure," Hari exclaimed.

David shouted: "Look, there's something more elsewhere!" The camera moved to a tree-lined neighbourhood, the screen showing scores of people running out of a temple and nearby houses from all directions converging on a cricket ground, and the voiceover: "This is the scene at the Hindu township of Dayalbagh, headquarters of the Radhasoami Faith. A part of this self-reliant Garden of the Merciful has been rocked by a series of explosions. Barely two miles from the Taj Mahal."

The voice went on: "Who could have conceived of this peaceful town as a target? Secular, serene, living in harmony with nature, mulberry trees and silk worms. Perhaps the most spiritual and morally upright community in the world, the Faith having a following of about two million globally."

David asked: "Why should a non-violent community be singled out for a brutal attack like this?"

"Precisely because it's harmless. Cowards fear retribution and non-violent neighbourhoods are the least hazardous for attackers," said Hari. "Who? We must expose the villains! I suspect that swine, Khalifa Ali!" David flared, pointing to a shadowy figure emerging out of a crescent-and-star doorway behind the bar.

"Khalifa means Caliph, which is the anglicized version of *khalifa*, meaning leader," Hari said; "Is this a coincidence or is this red-haired devil trying to revive the Islamic Caliphate?"

"There's certainly trouble wherever he goes. He was present at the religious conference where you were shot, Hari. Earlier, remember the Yehoodi Superstore blast in London last week? He was there! I saw him in Regent Street a few minutes after the nearby Oxford Street explosion. Look!"

The man was standing at the bar, walking stick in hand and unlit pipe in mouth. "Doesn't he look like Leucrota?" David asked.

"What's that?"

"Offspring of a hyena and a lioness with the worst traits of both." "Nonsense. The man looks like a teacher or some such."

"Believe me, Hari, he's evil, godfather of Jihad ! I heard him at an Islamic symposium in Oxford last week. His exact words were—'*If an eye for an eye leads to a world of the blind, so be it*'. Didn't you notice him at the Lotus Centre when the attempt was made to assassinate the Pope?"

"I can't remember," Hari said. He was still feeling low, not quite up to anything, feeling filthy, nauseated by the thought of the dirty cell and the stench of decaying corpses of human values in a democracy-bereft system. Besides, at that particular low point in his career, the challenge of reviving *Verdict Today* seemed to be beyond his enfeebled staying power. Even his ingrained resoluteness to save the 200-year-old institution was being shaken by pressures of the limits of human endurance. But his spirit was still intact and, with it, the passion to make *Verdict Today* the untarnished mirror in which humankind could see what it really looked like to itself despite the double-tongued deceit of the paper's managing director.

Parsi billionaire Wadia had drafted Hari as chief editor in the belief that the dynamic young man would breathe life into a gasping institution unable to stand up to an authoritarian regime and relentless competition from multi-media conglomerates.

Godfather of Jihad? What the hell! Listlessly, he took the elevator and started loitering while waiting for David, looking at knickknacks displayed by sidewalk vendors across the street. Unable to focus, he saw a Sikh extremist leader, Sant Nihal Singh Bawa, enter the pharmacy. The spurious saint had recently been appointed Home Minister by Mrs. Patel in order to appease him into mellowing his demand for an independent state for Sikhs.

Hari's blood boiled, his mind reverse-leapfrogging twenty years to the same spot on which he was now standing, visualising his own brother Krishna's brutal murder by two Sikh roughnecks right there because he was in love with the Sikh leader's daughter.

The bigoted creep must have ordered the hooligans to kill Krishna, kid Hari assumed at the time and still suspected, as the feeling of the supreme agony of helplessness enveloped him again. He was ten years old then and watched the killers plunge their unholy religious swords, *kirpans*, repeatedly into his body.

He wandered aimlessly along the sidewalk market, looking at the elephant-shaped structure. He saw anguish in one of the eyes of the jumbo and rage in the other, a furiously despondent rogue elephant. An impressive structure, complete with the tusks, seven-storied lair of hyenas. What was going on in there? David was still in there somewhere. A solitary Kwench aerated water van was parked outside the café in the no-parking zone. Similar to the vehicle which had dropped the two assassins twenty years ago.

Krishna had taken over the sidewalk shop after their father's death. Killed right in front of the shop as he waited for the girl he loved. In front of dozens of bystanders and two policemen, young Hari looking on, face to face with the indignity of the weakling, ashamed of his infirmity, the excruciating pain of helplessness still haunting him.

The Kwench van belonged to the Sant, the firebrand Sikh leader of the Khalistan movement, now seemingly mellowed, flowing *biryani* beard. What was he doing inside the pharmacy? The possibility of an unholy alliance between two unprincipled antagonists could not be ruled out. Hari was still wondering when David rejoined him, pointed to the building and snorted: "Strong evil vibrations all over!"

Hari stepped back hurriedly as he saw a girl running towards him with three men chasing her, all of them from the direction of Ivory Tower Heights. The girl's mini-skirt and translucent blouse were badly torn, revealing her ample bosoms and shapely legs, puffing, panting and shouting:

"Save me! Save me!"

She stumbled into Hari's arms, reeking of cheap liquor. The hooligans backed away as David moved threateningly towards them. "They were trying to rape me and make a movie in there," she screamed, pointing towards the beauty saloon next to the pharmacy. David hurriedly bought a pair of jeans and a top for the girl while Hari hailed a passing cab, pushing the girl in the back seat, signaling David to follow, himself sitting next to the Sikh driver.

"They were going to rape me and make a movie," she wailed, covering her face with her hands.

"Do you blame them, half-naked as you are? Even that Gandhi statue in the middle of the roundabout may be tempted to have a go at you," Hari mocked and David shuddered at the lack of genuflection shown for the mahatma.

"Stop making intemperate remarks about the father of your nation," he sneered.

The girl was affronted: "I am not that kind of girl. My name is Madhu, daughter of Mr. Kirpal Thapar, the industrialist. I just bought this outfit from a famous designer next to the parlor. I am participating in Urvashi Beauty Pageant being sponsored by Papa."

Her sobbing stopped. So did the cab, in the porch of Verdict Today House. Hari stepped out, asking David and Madhu to wait for a photographer.

Already waiting in his secretary's office was the larger-than life Dial Singh, his chief inquisitor earlier. .Hari sneered, making no attempt to camouflage his dislike of the domineering law-enforcer; "Please allow me to attend to a couple of urgent matters." His secretary, Mary Fernandez, had already served coffee.

David became extra-alert. "What brings the legendary crimebuster to the civilised world," he mocked, wondering if Singh had made any headway in his investigations into the attack on the Pope which might bail him out professionally for losing his own sources. "Have you been able to locate the two eyewitnesses to the assassination attempt, Mr. Singh?" he asked doubtfully.

The cop scowled: "No! Probably killed by the culprits, loudmouthed bums!"

"Bodies?" asked David.

"Not yet. We are still looking, Mr. Crawford. Don't pester me now!" Singh growled impatiently glaring at Hari who was giving instructions to his reporter Dev Bhalla: "Let's go, Mr. Rai. I'm getting late."

Hari snapped back: "I have just been released by you. Why don't you police leeches coordinate among your various amputated arms? I badly need a bloody bath to wash away police sins. What have I done now anyway, Mr. Singh," he said derisively."

David interjected: "May I make a call to London from your office, Hari, about your double detention in one day. Perhaps a world record."

Hari winked at David: "That's the end of your bottle party for me, buddy. Have a blast anyway!"

David asked Singh: "What's the charge, officer?"

"He is holding back information about the on-going terrorist attacks. If he is shielding someone, it may be serious, even treason."

Hari shot back angrily: "Goddamn you, Singh! Be thankful, I'm holding back information about *your* treachery because I have no evidence! Believe you me, I am seriously concerned about your highhandedness and perversions. But you don't have the bloody guts to silence me permanently, so you guys are doing your worst to soften me up! Once upon a time, I was colour blind, now my full vision has been restored. But you are still colour blind, Singh, like dogs who possess the admirable quality of faithfulness which tragically is lacking in you. Let's go, officer!"

Hari looked at Mary moodily chewing on a paper clip: "Don't worry, beautiful, garnish your dreams, everything is in place because there is a place for everything. That's the law of nature."

She stifled a sob. Hari added: "Call home and tell Usha to feed my Koel and to add a drop of honey in her water. I shall be back home by the evening." Turning to David, he grinned: "By everything I hold sacred, I will attend your bottle party in the evening, buddy." In the interrogation cell, Singh said: "You must be mad. What information do you have about me?"

"Nothing that you don't already know," he replied.

"What the hell do you mean?"

"Simple. Surely, I can't know more about you than you yourself, Mr. Singh," he said, grinning.

"Who tried to kill the Pope?" asked Singh.

"The Dalai Lama. May I go home now," he retorted.

"Why do you make life difficult for yourself by picking on powerful people?"

"I am a masochist, and I love drinking in solitary confinement," he said.

"Who is Koel?"

Hari laughed: "Scared of my tiny cuckoo bird, the singing black insurrectionist, symbol of the free spirit? Go get her, commissioner. She hates cages. Smuggled from Indonesia by me. Koel may be a Muslim because she comes from a country with the largest Muslim population in the world," Hari mocked.

"And who's Usha?" Singh continued, regardless.

"My sexy housekeeper, the explosive from Manipur. She's married to my cook. Will that be all? May I go home now? I must attend Mr. Crawford's party in the evening."

"Why do you have so many servants? You are single, aren't you?"

"Is that any of your business? My employer takes good care of my comforts! And I am required to give many parties."

"Mr Rai, I warn you! Tell me everything. Who told you about the terrorist attacks? What more are you concealing from the authorities? Fast, I can be a very dangerous man," Singh threatened.

Pain had returned to Hari's throbbing toe and back. A tornado of rage and disgust were churning his vitals. He looked at him scornfully. "Listen Singh, let's find out who is the more dangerous though I cannot handle firearms!" he yelled; "I am exasperated, buster. The sensitive information I have about you will be delivered to the Prime Minister if I don't return home in an hour," he half-bluffed without batting an eyelid.

"What do you have against me, big mouth?"

"You know well enough, officer, that you can't browbeat me. Meanwhile, a scheme is being hatched to assassinate Mrs. Patel and I will speak about it only to her. Tell her that I wish to speak to her tomorrow afternoon," he said coldly. Singh hurriedly went to his office to make the call to the PM.

"Tell Madam that plans are being made to assassinate her," he bluffed.

He also recalled overhearing someone utter one syllable when he was sitting in the pharmacy, the word "Jihad" was ringing in his ears. Linking the syllable to subsequent events meant a connection between the attack on the Pope, subsequent explosions and Ivory Tower Heights, specifically, the pharmacy and Ali. Even more mystifying was the Sikh leader's entry into the pharmacy. Could there be a chance of an unlikely alliance between militants belonging to opposing camps? Hari thought he must share his burden of thoughts with somebody. But who? Certainly not trigger-happy Singh. The PM? Logically, yes. But first things first. He must bluff his way out. He waited. Singh growled: "Well!"

"I will speak only to the PM. Personally. Make an appointment for me, tomorrow afternoon," Hari said firmly and closed his eyes, dismissing the super cop with an imperious wave of his hand. In the newsroom, meanwhile, Mary was close to tears when she failed to trace Karan, who was seldom available in an emergency. His secretary said he had gone out to meet someone in the Libyan Embassy. Mary contacted his wife, Roshan, who informed her unflappable father, who, in turn, instructed attorney Russi Modi to arrange bail.

Also in the newsroom, Dev asked Madhu to call her father and ask him to make an official report of her attempted rape to the nearest police station, which happened to be across the street from Verdict Today House. David concurred but Madhu declined with a delicate shrug of her dainty shoulders that sent a strangely pleasant tingling sensation through the young ace reporter's spine. "Coffee, miss?" he suggested; "At the scene of the crime." The girl nodded and Dev said: "Be my guest and let's walk to the café since I don't have a car." David suggested that they must first check out on her rape claim. Everything seemed aboveboard in the busy parlour. David was astonished to find his ex-wife Shanta Mitra attending customers at the next door Carnage Curves. He stormed into the boutique and confronted her: "Did you sell those sluttish rags to this girl?"

"What sluttish rags and who is this sexy dame?" she demanded. Madhu moved up defiantly and emptied a bag on the counter: "These rags, madam, you sold them to me this morning and took me to the parlour personally to that strange-looking man smoking a hookah beyond a hole in the wall."

David rushed out of the boutique and into the parlour, but found no hole in the wall. There was, however, a curtained door into a fully furnished bed-sitter which seemed like a knockdown movie set with cameras and lights. Sitting in the far corner on a plush couch was Ali, watching TV and contentedly puffing at a pipe attached to a hookah being refreshed by a puppy-eyed lad.

"Eyes!" David was struck by the opacity of Ali's eyes, no expression, no pain or pleasure. Frightfully fascinating looks: opaque eyes, rust-colour hair, pointed Kashmiri nose, Afghan freckles, coarse, taut acne-rough facial skin. David recalled his first meeting with him at an Islamic scholars conference in Oxford and the second time, a few minutes after the Oxford Street blast in London.

"What can I do for you, Mr Crawford?" Deep, slow mesmerizing voice of an accomplished soothsayer, the same he heard the previous week in Oxford, urging the west to adopt Sharia to curb lawlessness: "Deterrent punishment to offenders … if you cut off the hands of one thief, no one will dare steal in your neighbourhood. If an eye for an eye leads to a world of the blind, so be it. Allah *haafiz*! God be with the Faithful!"

David asked: "What punishment does your Sharia prescribe for a rapist, Mr Caliph?"

"Mutilation of genitals," Ali replied without batting an eyelid, ignoring David's hostile Caliph innuendo.

"This girl," David said, pointing to Madhu, "she says some hooligans tried to rape her right here this morning."

"Impossible!" countered Ali; "She must be hallucinating. Mrs. Crawford did bring her to the pharmacy earlier when the child was having an epileptic fit. Three pharmacy assistants brought her here and I gave her a heavy dose of barbiturates, left her to rest on that bed and returned to the pharmacy. I was later informed that she ran out through the parlour in a delirious state."

Madhu screamed: "This monster is a liar. He promised Madam Crawford that he would have me chosen Miss Urvashi and even telephoned Papa to give him the same assurance. Then he left after unleashing the three barbarian pharmacists on me!" David was perplexed. "I will be back, Mr. Ali," he said and beat a hasty retreat, fretting about his ex-wife's latest incarnation and the ultimatum from London about identifying the person who tried to shoot the Pope. At Police Headquarters, meanwhile, Singh left Hari in the cell and went away to his own office. Hari winked at one of the guards and started his introspection, planning strategies to break all barriers in his quest for excellence until he started getting apprehensive about the approaching darkness and sleeplessness in the cell which often turned him into an illnatured dyspeptic paranoid which forced him to reluctantly consume diazepam which helped him stay within the realms of normalcy in public.

Usha and Sheetal kept strict control of the dosage. He asked the guard to get some liquor, *any* liquor. The man already had a half-bottle of cheap whisky and took five hundred rupees for it.

"Alcoholism of a junkie is way better than the intoxication of power," Hari told the guard, who grinned blankly and pocketed the cash. However, he had no time to indulge in his favourite pastime of drinking in the solitude of detention to ward off the demon of depression and paranoia because his bluff worked on the psyche of an insecure leader scared of losing her grip on absolutism.

"Your appointment with Madam Prime Minister has been confirmed," Singh said, releasing him grudgingly. He reached home in double-quick time in an auto-rickshaw and went straight to Koel's barricade-free cradle. She cooed and performed a birdie rumba on her tiny yellow claws and flapping her velvety black wings as if thrilled to see her paramour: "I love you, cuckoo, free bird whose melody transcends barricades, borders, bondage." Usha went red in her face as Hari patted her tenderly on the shoulder and Sheetal, the eunuch butler, waltzed from one end of the room to the other. Prem Anand, the cook, face habitually drawn, rushed into the kitchen and brought a cup of steaming ginger-cardamom tea. "What's the news from your families in Manipur?" Hari asked the housekeeper and the cook, her husband. "The Manipur Liberation Army (MLA) has called for a state-wide general strike tomorrow if elections are not announced immediately," Usha said. Prem added: "The MLA has the support of China, Pakistan and Myanmar as well as of the Nepalese Marxists."

Hari made a face but said nothing. Instead, he scribbled a note and giving it to Sheetal, said: "Go to the offices of Pakistan International *JIHAD REDISCOVERED* 27 Airlines (PIA) and check on two look-alike European passengers expected in Delhi from Karachi."

He then dashed into the shower, feeling contaminated and wanting to throw up, spending more than an hour fumigating himself. After that, he sat down at his favourite antique desk he inherited from his first cousin Hira Lal Seth sentenced to death by the colonial government for being an arsonist. And he scribbled in long hand:

Again, I saw,
With my eyes
The stench of decay
Of human values.
I touched it and
Became unclean,
The lingering odor
Of suffocating souls.

And off he went with his driver Pande to David's bottle-party with three large bottles of Scotch, hobbled into the backyard, poured a large drink, rushed it through his parched gullet and said hello to no one in particular.

David tried to talk to him, but Hari was gazing fixedly at a white woman talking to Mary.

"What's *that*?" he asked, open-mouthed.

"That's the new American press attaché, C. Anne Spenser."

"Lead me to that stunning grace in simplicity in this day and age," he said, and floated towards her in a strangely oneiric manner.

Mary said: "Meet Mr. Rai, my boss."

"Pleased to meet you," said Anne, without extending her hand.

"Sand-bagged," whispered Hari, extending his hand: "Don't worry, absolutely hygienic, I've just fumigated myself completely."

Embarrassed, she took the proffered hand and giggled. His eyes lit up and he chanted: "Chimes at dawn on the banks of Ganges inside the Holy Trinity Temple." She looked at him, perplexed: "You do have a chip on your shoulder about the United States, Mr Rai."

He kept gazing at her as if in a trance. "Nirvana-like glow of a great soul on the face of a divine masterpiece," he murmured.

"Why do you hate America, Mr. Rai?"

He kept looking and said: "Wait! Your eyelash! Floating…here, it's landed on my palm, here, look, close your eyes, make a wish."

She laughed.

"Melody of a solitary snowflake tiptoeing down the slopes of Himalaya," he whispered.

She twittered again and blew into his extended palm. He sniffed, breathing in: "Divine! Sandalwood fragrance in Holy Trinity Temple at dawn."

She looked at him, quizzically: "I know about you, Mr. Below the Belt Rai. You do have a chip on your shoulder about the United States."

He said nothing, only smiled.

"Why do you hate America?" she demanded.

"I don't. The US thankfully is the only legitimate super power, a position it often arrogantly uses to prop up illegitimate regimes, the world's most vibrant democracy supporting tyrannies," he said.

"You have picked up one or two foreign policy miscalculations to base your habitual anti-American tirade," she exclaimed.

"You philanthropic Americans, madam, invariably back the wrong horse because of your obsession with balance of power. Example: India and Pakistan. You have supported successive despots in a country which should not have been created in the first place. Illegitimate regimes in an illegitimate country. That's your choice, Miss Spenser! Convince me!" He was angry and moved towards the bar, looking up at the cloud cover:

"Barefoot uncle moon frolicking with white clouds atop a fire-eating dragon descending, guffawing, confused, stopped by a giant two-horned spider weaving an intricate web, gobbling up the milky way...Give me a drink, please. Sorry, I've popped too many happy pills."

Anne burst out laughing: "Where's your uncle moon...it's overcast ... signs of a rainstorm."

"There!" he pointed; "That great bald eagle ... holding two doves in its claws perched atop the Olympic torch in the raised hand of the Statue of Liberty."

"You are drunk," she said softly.

"Say that again," he said looking at her dreamily.

A dozen pairs of eyes were watching the two.

A woman asked David: "Who's this handsome young man?"

"I am an alcoholic with a pickled big toe," Hari said.

Anne giggled.

"Don't do that so often, Miss. I feel like diving into that divine melody but I can't swim."

She giggled again.

"Chimes inside Holy Trinity Temple on the banks of the Ganges at dawn. One dip of immortality into those eyes and moksha."

"You must be Krishna's kid brother," the woman said.

He nodded: "How do you know my brother?"

"I am Neelam Bawa. My father had him killed," she said simply, gulping her drink, almost in tears, drunk, a graceful alcoholic.

Hari, dumb-struck, held her hand. Anne felt out of place, but David came to their rescue: "This clown saw your boyfriend murdered when you failed to show up twenty years ago."

"That agony of helplessness born out of infirmity is the most degrading experience of my life," he said; "Please meet me for dinner at my place tomorrow. Krishna left a last gift for you. Meanwhile, have a drink. I won't let you stumble. Make yourself miserable."

"That's cruel," Anne frowned.

"Bigotry," he said cryptically.

Just as David's party was beginning to get boisterous, the nearby Chanakya multiplex was rocked by a massive blast. Most of the guests at the party refilled their glasses. One of them said the Biblical classic *King of Kings* was being screened at the cinema.

"Jihad seems to be everywhere," David exclaimed.

"Muscle, money, marketing," said Anne.

"And madness! Explosions reported in more than a hundred theaters worldwide, all showing the same Biblical classic, the brutality condemned by the Vatican as an undisguised attack on the Holy Bible," Hari said. David added: "All suicide bombers! Internationalised martyrdom!"

"The world is up against forces of evil, corruption, bigotry and political chicanery. Let's declare our own holy professional war against Jihad! Cheers!"

"Cheers!" responded David, Anne, Mary and Neelam.

"Amen! Holy war against unholy Jihad!" declared Hari. Anne applauded.

Chapter - 15

Hellfire and Houris

There were too many loose ends for Hari to tie-up into his beyond doubt scoop of the century he was chasing about Jihad. He was also having difficulty extracting himself out of the quicksand of self-doubt about his ability to cope with the onslaught of an elusive polyhedronic evil force on the rampage for the obliteration of all non-Muslims.

Mercifully, he slept well the previous night, soothing thoughts of the classy American girl's fluty twitter acting as a divine lullaby. "Massacre, mutilation, misery! Snakes and ladders, oblivion for infidels, dizzying heights for Allah's indoctrinated crusaders. Islam is projected as a theology-based ideology by Al Jihad. Mosque is the base of Islamism. It is in the mosque where Islamic fanatics propagate their messages. There's nothing holy about militant Islam's bloodlust," Hari told David, who had become equally obsessive about Jihad, largely because it became imperative for him to urgently produce an expose about the attack on the Pope to put an end to the snide remarks being made by the Vatican linking the Archbishop of Canterbury with the assassination attempt.

"For my own emancipation, I must nail Ali, the catalyst for the revival of the Ottoman Caliphate, who promises *houris* and *Jannat* to *mujahids* and ordains hellfire and annihilation for *kafirs* and infidels," David said.

He had no evidence against him, but he saw him at the International Symposium on Saint Francis Xavier at New Delhi's Lotus Centre at which the Pope was the keynote speaker, and where a hit man had tried to kill the Pontiff. David had also seen Ali a few yards from London's Yehudi Superstore after it blew up in flames a few days ago. A day earlier at Oxford University, David heard him addressing an international Islamic scholars symposium, when he proposed the reestablishment of the Caliphate for the entire Muslim world and national caucuses even in countries having a single Muslim. "The man has a diabolical plan to militarize the entire Islamic world and to spread the Faith," he told Hari: "Call it the sixth sense of a Piscean psychic."

Ali was already on Hari's mind in any case as a credible threat to Prime Minister Mandira Patel. But he knew it would be difficult to convince the ruthless usurper of power during his afternoon meeting. Besides, that day, he did not want to be detained because he had a sort of date with the woman he desperately wanted to meet again, and again.

He seemed somewhat relaxed that morning, having slept through the night, thoughts of the American girl acting as an ethereal lullaby soothing his mind, inexplicably less disturbed by the prospect of an impending world war of religions.

The memory of the attack on the Pope three days ago served as a traumatizing reminder about his limitations as a journalist just when he was in the thick of a breakthrough interview with the serene icon of the Catholic world. The fact that Vatican investigators, led by a cardinal, had also drawn a blank so far was not a consolation for Hari because he believed that a much bigger conspiracy was behind the accidentally aborted attack on the supreme head of the Catholic Church.

David had his own reasons for his skepticism about the civilised world's inability to cope with the coming crisis because powerful nations were dominated by religious bigots and cowards devoting their energies on matters perceived by their myopic think-tanks to be more serious. Particularly disturbing for him was the media's lopsided projection of the incident as no more than an inter-denominational anachronism. Much more than everything else, David was under pressure from headquarters in London to produce a credible story relating to the abortive attack on the Pope to show that the Anglican Church was in no way linked to any parochial campaign to belittle Rome. Some of his bosses in London were discretely victimising him for being close to Indians in his lifestyle largely because of his failed marriage to an Americanised Bengali girl of dubious morals.

Indian media's coverage ranged from blaming Hindus for the attack to criticising the security regime without coming to grips with a semblance of reality. David was also confused, his mind having been influenced by his logic-propelled premonition about opaque-eye Ali.

At the other end of the city, Anne was cautioned by her boss, American Ambassador Dan Miller, against hobnobbing with Hari; "He is a womaniser and good copy for gossip columnists." Out of the blue, as it were, she thought, wondering if her former professor could read her mind. “He is also the brother of the country’s Air Force chief,” she retorted.

“But he is the rebel in the family and detests Air Chief Marshal Rajinder Nath Rai. In any case, that’s got nothing to do with your job, which is to favourably project American policy, not to interpret it, through foreign media, not to be chummy with dubious media men,” he said.

“What’s our policy on terrorism?” she asked.

“What kind of naive question is that? Of course, we have the finest counter-terrorism network and we are making speedy headway towards achieving our objectives,” he said, uncertainly.

“Why have we issued a US visa to a Khalifa Hasham Ali?” she demanded.

“He’s an eminent scholar and a successful entrepreneur.”

“I have heard some disquieting reports about Ali,” she said.

“Rumors?” Miller taunted.

Anne winced.

“Listen, Anne, please don’t misunderstand me. You have great future in the foreign service. This is your first important posting. Make the best of it, my girl. You will go very far. But be careful of charlatans like Hari Rai. Are you sleeping with him?”

“God! I’ve only just met him! What have you got against him?”

“I think he is too critical of US arms aid to some of our allies in Asia and Africa.”

“What about his consistent campaign against Jihad and our discordant threats against religious militarism?”

“I don’t think US policy is inconsistent with our overall objectives. Of course, we have always condemned such groups as Lashkar and Al- Qaeda, but…”

“But we still provide military aid to countries which are known to harbor Muslim terrorists who are openly against American principles of social justice and we know that such aid is misused,” Anne said, belligerently.

“Does your friend Hari know what the Prophet Muhammad meant by Jihad?”

“I don’t really know. I have met him only once and at a party,” she protested.

“The Prophet wanted his followers to conduct a holy war against injustice and oppression and against those who rejected the truth. He said 'holy is the warrior who is at war with himself'. Jihad can only be fought and won within, a kind of self-refinement, the eternal quest for excellence, the Holy Grail of Islam," said Miller.

Anne said: "Exactly what Hari told David. Islam does not sanction destruction of places of worship. After achieving perfection, a true Muslim donates all his belongings to the poor and becomes *Abdal*, the changed one, the Muslim equivalent of the Christian Enoch, who walked with God."

"Is that what your friend said?" Miller asked, surprised.

She nodded, all the time perplexed by Miller's apparently excessive interest in her career and his obviously subjective narrow-minded disapproval of a transparently sincere Indian journalist. She knew Miller was not a career diplomat but a political appointee who had often been bypassed for a much higher posting such as Permanent Representative to the United Nations Security Council. He was a highly-respected international relations theoretician who genuinely believed that the rich countries of the northern hemisphere must stop exploiting the countries of the poor South. Washington respected him as an academic but regarded him as a confused liberal unsuitable for a politically high-profile appointment. He was considered ideal in a cosmetic assignment such as Ambassador to India, a position in which he could do little harm to US interests in any of the key areas of socio-political and super power imperatives. India turned out to be an extraordinary setting for the thoughtful-looking ponderous Humanities professor with snowy hair and idealistic articulation of the American dream of egalitarianism. He was an instant hit as guest speaker at academic conferences in almost all Indian institutions of learning.

Miller wanted Anne to be his personal press officer to project his expansive excursions into a hands-across-the-sea approach to making a lasting impression on Indian academia of America's quest for excellence in arts and literature.

Under normal circumstances, Anne would have loved to play the role of a non-political propagandist to strengthen US-India socio-economic relations in contrast to playing the textbook role of a professional media relations manager cleverly doctoring the flow of information to project a positive image of the US.

She resented Miller's blatantly tactless attempts to condition her private life. His tirade against Hari seemed particularly offensive as she felt strangely attracted to the disarmingly outspoken clown with the faraway look in his drowsy eyes. Hari was perhaps the only media person who questioned the appropriateness of Washington's choice of a Cloud Nine humanist not having the foggiest about Ground Zero as envoy to India at a time when extremists were launching a global Jihad.

Halfway across the city, Hari was dreaming about Anne at a time when he should have been preparing for his crucial meeting with the leader who, as David told him, had the cunning of a fox to spot traps, the grunt of a lioness to frighten wolves and the lullaby voice of caring mother to hypnotise the masses.

"But I am neither setting a trap nor am I a wolf. Why should I feel nervous about my meeting with her? I must forewarn her. A concerted effort is being made to bisect the world into the Faithful and the Infidels," Hari told David just before leaving for the PM's residence, hoping he would again bluff his way out of a tricky situation.

However, he found himself strangely unable to concentrate on anything except the melodious aroma of the organic American woman he met at David's party whose subdued laughter seemed to penetrate his soul like the echoing serenade of a mountain stream zigzagging through the valley of flowers.

"I want to talk to her," he told David.

"What are you going to tell her?" David asked, thinking he was talking about the PM.

"I will listen to the rays of the sun," he whispered dreamily.

"And she will slap a permanent ban on the rag you call a newspaper," David warned.

To his surprise, Madam was more than receptive to Hari's warning about Jihad, but countered by saying that his fears about Muslim fundamentalists being on the threshold of victory were exaggerated.

"There are heathens in all faiths who habitually misinterpret Nature's laws and twist scriptures to hoodwink their gullible followers and to deceive their victims. They are the deceivers. We are their intended victims," said the PM.

"*You*, madam, are the target," Hari said.

"When? How soon?" she asked.

"Sooner or later."

"Levity will get you nowhere, young man!"

"My suggestion, madam, may seem farfetched, but it's worth looking into seriously. Khalifa's real name is Massey Dujjan, corrupted from the Persian Massih ad-Dujjal, the imposter Messiah, who, according to Islamic belief, is to appear before Qayamat, to wage a holy war against all Infidels, travelling around the world, causing havoc wherever he goes and preaching falsehoods."

"A brilliant new twist to *Arabian Nights*," she mocked.

"He is the last of thirty Dajjals predicted in Hadith. He has brought the gifts of paradise for holy warriors, the mujahids, and arsenal of hellfire against kafirs," he continued regardless.

"What gifts?" she asked, raising an imperious eyebrow.

"All pleasures associated with the Seventh Heaven, such as virgin maidens or houris and young lads," he said.

"Why the lads?"

"For the homosexual mujahids, madam," he grinned.

"How thoughtful, also taking care of perverts! What about eunuchs?" she asked derisively, hinting about Hari's eunuch butler Sheetal.

He winced.

"Quite a busybody, your majordomo," she pressed on; "There's a serious complaint against him of spying for the Special Branch."

"That's not true," he protested.

"He was caught snooping around inside the offices of Pakistan International Airlines," she said.

"Right, I had sent him to check on some arrivals and departures Harmless routine stuff."

"Well, he's being detained by airport police. I shall have him released if you tell me about your routine gibberish since your butler seems to be deaf-mute," she demanded.

He showed his annoyance by glaring at her: "Have him released immediately, madam. Hold me because he was working on my orders." "You really are a hot-tempered young rebel. Your turn will soon come. Tell me about your so-called harmless inquiries."

"Well, madam, if you must know, two professional hit men left Karachi a few days ago and my man was deputed to check passenger manifests of incoming PIA flights. They are the notorious twins Jim and Tim and they travel only on major assignments."

"Well?" she asked sternly.

"This time, you may be their target, madam."

"Are you sure?"

"No. But it's a wake-up call for your pretentious Intelligence Bureau, madam. These two professional assassins have been trained in South Africa. They are White mercenaries, not Pakistanis, who spent several weeks in Peshawar with the Inter-Services Intelligence (ISI) of Pakistan," Hari said looking straight into her twitching eyes.

"What makes you so certain?"

"Candidly, I don't know for sure. But I won't take any chances because of their reputation."

"What reputation?"

"The twins are precision artists, madam. I am surprised your overrated spies have not briefed you about them," he mocked.

"Who has hired them?" she asked.

"I'm not sure. My source overheard a couple of guys outside Parliament House, madam," he said.

"Who's your source and who are the two guys he overheard?"

"Your new Home Minister was seen talking about Jim and Tim to someone sitting in a car."

"Sant Nihal? Impossible!" she exclaimed; "Who's your source and what exactly did he overhear?"

"Madam, I have told you what I have learnt. And my source will remain anonymous," Hari said defiantly.

"Tell me, Rai, why are you always on a collision course with me?" She seemed determined to make him pay for his fearless opposition to her.

"I perform my duties honestly, madam," he said, avoiding a head-on confrontation because he had invited Anne over for a get-together with Neelam and some others. She must have sensed his reluctance to engage her in a battle of wits.

Pressing home her ascendancy over the impertinent swashbuckler, she asked: "Why are you so keen to foil any attempt on my life?"

"Simple, madam. You are the symbol of State, for whatever it's worth, and I am a vibrant part of that captive State," he smiled.

"Don't try to be cheeky. I agreed to see you because you told Dial Singh that my life was in danger, what information do you have?"

"None, madam."

"Let me tell you something, young man ... *your* life is in danger right now. I can have you shot dead and report an accident." She was livid.

"You can do nothing of the sort, madam. If I don't reach my office in the next twenty-five minutes, our correspondents worldwide will report that you have detained me because you have something to hide about the attempt on the Pope's life and to pre-empt disclosures about a member of your Cabinet being a comrade of Taliban," he bluffed, getting up defiantly.

Flustered, she exclaimed: "Sit down and tell me what you know."

"I have no idea if the twins have arrived in New Delhi. My man may have found out, but he will say nothing to your interrogators, madam. Let me talk to him. I assure you that I shall never withhold any information concerning the security of the State, but I will not divulge the identity of our sources," Hari said looking straight into her eyes.

The PM abruptly changed gears and switched to his personal life:

"Why don't you live with your brother?"

"My company provides me with a huge house and all other amenities."

"Like a eunuch butler, a pretty housekeeper, cook, driver, watchmen and unlimited entertainment allowance," she taunted.

He nodded.

"Why don't you get married and settle down. That will mellow you down."

"Thank you, madam. I think I have found the girl I would like to settle down with, but don't know her plans."

"That pretty American press attaché, is it?"

"So, you have informers everywhere, madam," he smiled.

She grinned: "It won't be easy. She's an heiress, her mom is politically ambitious and dad an alcoholic."

Hari kept quiet.

"So you are now proving that you decidedly are an Anglo-American stooge. Why don't you find a domesticated Indian girl to settle down decently instead of acting as a pretentious rebel for the sake of glamour."

He still said nothing, his mind focused on his presumed date with the most soulful woman in the world with mocking almond eyes, the whitest teeth, a twitter like a temple chime and exuding the fragrance of a sandalwood plantation.

"Make up with your big brother, the country's greatest fighter-pilot, and give up journalism." She was clearly trying to provoke him into committing an indiscretion. But he continued to grin.

"You should be proud of him, a national hero who won the highest gallantry award when you were a thumb-sucking toddler," she went on.

"Thank you, madam, I am proud of Big Brother's gallantry. The day he was awarded the Param Vir Chakra (PVC), our middle brother, an ordinary sidewalk garments vendor, was killed by men hired by that spurious saint who is now your Home Minister, madam, but Big Brother was ashamed of being seen to be related to us humble folk."

"So, that's why you want to implicate the saintly Sikh leader! What proof do you have against him?" she asked.

"Only that he is the father of the woman who loved my slain brother," he said angrily.

She shrugged, her eyes twitching thoughtfully. Hari knew she had the information she could use against the Sikh, who was anyway a compromise appointee to her handpicked Cabinet. He heaved a sigh of relief when she let him go without further ado.

His driver Pande, alert behind the wheel in the 7 Race Course Road parking lot, told him that David and Anne were waiting across the street outside the Flying Club along with some American and British media persons, providing another excuse to rival newspapers to paint Hari as an Anglo-American stooge, an accusation he found beneath contempt to deny. Hari was surrounded by the curious media persons. But Anne stood aloof as he could focus only on her smiling almond eyes and the infant rainbow glistening through her wind-swept honey-coloured hair.

"Well?" David asked finally.

"An entirely cordial meeting held at my request," he said aloud.

"Well?" said David again.

"The Prime Minister talked like the spinsterish widow she is, about match-making, gallantry and family harmony. She did not seem entirely convinced by my exposition of hellfire, martyrdom and heaven." He was visibly flustered because of the way in which Anne was gazing at him, a half-smile which said something he failed to understand. Perhaps she wanted to say something he wanted to hear as he saw a faint tremor on her lips.

He took one hesitant step towards her. She stiffened. He froze, torn between hope and doubt. He tried to move towards her but his legs became too heavy to lift his feet. Abruptly, he blurted out: "Your dress is an instrument of delightful torture," he said tremulously.

"Thank you," she said simply.

"Let's all meet at Seventh Heaven in half-hour."

He heard her twitter, and looked at her uncertainly. It didn't sound like a chime this time. After what seemed like an eternity, she hissed mischievously: "Living dangerously, *Harry*?"

"Hazards of the profession," he said tremulously.

"Aren't you scared?"

"Terrified. Of pain and discomfort."

"Of death?"

"No. I've been there. Had a fleeting taste of afterlife."

"How?"

"Drowned in river Jamuna in spate. Can't swim."

"Courage?"

"Bravado."

"Ambitious?"

"Audacious."

"What do you think of Jihad?"

"Carnage."

"Are we going to spend our lives in monosyllables?" she asked.

"Will you be my first real date, tonight?" he said.

She laughed. He closed his eyes, enjoying the symphonic rendition of an orchestra of flutes above white clouds. A dozen pair of clapping hands abruptly brought them crashing back on terra firma.

"I would like you to be my guest at the most disgusting place on earth," he said.

"Where?"

"Seventh Heaven."

"Enemy territory! Exciting venue for a first date."

"Shall we proceed to the hyena's dugout? In my car. I will act as your ladyship's chauffeur," he said.

"And the driver?" she asked.

"Off for the rest of the day from his tough duty," he said, opening the door of his BMW for her and saw her glide gracefully in, gently closing the door and pulling the seat belt with a single motion."

"You are an atrocious driver," she said as the car nearly missed an indolent cow. They arrived safely though and he parked the car in front of a sidewalk stall opposite Ivory Tower Heights. "Would you mind if I get a small gift for you as a first-date token?"

"How thoughtful!"

He purchased a pair of silver anklets from a young vendor and she accepted the gift quietly. In the lobby, she sat down briefly on a chair and fixed the anklets. He grinned appreciatively and she twittered. Inside the elevator, she whispered: "Negative vibes."

He nodded: "Undeniably repulsive."

"And expensive, I'm sure," she said, as he pulled a chair for her at a table near one of the windows overlooking the terrace.

"Revoltingly expensive. Let's order. But something to nibble first," he said beckoning a passing waiter and glancing at the menu. "Devil's Delight, please," he told the young waiter; "Plenty."

"Yes, sir," said the lad, about 20, green blazer, zombie eyes.

"You must be rich," she said.

"A comfortable coolie enjoying bourgeoisie perks. Not wealthy. Don't worry. The others will also be here soon."

"What's Devil's Delight?" she asked.

"House special, the menu says." Soon, the lad brought a sizzling dish; chicken wings. He took one. She took another.

"Delicious!" they exclaimed, together.

"This waiter reminds me of Colombian drug-runners," she said softly.

"Look! There are many more like him, right here, walking landmines!"

She looked around and saw a number of similarly-attired boys serving customers.

"Trainee suicide bombers," he whispered.

"How does anyone train suicide squads?"

"Haven't the foggiest. Indoctrination perhaps. Mujahids. Taliban. Madrassas. Hate campaigns."

David walked in casually, pulled up a chair and pushed aside the wings.

"Don't," he warned; "marinated in poppy seeds, rock salt and black salt. Bliss in a moment! Addiction in five days!" "Isn't there a law against such outlets.'

"Must be," Hari mocked; "The good news is that David and I are aware of the offensive being launched and the hypocritical tirade against terrorism by flat-footed world leaders, but wait... Ali is coming this way—huge ear-to-ear smile, hyena baring its molars..." David said: "Everything will turn out well. Eventually."

"Emperor of wishful thinking," Hari laughed, Anne stifled her twitter as she watched Ali pull up a chair next to her.

"Welcome to Seventh Heaven, Miss Spenser, Mr Crawford, Mr Rai," he said; "Very pretty, the anklets, miss. How are you feeling now, Mr. Rai?"

"Happy. Do you own this place, Mr Ali?"

"I'm chairman of Ivory Tower Holdings."

Hari thought he saw a triumphant glint in his inscrutable eyes. "What happened to Sant Nihal Singh Bawa?" David asked.

"He's the President and CEO."

Hari suddenly remembered Neelam: "I must pick her up before seven. Wait for me, please, Anne...David. Sorry, Mr Ali, I have a date with your CEO's daughter."

"A double-date, Mr Rai?"

"Living up to my reputation as a philanderer, Mr Ali... Do you mind, Anne?" he blinked, she smiled and he strode out.

David took over: "Where are you from, Mr Ali?"

"Afghanistan, Kashmir, Syria. You?"

"London."

"And Miss Spenser?"

"San Francisco," she said.

"Great! I'm planning a trip there."

Anne shuddered: "Business trip?"

"Sort of. To acquire real estate for setting up an institute," he said.

"What kind of institute?" asked David.

"Fatima Institute of Advanced Islamic Studies."

"Fatima ... your daughter?" David mocked.

He retorted: "Prophet Muhammad's daughter. I'm not married."

"Has a site been selected?" asked Anne.

"Dolores Park. Ideal for an open-air Islamic university, a high-tech theological *madrassah* incorporating the highest standards of a Catholic seminary and the finest armed forces training establishment in the west," he said.

"The notorious gay district of the city," she mocked.

Hari and Neelam walked in with an exaggerated display of arm-in-arm lovebird familiarity: "Meet your partner's alcoholic daughter, Mr. Ali."

"Hello," Ali said sternly, grabbed his walking stick, got up from the chair, glanced coldly at all four of them and hobbled away through the ornamental crescent door into his Penthouse Heaven.

"Who's that creep? Get me a drink, kid," Neelam lisped.

"Sure," he said and ordered drinks for all as Anne looked admiringly at Neelam: "You are a very beautiful woman … so graceful, so ladylike!"

Hari said sharply: "So drunk! She's drowning and you're describing the lake."

The drinks came and Neelam fumbled with her glass with a shaking hand, tried the other shakily and spilled the drink. "Life's too short to be drowned in regrets," Hari said, beckoning a zombie and placing another order.

"That's harsh!" Anne said testily, "Cheers!" Neelam said, raising her empty glass and suddenly flinging it away towards the bar counter: "What's dad doing in this hellhole!?"

"He owns the joint," David said.

Hari started feeling sorry for the woman who could have been his sister-in-law, "the girl who loved my brother and betrayed by her own father's murderous duplicity, a vibrant young beauty full of life afflicted by the tyranny of loneliness and forced to live in virtual widowhood with her lover's killer," he said.

"Her purposelessness compounded by self-pity," added Anne.

"You guys have got it all wrong," Neelam said belligerently. Her big black eyes blazing, she exclaimed: "You high and mighty Rais have absolved yourself of all guilt, haven't you!"

No one spoke. She added: "You saw the killers, kid, didn't you? And you told Big Brother, didn't you? What action did you take? Just abandoned me when I was pregnant, right?"

Hari was thunderstruck: "I never really looked at it that way. Really! Bloody coward! I am. And presuming to take on Jihad! A spineless infidel masquerading as custodian of humane sensitivities!" He moved over towards the edge of the roof and leaning on the parapet, he looked up at the clear sky wistfully: "Some pranksters have drilled so many holes in the heaven's floor," he told Anne, pointing to the sky.

"Let's go get lost in that void between a punctured paradise and the pulsating crowd of self-inflicted indignities here in the global hellfire," he said.

Anne looked at him balefully: "Are you scared of hellfire?"

"I think I will never be immune to the fear of agony, but I would sure like to tame it." There was steel in his voice.

"We have only just met and already I feel I can trust you more than anyone else," she said.

"I am flattered. That Sikh! I don't think Neelam knows how deep her dad is into this back-stabbing confrontation between blood-thirsty terrorists and the power-hungry tyrant.

"Are you always so intense, Hari?"

"Occasionally," he said, turning back to look at Neelam moodily: "A pathetic victim of the terrorism of theology-ism and hollow middle-class morality."

"What plans do you have for her?" she asked.

"I don't know. She has a nineteen-year-old daughter. My brother's child. I feel so terribly guilty," he said and lit a cigarette, trying to think, shrugged and crushed the cigarette with his fingers and threw it on the floor.

"Hari, you are so overwrought. Let's go for a drive … to relax … how far is your Holy Trinity Temple? That might bring back your sanity," she taunted.

He brightened: "Great idea to salvage a ruined first date!"

"Can we make a pact?" she said.

He looked at her quizzically: "Close your eyes and feel the profound melody of the void you just described. Only the two of us, on the banks of the sacred river inside the Holy Trinity Temple. In the arms of the prettiest Houri … perfect escape from hellfire. What's the pact?"

"That we meet again tomorrow, at your house," she said.

"Sure! Let's go. I know just the place …two hours drive, we shall be there by nine. Vegetarian dinner, booze in the car and surreptitiously along the banks of the sacred river, near the basement dungeons where Lord Krishna was born."

"I love intemperate devotees," she giggled.

"Let me first do something about the daughter of the bogus Sikh saint." Back on the table, Neelam was still sulking and David was trying to humor her. Hari held both her hands and looked into her eyes.

"Vengeance!" he said expansively; "I am with you, sister, all the way!" Neelam finished her drink in one gulp, grabbed Hari's collar and lisped: "Explain, kid."

"All four of us here are witnessing the most treacherous chapter in human history in the making and you, sister, have been a victim of the fanatics and living with Krishna's killer for twenty years," Hari said,

She flared: "I have never regarded that killer as my husband! I was pregnant, Krishna was killed and Papa arranged my marriage to conceal my shame from his hypocritical high society's middle-class value system!"

"Good night, I detest self-pity. See you tomorrow… let's go, Anne. I'll take you to my most favorite place in the world. You must meet my godmother, the River Jamuna … I died in her lap sixteen years ago and plopped out of her pulsating womb after a short while, following a brief blissful *moksha* in afterlife," he said.

"Do you expect me to believe this?"

"No," he replied.

"Then?"

"Apart from my schoolmates who saw me drown, no one knows about my unforgettable experience. I just had the urge to tell you and don't care if you don't believe."

"Aren't you a bit abrupt in your manner?"

"Sorry. I'm a private person, so I resent if I'm doubted. Believe me I've experienced the most horrible death—the agony of a helpless non-swimmer being swallowed up by an irate river, and mercifully a nirvana-like re-emergence following total surrender to the void of enlightened nothingness, what the Dalai Lama calls *shoonyata*, Swami Vivekananda's zeroism, the invisible void within and as a part of *shrishti* or cosmos."

She was moved. "Must have been agonising."

"Certainly not the best way to die and decidedly a memorable comeback from the dead at the very spot where newborn Krishna's biological father crossed the Jamuna to carry the infant to his foster parents."

"How exciting," she said.

He suddenly brought the car to a halt to give way to a speeding vehicle and made a note of its registration number.

"Would you like to make a brief stop at the prison where Krishna was born?" he asked and she nodded.

"Sleepless, restless stranger who keeps sipping from a glass and eating candy ..."

"What are you talking about?"

"The man in the back seat ... of the car which just overtook us ... custom-made Mercedes-600, only one of its kind in Delhi ... everyone knows the owner..."

"Who?"

"Bollywood super star Mazhar Khan. What's he doing on this road?"

"Do you know him?"

He nodded: "Professional hazard."

"Meaning, he's a Muslim and you hate him."

"I don't hate Muslims. Islam is a great faith. He just happens to be a Muslim and is an overrated pompous ham actor."

"But an overwhelming majority of Indians love him," she said.

"Forget it, let's get going ... to the spot where millions long for one dip of immortality."

But he headed first for the birthplace of Lord Krishna, "the multifaceted incarnation of Lord Vishnu", as he said; "ISKCON, the International Society for Krishna Consciousness, is inspired by his wartime philosophy of total commitment to righteous duty contained in *Bhagavad Gita* as well as his personal lifestyle."

Just ahead was a massive procession of saffron-clad Hare Krishna devotees, chanting and ululating, moving slowly towards the ancient palace-prison-temple above the now-holy basement dungeons of a mythical evil king, Lord Krishna's maternal uncle. Thousands of men, women and children, brown, white, black were moving forward: "Multi-coloured secular symphony in motion," Anne said.

"I'm afraid we'll have to walk all the way," he said. He could not find any parking on the narrow road in Mathura, so he reversed towards the Bharatpur bird sanctuary across the national highway and managed to park next to Khan's car, saying: "What's this creep doing here?"

Both seemed ill-at-ease, their first real date, alone, and the conversation focused mainly on Jihad and a passing mention of a film star.

"You don't mind walking, do you?" he said.

"Love it," she said.

"Actually, I hate driving in the mad Indian traffic."

"Me too."

"Oppressive July weather," he said, looking at the sky.

"Holes in the heaven's floor," she twittered.

He laughed; "Ice … breaking the ice … it's hard … very hard. I like your company … would like to have you around… always."

"Why?"

"Don't know … your eyes, smile, captivating almond oil…"

She giggled again: "An endearing … awkward clown."

She looked at him and grinned. He thought he saw more than affection in her entire bearing.

He had a sudden urge to kiss her, but a sudden tremor started affecting his limbs.

"Spineless crusader!" she said, held his unsteady hand, and squeezed it so hard that he winced.

"Crap!" he finally exclaimed; "I'm sure, now."

"About what?" she demanded with feigned belligerence.

"My feelings," he said hastily.

"About what?" she asked.

The two were so absorbed in their thoughts about each other that they failed to notice that they had reached the rear of the procession of thousands of singing and chanting devotees. Her question was answered by an ear-splitting blast followed or preceded by at least half-dozen huge mushroom flames about a hundred yards in front.

"Human bombs!" Anne screamed.

"Half-a-million sitting ducks roasting in flames!" Hari hissed.

"Makes my skin crawl," she said.

"Do you believe in omens?" he asked.

"Never thought about them. Why?"

"It makes me wonder. Our first date … tens of thousands of devotees reciting sacred mantras in the birthplace of Lord Krishna … and dozens of suicide bombers … murder and mayhem … survivors continuing to recite and moving forward ... free of all fear ... kind of mass Nirvana, just a step below *moksha*," Hari said in a state of suspended motion, admiring her serene dignity, eyes deeply troubled by the chaos just ahead.

"Is that a good omen?" she asked.

"I don't know and I don't care. I feel great in your presence," he said.

"Don't care!" she exclaimed angrily. But her expression softened as she watched him speak urgently into his cell phone and giving instructions. "Help is on its way," he said simply, looking ruefully at the carnage around, speechlessly furious watching a bleeding toddler crawling across the street and a young woman writhing in pain a few feet in front of Anne, who knelt down to have a closer look.

"She's pregnant," Anne yelled; "Help me. She's in labor." Hari picked up the toddler soaked in blood, and dragging a bulging diaper. "Mamma!" the infant squealed.

"Jesus!" cried the girl in distress.

"Relax," Anne coaxed her; "Hold her arms. Breathe hard, lady, and push. Please harder. She needs to be taken to hospital, Hari. Get the car, please!"

He ran, carrying the infant who had buried his head in his chest. "God protects only the strong," he whispered in his ear and saw a faint smile on his face. He reversed his car and noticed that Khan's car was no longer there.

The pregnant girl, Agnes, 18, was an African-American from Atlanta, Georgia. Her South African boyfriend, Mitch, was killed in one of the blasts. She was admitted to the nearby City Hospital's maternity ward. The infant was a white male, probably eight months old, and his parents could not be traced. Anne had him treated for superficial wounds and Hari decided to take him home.

"Let's now move on to the birthplace of Krishna and soak the vibrations of billions of prayers through the timeless past," she whispered as if in a trance watching the victims of Jihad, the dead, the dying, the writhing and the chanting hordes moving forward or attending to the wounded, a large number of them mourning the dead and the dying, some lost and others searching.

"I'm not superstitious. But is it the commencement of a new divine relationship in the midst of turmoil in a place sanctified by worshippers through the millennia and desecrated by the hellfire unleashed by the ungodly?" he said.

She didn't hear a word, too disturbed by the sight, anger welling up inside her heaving bosom, nauseated by the human agony around her, demonstrating the heartless bestiality of fanatics.

"Is this what you call hellfire?" she wailed, tears welling up beneath quivering eyelids.

"What a first date! Disastrous. I'm sorry, Anne, can we do it some other time, please?"

"Of course, romancing with Jihad's hellfire is beyond the nature of this particular houri. Turn around, please. This kid needs to be fed. Let's call him Krishna after the Lord!" she said.

Chapter - 16

Countdown to Jihad

"Lunacy of fanaticism is a soul-destroying paroxysm!" exclaimed Anne on their drive back, kissing cuddly Kris tenderly. Hari nodded absently, looking into the rearview mirror at Khan's fancy limousine approaching at breakneck speed.

"What was this pervert doing in the Hindu holy city?" he wondered aloud, his troubled mind focused on the disturbing ramifications of Jihad, including the plight of Kris, currently nestling soundlessly in the warmth of Anne's breasts. "What's Khan doing in the holy city?" he said again.

"Aren't you a bit prejudiced against the superstar? Millions of Indians love him and he is sure welcome everywhere," she said, moving her fingers lovingly on Kris's belly: "Pot-bellied divine kid dry without a diaper!"

"Child-molester!" he giggled.

"Isn't he cute? Chubby cheeks, dimples, big ears. Did Khan have a hand in the blasts?" she asked.

"Mass appeal is a great asset to legitimise his involvement in heinous activities," he sneered. "Remember there's also the giant oil refinery nearby. Why is he over-speeding? What's his hurry, steeped as his life is in intemperate languor?"

Anne said: "I heard what you *did not* say"

"What *didn't* I say?

"The countdown to Jihad has begun in earnest," she said somberly.

"It has started on a large scale and Khan is the new massappeal icon of the Muslim anarchist threatening the security of the world," he said.

Khan's limo overtook them in a flash and Hari suggested: "Let's take a break at this famous Shiva Temple for a glass of its soothing *bhang* concoction."

"What's that?"

"*Cannabis*, hemp, hashish, marijuana or such euphoric drink prepared to appease a temperamental Shiva. I can do with a few glasses myself of the great hallucinogenic and also a few drops for our bereaved Kris. I wonder who his parents are?"

"Or were?" she sighed; "What do you plan to do with him?

And Agnes?"

He did not have the opportunity to respond as the car stuttered to an asthmatic halt as if rocked by a high-intensity earthquake preceded by a volcanic eruption in the vicinity. Taken aback, the two got down and saw the oil refinery engulfed in flames and farting spurts of mini-blasts into the atmosphere, gusts of hot wind searing their faces.

"My scoop of the century is engulfing the world," he said; "Please cover the kid's face."

"And also swallowing you up," she taunted him.

He sensed resentment in the tone and was perplexed. He finally smiled after finishing one glass of holy *bhang*: "I'm truly swamped, not by the carnage but the contentment that strangely envelops me in your soothing presence."

She took a cautious sip of the concoction and asked: "Not bad. What does it contain?"

"*Cannabis* plucked from the bush, milk, almonds, cardamom, melon seeds, black pepper, honey, sugar, ground together in an earthen jar or mixer-grinder. Give a few drops to Kris." She dipped her index finger in the glass and placed it in his mouth. He licked it, reluctantly first and then greedily, uttering an eager burp and clutching the finger with his tiny hand.

"Why is it Shiva's favourite?" she asked, giggling and dipping the finger again.

"Haven't a clue. Anne, listen, I apologize for this harrowing first date, please," he said earnestly.

She gave him a kindred look and twittered: "Forgiveness is not a part of my job description … I like your boring company … so immersed in Jihad … and probably frigid … or gay."

He laughed so loud that almost all the Shiva devotees started looking at them. "Thanks for the vote of confidence. I love your body aroma, intoxicating, divine...Were you born near a sandalwood plantation...around a place called Little Rock. Never mind! No one gives a damn and I don't care!"

"I care!" she said with feeling, holding his hand; "Warm! Sensuous. Bulging mount of Venus. Reassuring. Nice. What do you plan to do with Kris?"

"First, get all his needs—diapers, clothes, baby foods, bath tub, pot, soaps and creams and what have you, and then try and look for his parents. But a nanny first," he said slowly, thinking.

"What if you had found a dozen toddlers in the same situation?"

"I don't know. Abandoned them? Unlikely. What can one do? Shit! Helpless in the face of carnage culture," he sighed.

"You are a good man, Hari," she said softly.

He whispered: "*I got love, I hope. True love I think.*"

She twittered, kissed the kid on the cheek and said: "Deliciously sour."

He kissed her hand: "Repulsive gunpowder. Time to go home and sleep after picking up the necessities for Kris." "Together? How disgusting!" she said; "Anti-climax after an eventful first date!"

India woke up in horror the next morning to experience and hear about an epidemic of explosions which rocked seven cities at seven o'clock. The blasts caused consternation in the Prime Minister's office:

Forty-nine explosions, seven in each of the seven cities, seventh day of the seventh month. The Prime Minister was livid. In her notorious "shift-the-blame" face-saving maneuver, she promptly sacked Home Minister Sant Nihal Singh Bawa and accused him of failing to act on warnings despite prior knowledge of terrorists' plans.

Air Chief Marshal Rajinder Nath Rai, the Chief National Security Adviser, was hopping mad. His kid brother, in his celebrated column, *Below the Belt*, had written that he, Hari, had personally informed the PM and the NSA chief of the presence in India of a dangerous Taliban leader. He accused Madam Mandira and Air Chief Rai of criminal neglect and demanded that they voluntarily quit posts too big for small-minded megalomaniacs.

Hari was also mystified by the Number Seven. He was also perplexed by eyewitness reports from all the affected cities about youngsters wearing green blazers with crescent-and-star badges on their breast pockets having been seen around the affected areas. A dusk-to-dawn curfew was imposed in all of the grieving cities of Delhi, Bombay, Calcutta, Madras, Bangalore, Hyderabad and Lucknow and, of course, Mathura—to prevent a Hindu backlash.

At seven O'clock in the evening, when Hari was heading towards Neelam's house, the PM, in a live telecast, accused Pakistan of the unprovoked "barbaric acts against innocent women, children and men". The Leader of the Opposition, Ram Kumar, accused a "slumbering" Mandira of paying greater attention to the intricate, hand-crafted embroidery on her expensive raw-silk sari than to the security of the State.

"She has become oblivious of the sufferings of the masses in her addiction to power," declared the President of the Masses Party. The American Ambassador to India, Dan Miller, was having a closed door meeting with the new head of the Consular Division, Thomas A. Pickering, the covert CIA super-agent in South Asia who had just arrived from Washington, D.C., to set up a new covert unit of the Counter- Terrorism Network (CTN).

However, topmost on their agenda seemed to be Anne's friendship with Hari, and the opposition to it of her mother, Alice Nielsen-Spenser, the influential California politician.

David was still desperately trying to locate two eyewitnesses to the assassination attempt on the Pope. Mr. and Mrs. Edgar Nandan had mysteriously gone missing without a trace.

The Associated Press was filing an "Exclusive" about the Taj Mahal being on the Taliban hit list. Dev Bhalla, the *Verdict Today* Insight Team chief, had already filed his "Exclusive" on the same subject. The *New York Times* had scooped them all: It quoted "reliable" sources as claiming that Khalifa Hasham Ali was seriously contemplating attacks on the Golden Gate Bridge and Pier 39 in San Francisco.

Dev was planning to execute the most daring story of his Insight Team's tenure. He was also excited because Madhu had agreed to have dinner with him to celebrate her victory as the inaugural Miss Urvashi. They went on a drive in his new company-gifted Honda Civic and were heading for Seventh Heaven to take advantage of his promotion to being an expense account media man.

A worried David decided to call it a day and sulk in the company of his dumb girlfriend, Bubbles, daughter of Deputy Police Commissioner Dial Singh, to be his date. She agreed promptly and they headed towards Seventh Heaven

Hari, meanwhile, pulled the *Vaastu-Shastra* chime-chord at the entrance to Neelam's house, 7, Ashoka Road, and was struck by the coincidence of Number Seven. A Sikh attendant dressed in a medical-green turban opened the door and hesitated. Neelam relieved him and welcomed the man who could have been her brother-in-law.

He grinned: "My sixth sense tells me I should be at the casino playing no-limit Lucky Seven on a medical-green table…Come with me, sister, my could-have-been sister-in-law."

"Please wait for my daughter Rani, Krishna's illegitimate daughter." The effervescent 19-year-old came dancing in and said cheerfully: "Mom! I just bumped into Mazhar Khan. The bastard made a dirty pass at me and I punched him on his face!" Then she saw Hari: "Who's this?"

"Your uncle Hari. Your Dad's brother."

Hari presented Neelam the pink jacket made for her by Krishna twenty years ago, but noticing she had outgrown it, suggested that she pass it on to Rani. "Great idea! After all, she's his daughter. She was in my womb when he was killed," she sobbed, tapping her tummy. She had probably been drinking since morning, Hari surmised, wondering if the daughter of the Sikh leader had become an addict. She hated her husband Rajbir Singh: "The bloody upstart can't stand Rani. Keeps talking about illegitimate bastards like this girl." She poured another drink for herself and gave one to Hari: "He's my husband only in name, literally. I refuse to share the bed with him, even the bedroom. His very touch is revolting."

"Why did you marry him?"

"Compulsion. He used to be Papa's muscleman, catapulted to his present position as chairman of Ivory Tower Holdings."

"Did he have anything to do with Krishna's murder?"

"I think so, but I can't be certain. He is clean-shaven now, but was a blue-turbaned Sikh not too long ago. Rani knows everything. She lives with Papa because Rajbir doesn't want her here:

"Mutual hatred! She's here because he's off to Africa to sign a joint-venture deal in Equatoria."

Hari called Anne to ask her to wait outside the entrance to her apartment complex. Rani readily agreed to stay behind and off they went, all three walking into Seventh Heaven, arm in arm. They were led to the casino by one of the zombie lads, from the main bar, and the restaurant beyond through a trapdoor-opening into the blazing lights of the Casino.

Suddenly, the casino was plunged into darkness. "Fuck!" said Hari. "Let's go back home," said Anne. "Get me a drink," said Neelam. The zombie shone a torch into Anne's eyes. She blinked and slapped Zombie hard in the face and snatched the torch: "Let's go get a drink. Torchlight boozing. Cheers!" "Cheers!" said Neelam. "What about my Lucky Seven in the Seventh Heaven on the seventh floor at 7 Ivory Tower Lane on the seventh day of the seventh month."

The lights came on with the whining of a super-generator. "I wonder if there are inverters and generators in heaven. I guess not… there are stars and moons and suns all the time. No artificial lights," Anne said. "Gift of paradise is the ultimate God has to offer to the mortals," said Neelam.

Hari thought about it and said: "In Islam, according to the false prophets, Allah has bought from the Momins, the faithful, their own selves, their belongings, their ancestors and their offspring in exchange for the gift of Jannat or Heaven. Every faithful is required to fight in the way of Allah; to kill and be killed."

"What's all this murder and mayhem on top of all the worldly sufferings we have to tolerate?" asked Neelam. "I'm not talking about normal life, my dear could-have-been." Anne chimed, and Hari said: "That sound alone is the Seventh Heaven for me, so childlike, so organic, so uninhibited."

"What about Lucky Seven, Hari?" asked Neelam.

"In a moment, please. I've got my flow going about heaven—Jihad is the surest means of access to paradise, the abode, like this prototype, of the choicest carnal delights after death; sex and violence combine to form the basic approach of Islamic fundamentalists to coax and cajole human beings into a simulated web of salvation," he said, as if in deep thought. According to the fanatics, Allah requires the Momins to fight those who do not believe in Allah and the Last Day and do not forbid what He and his Messenger Muhammad have forbidden. Fight those who do not practice the religion of truth."

"Have you brought us here to indoctrinate us against Islam?" asked Anne; "Remember, this is only our second meeting and you are already proving to be a bore and my boss and my mother have warned me against your sexual perversions." She chimed again.

"All right. One final remark: I believe that we are witnessing the beginnings of Jihad, fanatical Islam's Thousand-Year War against the Infidels and Kafirs. More after we tame the Lucky Seven virus."

"Do you like to gamble, Hari?" Anne asked seriously.

"God, no, never! I just want to check on something.

They had very little cash; only credit cards. Hari took out one of his and withdrew seven thousand rupees to start with. He tripled it promptly, and handed the winnings to Anne. Another seven thousand and again the same result. This time, the winnings went to Neelam, who played fourteen thousand and doubled it.

"Great casino," said Anne; "Let's go to Las Vegas."

"Beginners' luck," said Hari and won another twenty-one thousand. Then, he kept his own seven thousand in his pocket, placed all of the winnings on the table and told the half-naked croupier to roll the dice:

"Last bet, Triple Seven, please!"

There, he won again. He counted the counters: Seven hundred thousand. "All yours, ladies. I'm hungry."

Anne and Neelam, too, were ready to quit. "Let's go join the elite media force out there."

"Go ahead, I'll join you in a few minutes. Must pick up some stuff for Kris, milk, diapers, dresses and toys," Hari said.

Neelam asked: "Who's Kris?"

"Jihad-orphaned gremlin," Hari said. Both girls joined him in his quest and they were back a short while later.

"Let's party now." said Neelam "I'm thirsty, Champagne!"

"You are already drunk, dear could-have-been."

"Why do you keep rubbing it in? Why did your brother have to die on me."

"Ask your bigoted father and nominal husband…All right, let's order Champagne."

He crossed over to David's and Dev's tables and invited them over. "Get all the others and enjoy. I have just won a fortune. Whatever you want, boys and girls, my personal war has just started."

You are drunk, Harry," said David.

My name is Hari, as in hurry, not Harry, Dave."

"What new war is this?"

To get rid of the chips on my shoulder."

"How, sir?" said Dev.

"By drinking myself to oblivion." He made a face.

"It's a heavy day tomorrow, sir," said Dev.

"Every fucking day is going to be super-heavy from now on. Look at those young green blazers!"

"What about them?" asked Neelam.

"They represent the calm before and after the storm," said Hari.

"You are making no sense, Hari," said Anne.

"These zombies are the holy warriors, the Mujahids; it's their duty to carry the crescent-and-star to all corners of the world." Hari was being very serious and they urged him to continue.

"This is not the place to talk about it. Let's meet at my place tomorrow, 7 o'clock onwards," he said.

Anne: "Tomorrow is Sunday, seventh day of the week in the seventh month. But I have a problem tomorrow. My California neighbour Thomas Pickering is in New Delhi on a hush-hush mission and I have agreed to meet him in the morning."

"Bring him along. What does he do?"

"Ex-CIA, I think."

"Good. He may have a wealth of information about Jihad. We could sure use a professional spy as an adviser about Jihad, a binding contract between Allah and Muslims whereby He promises paradise to them in exchange for performing their ordained sacred duty to murder, plunder and seduce the women of infidels and kafirs. These green blazers are among the millions of foot-soldiers of Islam's holy war against non-believers."

Anne told him about her meeting with the Ambassador. She added: "I have a feeling that Dan Miller is determined to punish me for hobnobbing with you, to borrow his words."

"What hobnobbing? We have known each for barely a couple of days. I am too timid to try and come on to you. We have made no commitment to each other. We barely touched each other, much as I would like to do so right now."

She chimed and he said: "You are by far the most melodious female sound I have ever heard. Better than Ravi Shankar's sitar or Yehudi Menuhin's guitar or Lata's best. I feel like lifting you and placing you up on a pedestal where I can keep looking at you day and night."

Neelam coughed.

Anne said: "I am touched. But worried. You and I are on collision courses with our respective worlds. Perhaps not for the same reason. I don't know. But I do like you …very much. Do I love you? I don't know."

"Perhaps this is not the most opportune time for an international love triangle." he said.

"Are you always so enigmatic?" Anne smiled.

"I'm not sure. My gut feeling says that the countdown to Jihad has commenced."

"Why do you keep repeating yourself?"

Suddenly, he changed the subject: "Would you like to have corn on cob?"

"I would love it … here, in Seventh Heaven?"

"A cripple outside Parliament House is the world's best roaster of *bhuttas*, Hindi for corn on cob, the national snack."

"At this time?"

"Yeah, would you like going for a walk … ten minutes."

"Is it safe"

"No."

"Let's go."

In the elevator, she said: "I am very confused."

"Likewise," he said.

Outside, he said: "I think I'm attracted to you."

"I know."

"Would you like an ice cream cone?"

She nodded: "Sure."

"Never mind. Let's have a brief tour of what is left of India's life-sustaining system dented by the country's inept leaders. Here, to your left is Verdict Today House, the voice of freedom, haunted by the frightening specter of the coldblooded Media Strangler."

"That's your office, isn't it? Do you ever go there?" she asked and he chuckled, nodding vigorously. "Across the street, that's Parliament Street Police Station, alongside the Riot Police headquarters, the left arm of the tyrant, and to its right is the Special Branch, the eyes and ears of the oppressor."

"Where's the right hand?"

"The Research and Analysis Wing or RAW. Inside her office."

"And the cranium, heart and lungs and the digestive system?"

"Members of the Cabinet constitute the alimentary canal and she herself personifies the heart-lung-brain machine."

They walked in silence for a minute, then she said:

"Hari, you are in danger."

"Of what?"

"Of never recovering from your obsessive compulsive disorder," she mocked.

"I know, but not manic. Hate bloodshed, mortified of violence, searching for manna. Now, look to your left, the Reserve Bank of India, the Federal Reserve, the custodian of gross national product and all financial aid, of the misused wealth of a billion people, the national exchequer being methodically looted by greedy politicians," he said. "Extremely melodramatic," she mocked.

"And to your right, Broadcasting House, the well-oiled machine designed to transform a billion people into a nation of nincompoops."

She was not listening because she felt concerned about Hari's mental state in the face of his self-imposed challenges against Jihad and tyranny, the naïve idealist yearning for warmth in a cold-blooded world.

She grinned and said: "It's fun watching you try to cope with yourself."

He laughed: "Good ... we're there ... the *bhutta* specialist, slow-burning sandalwood fire ...fresh lemon and spices...three minutes from the main gate of the world's largest theater of marionettes, which, by the way, stands prorogued and is now the most spacious cemetery of democracy. You are right, Anne. Obsessive compulsive disorder, perhaps. This is my catharsis. Angry young man can't put this melodramatic reality in writing. Such stunts help me reinvent myself."

She thought over it and finally giggled. Hari sighed, a sigh of relief. "You really had me worried," she grinned.

"Now, meet Masterji, the *bhutta* genius. He occasionally helps me reinvent myself."

"Hello, Miss," Master smiled; "Long time, no see, Mr. Hari."

"Tell her your tale, sir," Hari said.

"No, sir, please don't embarrass me. Let me roast a couple of good *bhuttas*."

"Okay, Master. He used to be headmaster of an Old Delhi high school. Mostly Muslim pupils. Master Khan and his eighteen-year-old daughter Safiya were big international news for a day."

"What happened?"

"She was tortured and gang-raped by a group of Taliban and both his legs were decapitated with a machete during the school's morning assembly."

"Why?"

"Her Christian boyfriend Bobby presented her silver anklets, like the ones you are wearing, to embellish her pretty ankles for Eid and she was showing off her ankles to him. Indecent exposure! Whipped by fanatics, carried into a classroom, raped and killed."

Tearful Master Khan handed them their *bhuttas.*

Hari continued: "Master Khan is living testimony to the blasphemy of Taliban and hypocrisy of bigoted secularists as he suffered at the hands of both."

She twittered and gave a bite of her cob to Hari: "Amazing. He stands on his own feet… in a manner of speaking!"

"Master is also planning to participate in the paralympic games early next month," Hari said.

"Best of luck, Master Khan, and thanks for the best *bhutta* in the world," she said, kissing him on his forehead.

"Mr. Hari, I am really very grateful for everything you have done for me. Those killer twins are in Delhi, sir," he said.

"Keep it up, Master. The twins? Are you sure?"

Master nodded and asked: "How is Sheetal, Mr. Hari?"

"He is good."

Anne asked: "Who's Sheetal?"

"My inimitable eunuch butler, Master's student and his savior. He was himself gang-sodomized by the Taliban, but still carried his teacher to hospital."

At Seventh Heaven, each member of the media-plus soulsearching get-together found one thing or another to do probing the goings-on in Ivory Tower Heights.

Neelam, roasting in the solitariness of the stew served to her by her double-dealing father, was getting upset by the prolonged absence of the Xerox copy of her murdered boyfriend, the presumptuous kid who promised he would not let her stumble.

She ordered a bottle of Scotch and called Rani to say she would be late. Anne stepped out of the elevator, followed by Hari, who ran towards Neelam, stumbled on his pickled toe and said: "Sorry."

David, rushing in from behind, laughed: "A stumbling epidemic, I just stumbled on something frightfully interesting."

"What?"

"Come with me," David replied and led Hari to the basement, but not directly, elevator … stairs …service elevator … service staircase…until they stood in front of at least a thousand small wooden crates.

"Heroin," he whispered; "A billion quid, I'm sure."

"Let's get out of here … Fast!" Hari warned.

This time, they took the casino service elevator direct to the top floor, and joined the girls, Neelam still sulking and Anne staring quizzically. Irritated by Neelam's morbid attitude, he said: "Look here, sister! You can't live in your fatalistic memories!"
She screamed: "He loved me… I loved him. His memory is real… vibrant … pulsating in my veins … nerves … all over… And you, kid, saw the hit men! And what!?"

Hari closed his eyes, rocked by the vision of Sikh hooligans plunging their swords into his brother's body, and that unforgettable agony of his own infirmity-induced cowardice and helplessness in the face of a challenge he was unable to meet.

He felt Anne's eyes piercing through his forehead like the beam of a welder. And he spoke tremulously in a low but clear voice: "Look, I am also being tormented by the tornado of your emotional loss. It's also my loss. For twenty years, my soul has been fermenting in the pain of solitude, a lonesome wretch finding refuge in my work. I think I now have the physical and moral strength to do whatever might be necessary for redemption. Commit suicide, if you want! I will take care of your daughter. Understand! Or, Why don't you start acting as my eyes into the souls of your father and husband."

"They are soul-less beasts," she said, grabbing his hand; "Sorry, kid."

His 20-year agony suddenly started churning inside his entire system like a cyclone of emotional upheaval. Anne watched the changing contours of his face, beginning to understand the intense feelings that presumably lay hibernating within the seemingly flippant clown.

David, meanwhile, was getting jittery about the billion-pound heroin shipment he had stumbled into in the basement. "So, Hari," he finally said, "who's it going to be … the NSA or the Police Commissioner?"

"Neither," he replied.

"Why?" asked Anne, who had obviously been briefed.

"I don't trust any political appointee."

"You are out of your bloody mind," David protested.

"It's too big for wordsmiths, Hari. Please call Big Brother," Anne beseeched.

"The ace pilot is a political opportunist and the lady who controls him is world champion of sophistry," Hari said.

"What do you think of an NSA operation overseen by David and Hari," Neelam suggested.

"Brilliant!" said Anne, kissing her on both cheeks; "I will call the Big Bully… what's his direct number?"

David gave her the number, but Hari said: "Not here, Anne, go to the Ladies room, please."

Hari watched her go, honey-combed hair to sun-washed legs, moving gracefully like a gazelle in slow motion, tinkle, tinkle of the anklets compelling a passing zombie to gaze fixedly at her neat ankles as if accusing her of indecent exposure in a public place.

David looked worried, watching the zombies move purposefully from table to table and inching towards the restrooms. Finally, he requested Neelam to go after Anne, who came out in a hurry and signaled Hari to rush towards her.

All four rushed towards her and she led them into the Ladies room. Two waiters were sprawled on the floor: "Sex-starved *mujahid* rapists bungled into a black belt!" Her triumphant twitter seemed to Hari like the melody of the moment encompassing an entire lifetime.

"Our fragile fairy also knows how to get tough," Hari said, amazed. In a matter of minutes, the whole building was surrounded by several contingents of the Special Security Brigade. The entire basement area was sealed off and declared as a bonded warehouse. The two goons who tried to molest Anne were taken away to the nearest police station and locked up.

David and Hari were picked up for questioning and taken straight to the NSA chief, but not before Hari had requested the girls to join him at his house the next evening.

"What is the meaning of this attempted blackmail?" Air Chief Marshal Rai growled.

"I don't trust your extra-constitutional administration, sir," Hari said simply.

"That's treason," he glared.

"That's what I mean … you specialise in growling and glaring and she is an expert in choking the deprived masses," Hari said.

"Small-minded megalomaniacs, according to you, right? So, you want to establish a parallel administration, kiddo, don't you?"

"That's not true, and you know it."

"Then what?"

"Arrest all directors and senior officials of Ivory Tower Heights right now wherever they might be," said Hari.

"Consider it done," said the NSA chief.

Hari said: "I hope that you will arrest your devious and deceitful Home Minister, his son-in-law and Ali forthwith and reopen the case about your brother Krishna's murder."

Rai retorted: "You still think with your heart, kid. Ali, Sant and Singh can't be detained on the basis of whim and it's not easy to reopen a twenty-year-old case. We do have an open-and-shut case against those two goons who tried to molest the American girl. The heroin has been seized and the pharmacy owners are being interrogated. There's no evidence or complaint of misdemeanor against your three suspects."

"I don't accept your verdict, sir," Hari said, on the verge of losing his temper.

"You are an inveterate rebel, popping Diwali crackers in your mouth like a kid masticating candy as you talk and spit fire at invisible terrorists," said the NSA chief.

"What was Khan doing in Mathura at that time?" Hari persisted.

"It's a free country. What were *you* doing there?"

"Romancing with Jihad!" he sniggered and went away.

Chapter - 17

Two-Sided Triangle

Thomas A. Pickering looked and behaved like the perfect easy-going and languidly inquisitive American tourist on sabbatical from the rat race who was superficially impressed by everything he saw and liked everyone he met. He was the ideal American spy because hardly anyone could pierce the daredevil secret service operative's veneer of a fun-loving extrovert.

Pickering was not a regular churchgoer. But that Sunday morning, his first in New Delhi, he asked Anne to accompany him to All Saints Cathedral in accordance with her mother's plan to enable the dynamic undercover CIA agent to put his best foot forward as a suitor for her heiress daughter.

He had already taken over as chief of Consular Division at the Embassy in New Delhi as a front for his *de facto* position as head of the new covert unit of the Counter-Terrorism Network (CTN) on a top secret mission officially precluded from his ambivalent job description.

He arrived at Anne's duplex exactly half-hour earlier than the appointed time. He was peeping through the keyhole when she suddenly opened the door, he lost balance and fell flat on his face on the patio carpet sending Anne's pet, quietlyperceptive Snow White, into a frenzy of angry barking reserved for hostile intruders.

"Peeping Tom," Anne mocked, giggling.

He was instantly back on his feet and mumbled something incoherently as Anne continued to giggle while controlling Snow White. He laughed mirthlessly to cover his embarrassment and tried vainly to pat Snow White on the head, hurriedly withdrawing a reluctant hand and stepping back. "Sorry," whispered the tall, fair, handsome buccaneer who had always admired Anne, the sprightly next-door girl with the pearl-smooth complexion, and an enticing smile which taunted him day and night.

Her control-freak mother had good reason to act as matchmaker on behalf of Tom, whose father, an influential lobbyist in Washington, D.C., had helped her through divorce and ruined her father. Alice wanted Anne to make a career in politics, especially when she inherited a fortune after her father-in-law's death. Alice became even more ambitious after divorcing Anne's father, Richard Spenser.

Richard "Dickhead", as he was derisively referred to in the neighbourhood watering holes, took to the bottle after a series of upheavals, namely, alimony-pauperisation, and nervous breakdown brought about by his inability to come to grips with his morbid loneliness without a family he had nurtured in a winner-take-all society bereft of emotions.

Richard missed his daughter most of all. Anne was the only one who could effectively save him from himself and his self-destructive mood swings. He craved to sleep, for that was perhaps the only mode in which he could get interim solace. But he was unable to sleep without heavy doses of prescription pills which deadened sensation in dreamless slumber. Anne, too, missed the warmth of her papa's meaningless non-stop chatter, his venturesome spirit and, most of all, his ability to poke fun at himself for his clumsiness and his hilariously fruitless fishing trips during which he strutted like a man-eating lion pretending to be a shark. Her thoughts were now focused on her papa's abysmal decline and fall from a stuffy millionaire's fully three dimensional son to a claustrophobic amnesiac alcoholic.

The drive to the church seemed to be taking too long as Tom talked vaguely about the "exciting" world of espionage, deadly nuclear secrets, drug-trafficking, money-laundering, corruption at the highest level in the United States government. He was particularly apprehensive of the growing threat of Islamism following the US-engineered demise of the Soviet Union. Tom inadvertently blurted out that an elite cadre of assassins was being put together somewhere in the Indian Ocean region. "Militant Islam is threatening to bifurcate the world into rampaging fanatical hordes of unified Taliban and the rhetorical secularists divided against themselves," he said, moving closer to Anne in the back seat. He was particularly harsh on the ineptitude of the partisan mass media owned, controlled or manipulated by big money and the soulless mafia, and fearful of Taliban's retributive *fatwa*-driven terror. "Terrorism has become the biggest single threat to the civilised world. Religious fanatics now are acquiring stocks of all kinds of weapons. Nuclear corruption has become big business in America. Weapons of Mass Destruction (WMD) have acquired nightmarish proportions for humans and the environment everywhere in the world," he said, as Anne yawned and moved away; "Bioterrorism, electronic espionage of computer communication and..."

"Infamous game of one-upmanship being played between emasculated superpower heavyweights and dehumanised terrorists, the Third World's suicide bombers enjoying their moment of glory when they explode in the midst of innocent people," she said with such intensity that Tom was taken aback.

She suddenly exclaimed: "Suicide! Your Mom! Didn't she commit suicide, Tom?"

"Lord, no!" he retorted; "She was Jewish."

"What's that to do with it?" she demanded.

"Suicide is the lowest sin for Jews. Suicide, premeditated murder, adultery. Idol worship are looked upon as evil by Jews."

"What about Jihad?" she scowled.

"American society is in upheaval, crime rates are skyrocketing. Roving gangs of non-whites and blacks rape and pillage at will, gangs of browns and blacks invade white homes, seize their cash and belongings and generally go on the rampage with impunity," he replied.

"Why do I get the feeling that you are making a rehearsed speech? Whose idea is this, Mom or Dan Miller?" she asked pointedly.

"What do you mean? Your Mom only thinks about your wellbeing, and Dan, too, has your interest at heart when it comes to that notorious playboy wordsmith."

"Enough, Tom!" she flared; "I've met Hari only twice. There's no hanky-panky, not yet, at any rate. I like him. He's attractive, ... and ... and flippant. Not frivolous. Proud. Good journalist. Honest ... not hypocritical, He has convinced me that we are witnessing the beginnings of Islam's thousand-year war against non-Muslims." She was surprised at her own fervent, incoherent protest against Tom's insinuation against Hari.

Tom was taken aback: "I didn't mean to hurt you, Anne. I have known you for so long and admired you secretly." "Let's not go to the church today," she said curtly; "Some other time. Would you like to meet Hari if you are free this evening. I'll pick you up at six-thirty. Wait for me at your hotel entrance. Drop me here. I will take a cab," she said abruptly and went away without waiting for his response.

If American society was in upheaval, her own mind was in turmoil, torn between her baffling feelings for the devil-maycare prodigal Indian and her own attachment to American values. She did understand why so much fuss was being made about her acquaintance with him and she was determined to defy all such opposition. She found Hari eminently presentable and successful and decidedly better looking than most of the men she had known. But there was much more to him than met the eye, other-worldly with his feet on the ground, living life large and recklessly but purposefully, may be not a man of success, but certainly a man of value.

Was it a sin not to be American? Not in her book. In any event, one could hardly call it an affair. She understood why her mother disapproved of him: Her profile as a candidate for the House of Representatives would be tarnished if it said her son-in-law was an Indian-Indian from the famished land of slums and snake charmers.

She punched mom's number in her cell phone and came straight to the point: "Did your boyfriend's wife commit suicide?"

"What are you talking about?"

"Your sexy neighbour Joshua Pickering's wife Daphne. How did she die, mom?"

"Cardiac arrest ... when she found another woman in Joshua's bed on return from the synagogue early," Alice said.

"Are you that other woman, mom?" Anne sneered.

"What are you talking about, my child?"

"Don't try and control me with your deviousness, mom! "Hari is a very good friend, not the Boston Strangler or Jack the Ripper. I like him."

"There have been cases, dear, of sex-starved Indians going hammer-and-tongs at pretty white girls..."

"Believe me, Hari and I haven't met for more than a few hours and mostly in public. There's nothing going on between us, not yet. Please also inform your friends Dan Miller and Peeping Tom not to bother me." Hari was going through one of the rare phases of his anxiety syndrome for no apparent reason, the one phobia that was perhaps his driving force that was turning him into a hypochondriacally legendary editor in a Third World society suffering under the tyranny of self-righteous stupidity.

He first called the Mathura hospital where Agnes was admitted. Said the matron: "Messy! the ovary has somersaulted inside the womb. She eats the rain moths. Raw, with wings. Massive nervous breakdown interfering with her pregnancy, inconsolable, claims she saw the man who shot Mitch after he was unhurt in the suicide blasts." Hari asked a senior reporter to interview Agnes to identify the assailant.

Then he called ISKCON and discovered that there were no inquiries about a missing infant, Kris, who seemed to be having fun in the front lawn, gleefully watching a squirrel frolicking around a tamarind tree. He rushed out and brought the kid back into the house and asked Usha to give him a bath, feed him and dress him up with a saffron gown for the evening party.

Uppermost on his mind, though, was Anne in view of her clash with her boss and the storm being churned in her mother's high-tech sociopath high society. Using his habitual fail-safe acumen, Hari got involved in instructing the domestic help about preparations for the evening party.

Usha promptly got down to making arrangements. She enjoyed doing the chores because she was virtually the hostess and secretly in love with her employer. She wanted every single thing to be spotlessly clean and absolutely free of Delhi's proverbial dust and cobwebs that sprang up like wild mushrooms, the pollutants to which the asthmatic Manipur mannequin was allergic.

Even his pet and precocious cuckoo bird Koel on her steelbar swing must be taken care of: her food and drink and an occasional worm. "Coo oo," jeered Koel as Usha cleaned her open-ended golden cage. Her husband, Prem Anand, the cook, resented the lewd expression he thought he saw in her eyes whenever Hari talked, so much so that he used his own suspicion about her adulterous inclinations as an excuse to beat her up whenever he was under the influence of alcohol, which was often since liquor was freely available in the house.

Sheetal, the eunuch butler, wasn't his usual cheerful self that day. He had just been released by airport police and his best friend was killed while watching *King of Kings* in a theater. Sheetal even forgot to brief Hari about Jim and Tim, the terror twins who had already arrived.

Usha was in an ecstatic mood. Hari had patted her on the upper arm, almost touching her nipple, making her wish to scream in orgasmic glee. Usha felt safe with Sheetal. She could easily narrate to him her ordeal with her gay and violent husband without inhibition. Even Sheetal felt tickled when she referred to his neuter gender as "it".

Right now, when she found him in abysmal spirits, she tried to humor him. She told him that she had learnt another word of English. "Hari sir told me that you are not a faggot. 'He' also said Sheetal is not 'he' or 'she' or 'him', but an 'it'." And he actually burst out laughing when she called him "Miss It" when "Mr. Hari" was nodding meaninglessly into the telephone, listening to Big Brother's bellow: "How dare you embarrass me like this?"

"What have I done now?"

"That crappy column of yours—Couldn't you have been discreet about what you told me about Jim and Tim?"

Hari had a sinking feeling that he was going to go in for another round of detentions. Breathing spasmodically and moving his foot from side to side, he put the phone down gently, swallowed a couple of pills given to him by Ali. Usha noticed the pain in his voice and rushed to help.

In another part of the city, Ali secretly moved out of his Penthouse Paradise to a little-known hotel in the Jamia Mosque area minutes before the arrival of plainclothes men belatedly deputed by the Chief National Security Adviser to surround Ivory Tower Heights.

But Insight Team reporter Raju Chetan followed him to Jannat Lodge next to the fish market and called his boss Dev on his cell phone. Neelam was creating yet another scene at her father's house about Krishna's murder, her insistent questioning making Sant Nihal very nervous. "I am finally going to call the media and expose you and my grimy husband. How could you have me married to that killer of the man I loved," she screamed.

"That was two decades ago, girl! Get over it. I had nothing to do with that vagabond's death," Singh shouted.

"Lies, nothing but lies. And Krishna wasn't a vagabond, Mr. Home Minister!"

"You are drunk. You are always drunk," complained the father.

At about the same time, Anne was again arguing with her Mom: "These are three straight lines, Mom, not a triangle. I don't like Peeping Tom anyway and I have not made up my mind about Hari." She banged the phone, grabbed a sandwich and a cup of coffee and dozed off at the dining table, exhausted.

Too many people had flooded into Hari's life in his brief tenure as chief editor of *Verdict Today*, he reflected as he allowed Usha to lead him to his bedroom. She was a qualified nurse who used to work at Wadia Hospital, and was temporarily posted as Hari's housekeeper by Wadia immediately after his appointment as chief editor of the two hundred years' old newspaper which was finding it hard to cope with the twin challenges of competition from other established dailies and excesses of a dictatorial regime.

Usha loved the job and refused to be sent back to the hospital. She watched Hari as he dozed off. In fact, she loved the boss more than the job. She sat at the corner of the bed and kept looking at Hari: "I want to worship you, sir," she whispered; "The North Star, constant, unwavering, steadfast, shining always."

Then she went to the kitchen and asked Prem to make chicken soup and toasted cheese sandwiches for Hari. In reply, he hit her hard with a hot ladle. She screamed and staggered back, but straight into Hari who rushed to help after hearing the scream.

"My life is like a broken thermometer's mercury on the floor of your house, sir," she sobbed. He smiled and patted her on the shoulder: "You are a brave girl, Usha. Pull yourself up. Pick up that ladle, dip it in hot curry and hit the faggot hard."

"Repeatedly, the sterile wife-beating coward. Give him a taste of his own food. After you are through, give *me* a cup of tea on the dining table."

"Why did you get up so soon, sir, for me? This is my daily dose," she said.

He finally sat down to type some notes about Ali, who, according to Hari, professed that Jihad was a binding contract between Allah and all Muslims or *Momins*. Under the contract, Allah promised *Jannah* or paradise to *Mujahids* or holy warriors who must feel honour-bound to kill or be killed for His pleasure. Jihad automatically became obligatory on a Muslim when people "do not practice what Allah and Muhammad have prescribed it, according to the *Manifesto* of Ali's Al Jihad Party.

Registered office not stated, believed to be somewhere in noman's land on the India-Pakistan border, with branches in Equatoria, London, New York, San Francisco, Los Angeles, Las Vegas, and "Wherever there is a population of even one Muslim". The *Manifesto* says: "Jihad is all about massacre, mutilation and misery", not about moral, social or humanitarian service. Says the confidential document: "Everything a Momin possesses, including his life, belongs to Allah who promises Paradise in exchange". All Muslims "are required to fight non-Muslims—all those who do not believe in Islam, the religion of truth". The *Manifesto* adds: "The people of the *Book* (meaning The Bible)—the Christians and the Jews—are equally infidels like the Hindus, the Buddhists, the atheists, the Japonicus and the Cynics". All of the Infidels and *Kafirs* "must be killed unless they submit before the Islamic gun and live as tributaries (*zimmie*) and acknowledge their humiliation by payment of *Jizya* or Poll Tax". It says: "There is a direct connection between Jihad and Jannat, the provision of the choicest *sex-after-death* in the most hilarious settings ebullient with pleasures, presents and pleasantries."

Hari grinned as he underlined "hilarious", "ebullient" and "pleasantries". Lunatics, he said to himself.

But Usha, admiring him, said: "Sir?"

"Where's my tea?" he asked.

"You have already finished it, sir."

He started typing on his portable old Olympia again: "Having sex after death is a novel concept, which can be realised by terrorising, tearing and tyrannising non-Muslims. The commission of atrocities against Infidels makes Allah honourbound to offer paradise as a gift to a Mujahid, empyrean, the highest heaven, the realm of pure fire and light."

The *Manifesto* concluded: "Islam is the only true way of life; the rest is fake; unpardonable heresy. Infidels must be murdered or enslaved." Hari sighed and took out the typewritten copy and asked Usha to make photocopies to be distributed among the guests in the evening.

Time to place a call to Anne: "Good afternoon, My Lady. This is your slave, no need to execute this *Kafir*. I'm willing to part with all the *Jaziyah*, in cash as well as kind, in exchange for a drop of honey from your juicy lips."

She chimed: "What are you talking about."

"Ebulliently hilarious pleasantries of a humble *Mujahid* looking for the Seventh Heaven, Madam."

"How idiotically unromantic! You have lost your way and failed significantly to sweep me off my delicate feet. Mom is trying to make a love-triangle out of three straight lines. I'm ready to partially submit to her command—how about a two-sided triangle?" She chimed again.

"Listen, Koel is getting jealous. So is Usha. Say yes and I'll go get an engagement ring from last night's winnings."

"How's little Kris?" she asked.

"God! The imp has just crawled out into the backyard!" he screamed, gesticulating feverishly towards Usha; "The gnome is really adorable."

"May I bring along your rival Peeping Tom?"

"Of course. See you later, I think my employer's daughter Roshan is at the door. We are on course to make a hexagon. You too have plenty of competition. I want only a drop of nectar, not the beehive."

There was something compelling about her twitter, a soothing melody he wanted to record, replay and keep replaying with his eyes closed. Simply ethereal! Again, the mutilated toe and backache shooting through the spine and from head to toe caused him to camouflage a gasp with a hollow guffaw.

"Hazards of my antiquated profession," he said into the phone.

She laughed again. "And the perks," he added.

Again two more of the happy pills given by Ali. He kept them handy. Made him pain-free, light-hearted and flippant.

Roshan was in an awful mood. Karan had gone missing again: "Where could he have gone today?" she asked.

"Haven't the foggiest. He has made a habit of it of late." "Strange. These days, he also wears a special kind of perfume, **Itr**, he calls it. Real organic scent, not synthetic. Strong, pungent, quaint, exotic, says the deviant, my homo hubby. Sissy! Pooh!" She was hysterical.

"What's the matter? Seriously. It was love marriage, wasn't it? And now ..."

"I hate him. Impotent rogue. Sterile, your MD, Hari. Sells newsprint on the black market to buy gifts for his Pakistani boyfriend! Why don't you keep a tab on the creep."

"He's my boss, you know. And my employer's son-in-law," he said.

"Who's the Pakistani?"

"First Secretary in the Embassy, Yusuf," she said and asked for a drink.

"What's happening to our womenfolk," he said, and poured Scotch for both as Usha watched disapprovingly.

"Not good, sir, with those drugs you are taking," she spoke like a matron.

"What drugs?" asked Roshan.

"These, madam." said Usha. Roshan glanced at them: "Midazolam and Laudanum! For what? Throw that drink, Hari! My mother took an overdose of Laudanum and died." She tried to snatch the glass from his hand, stumbled on the carpet and fell into Hari's arms just as Anne floated in with a twinkle in her eye, stopped short of saying something, glided towards Koel's barricade-free cage and said: "Thrilled to make your acquaintance, birdie. Sing for me."

Koel skipped on her swing and said: "Coo ... Coo."

"Happy bird, don't you miss your mate?" Anne said extending a candy on her palm for Koel to pick up cleanly with her yellow beak.

Tom followed Anne into the room, smiled cautiously at nothing in particular and looked disapprovingly at Anne chirping in gay abandon with the bird and the diminutive girl with chink eyes. There was tension in the air. Tom's body language exuded vanity and David saw through the superficiality of Hari's buoyancy.

"Welcome, Mr Pickering. Welcome to India. Make yourself at home, please," Hari said.

"Thank you. Quite a place you've got."

"Luxuries of vulgar *nouveau riche* affluence," Hari grinned, trying to conceal his adversarial manner.

Dev burst in with the news that Raju was in hospital after being beaten up by a mob for teasing a burqa-clad woman near Jannat Lodge, where Ali was staying.

"*Dozakh* to Kafirs!" That's what they chanted while thrashing the reporter," Dev said.

"What's that?" Tom asked.

"Hell to Infidels!" Hari translated.

Dev whispered something in Hari's ear. His face fell, but he moved quickly to the liquor cabinet and poured a stiff drink. Anne noticed the look of anguish and asked: "What?"

"Liquor, the moribund refuge of a helpless coward in distress," he sighed.

She grabbed his arm and took him aside: "What's it?"

"Catastrophe!" he whispered.

"Where?"

"Poison gas threat over Delhi!" he hissed: "A million dollar scoop for an evening tabloid or unprincipled newsman which will cause cataclysmic panic," he said.

She grasped both his hands, brushed her lips against his. "Distillery stench!" she chortled.

Not being too technical, he was confused: "I need your discreet advice, Anne."

"Tell the Prime Minister," she said simply.

"I can't imagine a city like Delhi vanishing in a cloud of poison gas. But the information is reliable and I will have to go against my instinct and inform Big Brother hoping he will act promptly and pragmatically, not ponderously and politically," he said, went to the bedroom and spent twenty matter-of-fact minutes briefing the NSA chief.

He heaved a sigh of relief when the highly-decorated ace pilot, the stiff-upper-lip editor's routinely officious Big Brother, assured him that everything possible would be done to foil any poison gas invasion of the capital.

A huge weight off his chest, Hari rejoined the group, patting Tom on the back and winking at David: "Is it true that you can hear lobsters scream when you boil them?"

David winked back, Tom frowned, Anne twittered, Neelam poured herself another drink, Dev and Madhu smiled at each other and Usha placed a plum in front of Koel as toothless Kris tried to swallow an apple and lost his temper.

Hari said: "I hope you guys are taking care of yourselves. Sorry, I'm a lousy host. This get-together has been arranged to welcome Mr Thomas A. Pickering, the new American Consul, in the hope that he would overlook our frailties when we apply for US visas."

Anne's twitter prompted Usha to applaud as Tom scowled. Addressing Tom, he added: "Levity aside, please treat this as a kind of orientation session for you as well as an introduction to the proclivities and propensities of Jihad."

He heard Anne's chime and closed his eyes. "Long-winded Indian editor," she said. Koel cooed, Usha laughed, Madhu sniggered and Roshan clapped. Kris grabbed Anne's knee and used it as support to stand and giggle in her face, drops of milk suspended at the corners of his mouth. She picked him up and started kissing him from head to toe: "He's hungry."

"Mother's milk is best, says pediatrician Aryan," Hari grinned, looking at her heaving bosom.

"The fact, friends, is that there has been a deluge of disconcerting events all around us in the past few days. I have placed in front of all of you a rough draft concerning Jihad and its link with Jannat or paradise. Please go through my superficial observations and add your comments."

Sheetal and Usha, meanwhile, continued serving drinks. Pande, the driver, was drafted to help and his wife Laxmi was deputed in the kitchen in place of Prem, who was sulking in his quarters.

Tom thanked Hari for the "honor".

"It's all right, dude. I'm only trying to connect three straight lines to make an obtuse triangle," Hari grinned, and Anne twittered. He told him that the guests generally did not represent a cross-section of opinion-molders in the capital: "Just a bunch of naïve idealists."

"I have also invited my brother and his wife, representing the ruling elite, and Ram Kumar, for the opposition. "All the ingredients for a lethal showdown will be here when BB and RK arrive."

But neither of them came. No apology either; the Air Chief representing addiction to autocracy, and RK standing for virulent opposition to absolute power.

At the back of Hari's mind was his desire to make life less unbearable for humankind. Anne was perhaps the only person who could see through the veneer of Hari's clownish behaviour.

"You are caught up in your love affair with doing noble deeds and pursuit of unachievable goals," she told him.

David concurred: "Your impractical plans are much too good for the world, buddy boy, but you never waver in pursuing causes you consider good or just."

"Let's party!" Hari said; "Let's upload the Seventh Heaven for posterity, as exemplified by orphaned Kris, while the going is good!" A sudden explosion in the kitchen shook the house and brought the frolicking to an abrupt end.

"That's the essence of phony Jihad," Anne's voice rose above the pin-drop silence after the blast. Hari, Sheetal and Pande rushed to the kitchen. Laxmi was badly wounded. Dev called an ambulance. Hari and Sheetal accompanied it to Wadia Hospital, followed by Pande in Hari's car.

"This is the true face of militant Islam," Anne told the guests; "Islamism reigns as the most powerful ideological force across the world, the most dangerous anti-democratic movement."

"I agree," said David; "In the Muslim world, religion has become all encompassing in the last few decades—the fanatics represent the cutting edge of the culture. The world of Islam has been least penetrated by irreligion."

Tom drew attention to the internal contradictions of Islam in the face of socioeconomic realities which would not change poverty, crises in values and identities, the decay of the educational systems, the North-South conflict, and, above all, the problem of immigrant integration in host societies.

Everyone agreed, so did Hari, who had just returned with the news that "Laxmi could survive if the hospital could get some people to donate five pints of ABH blood group". Neelam promptly volunteered and Dev drove her to the hospital.

Hari felt exhausted. "It's only the beginning, crusader," Anne chimed; "You are trying to churn the mythical ocean at the beginning of time according to your Hindu scriptures."

"I know. Hilarious. A single journalist committed to defeating the green-blazer force of indoctrinated zombies or a group of idealists trying to save humanity from countless monsters," he said.

"Pen is mightier than the sword," she chimed.

"This is not the age of the sword."

"Nor is it the age of the pen."

"It's the age of deceit and perversion," said Roshan.

"It's the age of love. I can hear time go by stealthily, footsteps on the sands of time challenging us to stay on course as we try to divert a sandstorm into evil eyes," Hari said with a distant look in his eyes.

Anne glanced at him and twittered. Tom moved uneasily.

"Your fragrance touches my eyes, your chuckle caresses my lips and your breath intoxicates me," Hari said dreamily.

"What kind of Oriental poetic nonsense is this?" Anne said, amused, as Tom stared open-mouthed.

"Will I remain suspended forever within that fleeting moment between hope and despair," he said, and turning to Koel, added: "O' little bird, stop regurgitating kernel, convey my message to the angel, tell her that without her giggle, life's unbearable."

This time, Anne moved. She giggled, he chuckled, and an embrace with a pent-up kiss lasting an eternity followed. Tom squirmed, Roshan, Neelam and Usha applauded in unison.

"This is my Seventh Heaven," Hari said, his limbs quivering, sensing a confluence of two souls.

"Mine, too. And I don't need a Jihad fanatic to define Jannat for me. Believe it or not, the triangle is complete," she twittered.

"To hell with Jannat and Jihad!" David exclaimed.

"No matter what happens, always keep your childlike innocence intact, pure, noble, my real new world," he said and kissed her again, tenderly.

Koel seemed ecstatic, fluttering her velvety wings excitedly:

"Coo…coo," she sang fervently.

Tom wasn't amused. He glared at the tiny cuckoo bird with a big appetite as he found her gobbling up an apple and regurgitating the pith.

"Has somebody notified the bomb-squad?" he asked.

Chapter - 18

Below the Belt

Dev came rushing into the newsroom and walked nervously into Hari's private office: "Sir! A Taliban group in London has issued fatwa against you!"

"Do you have the full story?" he asked. Dev nodded. "Let me see it after you have done it. By the way, Dev, try and do a small sidebar on the legal intricacies of fatwa under sharia," the chief said, and picked up his ringing telephone. A voice said: "This is Parliament Street Police Station. There is a woman here who wants to tell you something important about the Madhu case. Only you, no one else. Immediately, somebody is chasing her."

Hari could not help feeling that some unseen force was out to make a sucker out of him. First, the fatwa. Then, the anonymous call about a mystery woman with a secret. "Only the chief, not anybody else," the voice insisted. Hari dropped everything else and rushed to the station across the street only to be told that no one had called him and that there were no new leads on the Madhu story. Annoyed but unconvinced, he looked around suspiciously and saw a glimpse of interrogationist Dial.

Singh entering one of the offices. "What's the super cop doing here?" he asked a constable.

"I don't know, sir," the cop replied. Hari stopped to think about the goings-on and wondering about the presence of the scapegrace scoundrel who was disliked by most people and for good reason. He shrugged and started walking back, his mind focused on the fatwa against him and the ongoing carnage and the threats ahead, his overdue scoop of the century. At the zebra crossing, he mechanically looked left, right, then left and started crossing the road watchfully. Straight ahead, he saw Anne step out of her

Toyota Highlander outside Verdict Today House, His mood changed instantly, his heart missed a beat as he saw the silver anklets glittering around her tantalizing ankles. He started cavorting merrily across the road unmindful of a speeding truck coming straight at him. He swayed from side to side, backed away, but the truck kept coming at him, and he started performing an impromptu Swan Lake ramba nervously in the middle of the road, trying in vain to avoid the maniacal vehicle.

Anne saw the truck swerve wildly out of control and crash into a stationary bus. She ran towards the site as she could no longer see Hari, who was lying flat on his back, unconscious, surrounded by curious onlookers doing nothing. She pushed some of them impatiently and was relieved to see he was breathing, asked a couple of idle cops to help her lift him to her car. "This is the only state in which he can be brought under control," she said to no one in particular and drove him to Wadia Hospital about a block away.

When Hari came to, Anne was arguing with a nurse. "You guys have no sense of cleanliness and comfort. Look at those bloodstains on the bed sheet and cobwebs on the wall!"

"Sorry, madam," said the nurse.

"Dusty cobwebs, rusty bloodstains, green mold, oxidized candelabras, reverse swastikas, gloomy pentagrams, gaping skulls and gay zombies, wet sand in the hourglass of life and bloodthirsty Jihadis," Hari groaned.

"And long-winded editors!" said Anne, visibly relieved; "What are you going to do about the fatwa, dear?"

"I must go to the office!" he shouted, trying to get up from the bed and groaned: "Some components are already broken? Extremely painful. That bastard kept following me!"

"Shoulder and thigh, fractures and slipped disc," said Anne; "Big Brother has been appointed Principal Martial Law Administrator. India is bleeding. Lunatics on the rampage."

"Gosh! My brother! Shit!! Tranquilize me to oblivion!" he sighed, and then pulled himself up: "Where's Dev? Please get to the bottom of the carnage. Coordinate all sources. Do it fast before it's too late. My brother takes his job seriously!"

"Runs in the family," grinned the Insight team chief.

"No bloody clowning!"

"But the Air Chief will soon control the situation, sir," Dev said.

"That's my fear! He'll do it too fast and perhaps too well, that son of...my father, I'm sorry to say. No Muslim is safe.

Please connect me to his wife," he said.

"She's already here, stupid," Anne twittered holding Yukta's hand, who said: "Send this dazzler to reason with him. He has accepted her as our daughter and no Rai can decline a girl child's request."

Hari followed the advice and Anne reluctantly agreed after a great deal of humanitarian reasoning. Anne requested an appointment and Rai agreed to meet her right away. Then, Hari suggested to Dev to get in touch with the Imam of Jama Masjid in Delhi and the heads of Hazratbal in Kashmir and other Islamic leaders. "Provoke them to come out with their statements."

"Trying to engineer a Hindu backlash, sir?" he taunted. "The price we are paying for accepting the two-nation theory of the founder of Pakistan, Mohammed Ali Jinnah, not even a proper Muslim himself," he lamented, almost in tears. Mary, astonished, said: "I had no idea you could be so emotional about anything."

"I've seen much turmoil during the partition. Tragic.

Massacre!

Genocide! These are not just words. They are bloody sores on our nation's collective soul. I still get nightmares about it, years after the bloodbath of Indian independence. I saw with my own eyes my first cousin, Hira Lal Seth, being brutally murdered by Muslim fanatics. Even today, a part of India is ablaze."

Dr Ali Chughtai was summoned. "Hallucinating," he said.

By now, Usha had also arrived. Looking at the bedside chart, she asked for the file. Examining it, she tersely asked: "Why is he being given Pethidine and Midazolam?" The duty nurse kept quiet. Hari was now fast asleep, but still mumbling: "Please prevent a Hindu backlash."

Usha said she did not understand what he was saying. But Dev said he did: "He's making a lot of sense and we don't know what to do to prevent a majority backlash. I am worried about the fatwa, but why isn't the chief scared?"

"I am mortified, Dev. What can I do? Go underground?

Never! Is it a Sunni fatwa or a Shia fatwa? Who has signed the order? Anyway, it doesn't apply to me. Islamic jurisprudence has no jurisdiction over a Hindu," he grinned.

"Sir, an attempt has already made on your life. The truck driver has confessed that Mufti Faqih of Madrasa-e-Rehmat ordered him to slay you," Dev said.

At about that moment, Anne arrived at the Air Chief's operational headquarters, and BB courteously bowed and said: "What can we do for Queen Cleopatra?"

Anne reasoned with him for ten minutes and got him to do what Hari had carefully coached her to demand. "My worry, sir, is that all martial law administrators around the world throughout history and today have been notorious for their bloodlust! I don't want my own oldest relative-to-be to follow in their bloody trail!" she said, touching the sentimental chord in the ace pilot.

"How touchingly eloquent! Do you mean no bloodshed at all?"

"Yes, sir."

"But there will, of necessity, have to be some bloodshed in a highly charged situation such as this."

"That's understood, sir." "All right, sweetheart. Your word is my command. I will issue the necessary orders right away! Go and tell my kid brother. He hates me, that rascal, but you are finally the daughter the Rai family hasn't had for five generations because of a curse!" he said, and gently kissed her hand. After thanking him with a kiss on his cheek, she rushed to the hospital, to tell Hari. He said he knew, and then told her about the curse. "It's like a fairy tale," he began; "I can't vouch for it's truth, but I still believe it because it's corroborated by several independent sources."

"Will he keep his word?" a fascinated Usha asked.

"Of course, he will! He will do everything possible to keep his word, so keen are the Rais to have a daughter. Five generations and no girl child. You are the fulfillment of the Rai dream!"

"Really! Am I so loved?"

"Even you? Do you love me as a daughter, you numbskull!"

"Well, we shall learn about that part too," he smiled.

"Eventually!"

Tell us the whole story," Anne said.

"First, I believe in my version, my interpretation, of the fairy tale. And that does not make me very proud of our aristocratic ancestors," he said.

"What's that?"

"All right, there was once a nobleman in Lahore—my ancestor five generations ago, I've forgotten his name. He was a senior courtesan of the famous Maharaja Ranjit Singh of Punjab and probably very corrupt and rich. But there was no heir to his immense ill-gotten wealth. So, he married again. No luck. And again. Still no offspring. Then, another courtesan told him about a Muslim holy man who granted boons to his followers. Thus, the story goes, my ancestor and his three wives went to see the holy man, who, after much ado, predicted that if the nobleman submitted to his, the holy man's condition, he would soon be blessed with a son."

"What condition," asked Usha, her chinky eyes becoming bigger.

"The condition was to name the male offspring Mehboob Rai."

"What else?"

"He also predicted that the nobleman will beget a girl child and that he must name her Fatima after the Prophet Muhammad's daughter. And that's where the curse came in. The nobleman did not name the girl Fatima, and gave her a Hindu name. The girl child died before her fifth birthday just as the Muslim holy man had said. He had also cursed that failure to give the girl child a Muslim name would mean that no female child would be born into that family for a certain number, I don't remember, of generations."

Anne said: "So, it's five generations since you guys haven't had a female in your family. That's your story?" said Anne.

"It's more to do with logic than skepticism Or logical skepticism, if you please. I accuse my ancestors of the most heinous crime: doing with newborn or infant female children as a number of Hindus, the less well to do or poor Hindus, do not want a girl child because of the dowry system. I guess my ancestors too may have been poor until this one who became a sycophant of the ruler of Punjab," said Hari, now animated.

"Please tell us more, sir," Usha beseeched.

"Later, right now, several parts of India are bleeding. Religious riots. Arrests of so-called anti-social elements. Hate crimes. Arson. Looting. Brutality everywhere. That's a heavy price this nation is paying for it's chosen leaders' blunder of accepting the two-nation theory. Only two nations? Screw you! A billion lunatics involved in an orgy of raping the country in a pornographic tandava," said Hari, breathless, asking for a cup of tea.

His secretary brought a transcript of the statement the Air Chief had just made to a crowded news conference. A little bleary-eyed. Hari asked Mary to read it to him: The report follows: "I have called you, ladies and gentlemen, to make a humble request and to make one statement. I implore media to refrain from publishing news that might incite communal violence. That's the request. The announcement is that no one will be subjected to censorship during the martial law period. Please exercise self-censorship in the national interest."

He added: "You will be pleased to know that I have ordered the armed forces and other law-enforcement agencies to refrain from using force against enemies of the State except in cases of extreme provocation. But please do not consider my call for peace as a sign of weakness. If you don't heed my request, please be warned that the authorities will use all means possible to stop any threat to peace and stability in this country. And finally to the foreign terrorists operating in the country, this is my final warning: Surrender, or be prepared to be crushed. Don't even try to escape across the border. Don't make that mistake! We will shoot first and ask questions later.... Thank you, ladies and gentlemen Jai Hind!"

Some reporters wanted to know about the action being taken about Hari's accident. He told them that the rogue driver was seriously injured and that he had admitted his links with Jihad. "Police are following up on some vital leads," he said cryptically. Hari said he was ready to make a statement about the Muslim holy man.

"Are you mad!" Anne demanded; "An open invitation to assassins! Please don't do this," she beseeched.

"Don't be afraid. I have just remembered the name of the holy guy."

"What!"

"Rai Ali Hassan...That's where we get our family name from—a Muslim witch doctor!" he laughed; "Who says the Rai's are not secularists?" And Hari laughed; "Frankly, my dear, secularism is the curse of the humanitarian world!"

Anne was exasperated: "You know, you are blabbering like a lunatic under the influence of the drugs you are apparently being given." "Yes, why am I being given these drugs and by whom... oh, yeah, Dr. Ali Chughtai, is a Muslim! I know he must be mixed up in this, too!"

"Now, that's enough! Either you are very ill or something terrible is bothering you. Why don't you go to sleep," she said. "No, I can't! A lot of things are, indeed, troubling me and I am helpless in this bloody bed! Please get me out of this hospital," he pleaded.

"In due course," said Dr. Chughtai, who had walked in. Hari gave him a strange look:

"Why are you trying to turn me into a junkie, doc?" he demanded.

"What are you talking about, Mr. Rai?"

"The strong drugs. Heavy doses? Why?"

The doctor turned to the matron: "What is being given?"

"Pethidine, and Midazolam 15 mg. Every three hours," she said.

"On whose orders?"

"Dr. Bansal, sir," she said.

"Who the hell is this Dr Bansal … Never heard of him! God! Stop all medication. Remove the drip. There's been a breach of security, sister; call the police fast and perform all the conceivable tests on the patient. Fast." A virtual state of emergency was declared in and around Room Five in the VIP bloc of the hospital.

Anne was flabbergasted. Hari was aghast in a drowsy sort of way: "It's so funny. I have suddenly become so important for criminals to hire hooligans to eliminate me! What have I done! Come, get me, you illegitimate bastards of whores! Too many adjectives! So what? I am the Chief Editor, you mongrels!" He was delirious. The matron, Annie Mathew, ordered all visitors to get out of the room. But Anne and Usha declined to leave, and the matron relented: "It's important for him to sleep. Please try not to agitate him." Hari slept for about forty minutes, woke up with a splitting headache and mumbled: "Hangover. I just had a nightmare. An overgrown child resembling our Kris sitting on my chest and strangling me with hairy hands and breathing foul breath into my face while I am lying motionless on a barricaded bed and a ceiling fan is expanding like a multi-armed balloon. What can that mean, my dear girls?" he said and dozed off again.

Dr Chughtai tiptoed in and said: "He has been heavily drugged by some miscreants. There was cocaine even in the drip. We are giving some antidote, but that will take some time to take effect." He also suggested that they take rest for a while, but the girls declined: "We must personally guard against any more intrusions," Anne insisted, firmly.

Meanwhile, Hari came to again and complained he had not had a bath for a year. "I'm feeling very dirty, unwashed, unbrushed, unshaved, unfed, undressed, unclean," he mumbled and dozed off again. Usha burst into tears and ran out.

It turned out to be night-long vigil. The two girls were relieved by Mary, Yukta, Roshan and Sheetal. Early morning, Hari wanted to be helped to sit up, but tight bandages prevented him from doing so. His bandaged leg zipped up in a tight bandage and his left arm in plaster in a fixed position tied to a stand, and his right arm taped to the bed because of the drip, he had to contend with only a little bit of leeway. So he gave up and laughed in his usual good-natured way. But everyone saw that he was fully alert. The smile was back and the delirious cynic was no longer there.

"Let's do some hard thinking, sister," Hari said, looking at Roshan, "About what? she asked.

"Everything."

"No, you must rest and it's too early to strain your mind."

"All right, get the senior editors to come around, so we can have an early morning editorial meeting," he said.

"They have only just gone home. They also need to rest," he said. "All right then, only you and I. The fatwa, issued in London, orders given by the mufti of Mecca Mosque in Delhi. All oral. Who paid the stupid driver and who made the fake call? Why can't extremism be abolished. I don't think I'm a rabble-rouser. Not even a crusader. Not even a righter of wrongs. No sermonizer. Only a fact-finder and presenter of truth without value-judgments. An honest interpreter of facts without bias." He was talking aloud. "Not big enough to be assassinated, an intense wordsmith who wants to prevent bloodshed, a fact-finder intending to hold the mirror to fanatics to show them as what they really are, not martyrs but brainwashed obnoxious creatures due to no fault of their own."

"Perhaps these are the very qualities that have earned you the wrath of some people. Your honesty and relentlessness lead you to the pursuit of truth which somebody may be finding dangerous. Tell me, what are you feverishly working on right now and pushing your team to accomplish? You are a very irritating pusher, you know," said Roshan.

"What really are you pursuing?"

At that point, Anne stepped in to bring "sunshine" into Hari's eyes. "That," he pointed to her; "That's what I'm pursuing with all my heart and soul," he said.

Meanwhile, some of the senior editors came in and Hari signaled the start of the meeting: "Tell me, boys and girls, what are we chasing as the most crucial stories," he asked.; "I am now back on terra firma, please.

Let's begin…"

"Pornography. Wildlife-poaching and diamond deals. Race Course jackpot scam, cricket gambling. Afrikaner Broederbond or the Brotherhood of Power. Gun-running to Africa. Terrorism network. Corruption in high places. Drug mafia. Indians spying for Pakistan," he started.

"From the Kama Sutra of Pornography to enemies within and human-organ supermarket to the Brotherhood of Power and overthrow of African regimes. These are among the matters on our docket," said Hari.

"Where are we on Muslim Africa's war against the US and Israel?

"That's waiting for proper execution by you." said his deputy, Ramesh Gaur; "Islam versus the rest, your scoop of the century!"

"What about the attempts on your life?" asked Anne.

"And Roshan, I'm angry with your husband for not visiting me in the hospital. Anyway, let's all have tea if someone will organise it," Hari said, thanking everyone for their hard work "in keeping *Verdict Today* in contention" in his absence.

In the general ward, trucker Imran Sultan admitted trying "to crush the kafir Hari on the orders of Dial Singh" and that he was to receive payment from Hamid Mirza, owner of the trucking company. Sultan lived in a small room in a three storey building rented by eunuchs, who did not charge him any rent because he gave them protection against hooligans. He also acted as a pimp for the eunuchs, some of whom functioned as male prostitutes. "A strange world," said Hari when he was told all this. Eunuchs, rapists, killers, movie extras, a superstar. What else? Carry on inspector. Is Sultan also a eunuch?"

"He does not appear to be sexually weird. Strong as an ox. Besides, he is also badly injured in that hit-and-run and is being treated at this very hospital. Hordes of ungainly eunuchs visit the muscleman at all times and they are very chummy with him."

"Interesting," said Hari; "So, we have a full-fledged Eunuch Force on our hands!" The police officer laughed. So did Dr Chughtai who had stealthily walked in; "Were you eavesdropping, doctor?" Hari asked, a cunning smile on his face. The doctor grinned, possibly embarrassed, Hari noted.

"How are we feeling, Mr Rai?"

"I feel like a fragile snowflake rolling down the slope of Kanchenjunga desperately looking for Mother Ganga, lonely, fragile, melting, dizzy, shattering," he said; "Tell me, Dr Chughtai, your name sounds familiar, like I may have read it somewhere in connection with a historic event ... Let me think ... Tell me, doctor, please, how did Prime Minister Lal Bahadur Shastri die? Heart attack? Or poisoned? In Tashkent, you know, shortly after signing the peace agreement with General Mohammad Ayub Khan of Pakistan after the 1965 war," said Hari, very slowly, emphasising every syllable Dr Chughtai was taken aback: "Of course, I remember," he stammered; "I was his personal physician, you know."

"So?" asked Hari.

"You know, the PM was already dead when I arrived in his suite. The Shastri family accused the cook of poisoning him. But I don't know. No post-mortem. All hush-hush. I was scared," he said, moving towards the door.

"Please don't go, doctor. I want to talk to you about something else.

"Never mind Shastri. Who's Dr Bansal," he asked.

Once again, Dr Chughtai was uneasy: "I don't remember."

At that precise moment, Usha walked in, holding the hand of a nervous young man: "This is Dr Bansal, sir. I just found him waiting for a bus outside Talkatora Club across the street, sir," she said, triumphantly.

It became clear that young Bansal was an intern attached to the VIP unit. He admitted that he was sent by Dr. Chughtai to administer the pills and that he had no idea that the medicines could be lethal, especially if given together. Midazolam, researchers found, was a potent amnestic, hypnotic, anticonvulsant, muscle relaxant and water-soluble sedative. Pathedin was an opiate painkiller. Both, administered together, could be fatal. Flumazenil anexate was the only known antidote for an overdose and it was not available in the hospital pharmacy. It was hurriedly obtained it from another institution and Hari was well on his way to recovery to go on the world's most intoxicating binge of risk-taking in a face-to-face with fatwa-wielding Jihad.

Hari now had a self-satisfied smile on his face. "Tell me, my dear doctor, who won the 1965 India-Pakistan war? Your Pakistani cousin, Shaan, editor of a Pakistani newspaper, boasted that Pakistan won its Jihad hands down and that the Indian armed forces surrendered like cowards before the brave Pakistani mujahids. You may not be pleased to know that I have personally done a great deal of truly objective research into Indo-Pak conflicts. At this stage, all I want to tell you is that the 1965 war was, indeed, won by India although casualties on both sides were very heavy." said Hari; "But you are absolutely right in assuming that one Wing Commander RAI, namely my elder brother, did run amuck over Lahore and heavily bombed a mansion known as Mehboob Rai Palace, our ancestral home, and inadvertently caused the death of your aunt's entire family! I am sorry for that. My brother became very emotional at the time and, in his mind, he was destroying his own ancestral property occupied by Pakistanis! I am truly sorry, but I still cannot condone your vindictiveness against me."

"Who killed Shastri and why?" asked Anne.

"Don't worry sweetheart, it wasn't President Lyndon B. Johnson of the United States. True, American sympathies were with Pakistan.

Below the Belt Indeed, the USA had supplied the most sophisticated arms and aircraft to the Pakistanis, but they had no reason to kill the Indian PM. The peace broker, Kosygin, also had no motive. However, I did suspect China, because, at about the same time, the People's Republic had made noises about Indian incursions into Chinese territory, but Shastri had declared that India would throw out all invading enemies, meaning both Pakistan and China," Hari added.

"So?" Anne interjected.

"So, it leaves both India and Pakistan. And I have enough circumstantial evidence to show it was retribution by Jihad fatwa executed by…"

"Stop! That may well be the motive for the attempt on your life!" she said, her eyes widening in horror; "For my sake, Hari, stop trying to make your paper the greatest overnight. You are being unfair to those who care for you. You are a lunatic."

Hari retorted: "True, I am mad! But I am not chasing these issues; they are chasing me, staring me in the face, glaring at me as I lie helplessly in bed! Yes, I am a lunatic, woman! Go back to your comfortable lifestyle to live the American Dream, and leave me alone to struggle to chase the Indian nightmare."

Anne, finally, smiled: "What an impassioned speech." She got up from her chair in controlled slow motion, planted a kiss on his mouth and giggled. He tried to sit up, but writhed in pain, and said:

"What's the date today?"

"Why?" she asked.

"The first kiss! Divine! An historic event. Must make a note of it in our anniversary calendar, First meeting. First time you melted in my arms, first fight and first kiss."

"Let's postpone the argument. Change the subject now. By the way, I saw your Mazhar Khan today. At the Embassy this morning, waiting to meet visa chief Tom Pickering. Perhaps planning a trip to the US," she said.

"Really? Interesting," he said without enthusiasm.

"Why? Not interested?" she taunted.

"I'll leave this to the boys. I feel tired right now. Try and get me a drink, please," he said.

"Oh yeah?" she sneered; "You do think you are the centre of the universe, don't you?"

"Please! I'm thirsty. You *are* the centre of my universe. You know that."

"But this is not the residential wing of your India International Centre. No liquor, mister!"

"Heartless American! Ku Klux Klan (KKK}!" He made a face, and showed her the middle finger.

She was genuinely annoyed: "Where does KKK come in!"

"Why? Aren't you a member of the Church of Fiery Cross?" he mocked.

"Certainly not! I'm not a southerner, lunatic!" She glared at him.

"For God, Race and Nation—the politically incorrect Christian outreach ministry to God's chosen race—the true Israel, the White, European peoples," he taunted.

"What are you blabbering about. You really are mad. How low can you stoop to provoke me to give you a drink, you alcoholic womanizer!"

She had now understood what Hari was getting at. Even so, he was conducting some superficial research on the KKK to discover its connection, if any, with the Afrikaner Broederbond. Thus far, he had not found any link, but his findings were as yet inconclusive; good enough for a couple of drinks. She continued to pull his leg for presuming himself to be the centre of the universe, and Hari, on the defensive, contending that, as the youngest national editor, he had to make *Verdict Today* a good, untarnished, mirror through which the readers could see the world as it was, untainted, tarnished or untarnished, as the case may be. Ironically, his own managing director, Karan, was at that very moment sweet-soaping Wadia with his cunningly disparaging innuendos about the chief editor: "Hari's pornographic inclinations may prove counter-productive in the not too distant future."

The shrewd tycoon shook his head: "I see nothing even remotely erotic in the paper. What makes you feel that way, young man?"

"I'll tell you what, papa. He says the great temples of Khajuraho are obscene tributes to Hindu gods in profane sculptures by perverts," Karan said; "He is also planning to seriously defame some film stars and producers by reporting that they are making big-budget lewd flicks besmirching Hindu epics and the Old Testament by selectively picking tales from the scriptures and giving them modernist twists."

His wife countered: "Hari has talked to me about this. The fact is that police have caught some actors in compromising situations and that some of them have made incriminating statements against my sweet husband's buddy megastar Mazhar Khan, who, they claim, is contributing to the Jihad kitty. It's going to be a mammoth multi-dimensional campaign to ridicule

Hinduism, Christianity, Buddhism and Judaism. The Insight team is looking into the economics of Islam's pornographic misadventures, which also involve bootlegging and drug-running. Revenue, you know, papa. For conducting Jihad."

"I understand, baby. Our Parsi community has also been asked to pay jizya as protection money to Mecca Mosque. The message was brought sweetly by your husband on the pretext that he had intercepted a Taliban message meant for Al-Jazeera TV."

Around that time, a restless Hari called Wadia and urged him to have him discharged from the hospital: "I am better. No pain." Hari was surprised when Wadia readily agreed. Anne drove him to his house, where he found that all arrangements had been made for him to function comfortably. A party was already in progress and Wadia made the announcement immediately after Hari was wheel-chaired in by Anne.

"Global Media Freedom House, New York, has chosen Hari Journalist of the Month," Wadia said.

Hari screamed: "Somebody, please give me a drink!"

Sheetal brought his drink: "We are proud of you, sir!"

Deputy editor Ramesh said: "Circulation has crossed two million. And Karan complains about newsprint shortage."

Wadia asked: "What's happened to our own newsprint plant?"

"Raw material shortage, sir," Ramesh replied.

Wadia was livid: "Call Karan, please. Have we sunk a million dollars in the new factory? Where is Karan?"

"He is attending a reception at the Libyan Embassy, sir," said Mary. Anyway, Hari's home-coming was turned into one rocking party in which the host could not dance because of his fractured femur. Even so, he joined in the merrymaking by over-drinking and falling asleep in the wheelchair and Anne moved him to his bed as the guests departed. "You are in grave danger, Hari," she whispered.

"I'm not worried about the danger about which you are talking. The greater danger is from within. From my damned MD, who's sabotaging the paper and I can do nothing about it because the creep is my employer's son-in-law," he sighed. "I'm surprised. It's not simply a question of nepotism. Karan is in regular touch with Libyans and Pakistanis and God knows who else," she said.

"So?"

"Why Libya? Is he somehow linked to Jihad?" she asked.

"Never mind. Will you marry me, Anne Spencer? I will make you the most miserable fairy in the cosmos," he stammered, looked intently into her eyes.

"Why?" she ejaculated, surprised, open-mouthed, and whispered: "I thought you'd never ask; "Of course, I'll marry you and then kill you ever so slowly in a hundred different and delicious ways in a hundred years so you can rewrite Kamasutra and build another Khajuraho!" They kissed passionately for an eternity, oblivious of the trials and tribulations ahead.

But they were reluctantly interrupted by Sheetal: "Mr. Wadia is here to see you, sir."

The tycoon seemed preoccupied: "Something bothering you, sir," Hari asked.

"Your MD, Karan seems to have a Libyan connection."

"Oh, the Great Socialist People's Libyan Arab Jamahiriya, sir, and Colonel Muammar Qaddafi's veneer of democracy concealing his Jihadi inclinations," Hari said.

"Exactly, he's my son-in-law and I can't sack him, so he is being transferred to the cosmetics division," Wadia said and left.

"This man, Anne, is the catalyst in India's industrialisation. Oil, steel, locomotives, textiles, pharmaceuticals, media, food processing, textiles, hospitality, aviation. Excellent quality in every product and service. Healthcare. Charities, Education, Social welfare, Humility is his second nature," Hari said.

"Why is he unhappy with Karan?" she asked.

"He must have found out something. I wonder if he already hinted about his decision to anyone. I hope not. He must make a surprise announcement at tomorrow's general body meeting," Hari said, looking worried.

"Are you well enough to attend the meeting," she asked.

"I think I'm quite fit, but I won't attend. But I will go to the party. And I would like you to be my date. Would you mind if we take Kris to his first big national party?"

"Where is the imp? Haven't seen him all evening," she asked.

"A lady reporter has taken her to Iskcon headquarters to locate his parents."

"Let's take him along. He will enjoy," she said, but was surprised to see Hari get up effortlessly from his chair, and perform an intricate Kathak dance move involving a warrior riding a chariot, whipping the horses in one miraculous movement. The next day was hectic for Jal Dastoor Wadia. He presided over half-a-dozen meetings, an international conference of development economists and an extraordinary general body meeting of *Verdict Today* shareholders, his last professional engagement, just before the cocktail party to honor Hari. There was an undercurrent of moodiness in Wadia's bearing as he shook hands with the shareholders on his way to the podium. All through, he was thinking about her daughter's happiness and the ultimate meaning of her so-called "love marriage" with Karan.

How much of love was enough for a happily-married life? True love, if there was such an emotion, was not like sexual orgasm which was enough when it happened. His ultimate goal in life was total satisfaction, bliss, continuous, uninterrupted lifelong orgasm, as he was to tell his son, daughter, Hari and Anne before the cocktail party.

Roshan was looking for Karan at the party, not knowing that the saboteur suspected that Wadia was planning to disinherit him and was trying to make arrangements to prevent him from doing so. He drove his Range Rover madly towards the Friday Mosque area to a herbalist's clinic and confided in a bearded practitioner of leech-craft, who said: "Don't worry, son. Go attend the party. Your problem will be taken care of."

He arrived at the party an hour late in much better humor.

Apparently, he had blind faith in the witchdoctor. Mingling freely with the guests, he even greeted Hari warmly and paid abundant attention to Roshan. Wadia was surrounded by several admirers.

"Who's he talking to?" Anne asked.

The man's back was towards them; broad-shoulders, taller than Wadia, henna-dyed hair, green blazer, gray trousers, no necktie. The two started advancing towards Wadia, but stopped short as they heard a muffled scream and saw the tycoon slump to the floor. Hari rushed to the spot. Wadia was lying in a pool of blood, gasping for breath, dying, dying, dead. Pandemonium. The richest man murdered, stabbed. Hari noticed Karan move gingerly towards the bar, pick up a glass and gulp the drink before rushing towards the scene of the crime, stammering and grasping Rustom's arm in simulated grief.

Hari and Roshan watched in disbelief, devastated by the murder most foul having snatched a great employer and the best father who was too busy with his full life to fear death. "Death has taken him by surprise although he was always ready for a new adventure in afterlife," Hari said, wiping Roshan's tears.

Police arrived within minutes and all entrances and exits were sealed as assistant commissioner P. S. Aurora took charge. Hari was shocked to see the dirty cop. Anne was the first to approach him. She told him: "Mr Wadia was talking to a man with henna-dyed hair who was wearing a green blazer." Aurora waved her aside and glared at Hari: "Where were you at the time, mister?

Hari was livid: "Don't you screw up this time, bully! Find the green blazer, tall, broad shoulders, henna hair. Now! Be warned! No more pickling of toes!"

Aurora barked: "Didn't Mr Wadia threaten to dismiss you for defaming Khan?"

"Not at all! I haven't defamed anyone, but I am eagerly waiting to expose you and your traitorous chief, paramour of the Iraqi dictator's kin! Don't slander me this time, Aurora! Be warned! Mr Wadia was a man of great integrity, a towering icon of global eminence. Don't you mess it up."

Rustam brought the situation under control and requested Hari and Anne to go into the house. She mentioned a scar on the face of green blazer. Hari looked doubtful: "We only saw the guy's back."

"I could see a part of his face from my position," she said; "I have a feeling that I have seen the scarface somewhere else…"

"Try to remember. Concentrate. Close your eyes, yoga-like, and concentrate hard. Don't get tense. Just relax and concentrate. Finally, she said: "Yeah! It's Karachi! The airport… baggage counter… No … Immigration …cubicle — henna-dyed hair, Scarface! Got it!" she jumped triumphantly: "An Immigration Officer at Karachi Airport at the enclosure for diplomats and VIPs. Broad smile, filthy teeth, smell of cheap tobacco. Now, what should I do?" she asked.

He advised her to check with an appropriate Embassy official about the protocol in criminal investigations. "Don't go directly to the police. Besides, you never saw anybody stab Mr Wadia. You have no reason to believe that scarface is the killer. Just because the man's teeth are dirty and he smells of garlic does not make him the murderer, young lady. Besides, it's possible that someone has already given description of the suspect to the police. After all, Wadia was surrounded by several people at the time of the murder."

"Wait, do you want to run a parallel investigation?" she asked.

"Perhaps," he said.

"All right. Do you have someone at the Embassy who could draw a sketch of scarface according to the description you provide. We have our cartoonist and an illustrator. But they are no good for this purpose. Someone with CIA or FBI background?"

"Yes, there's Tom."

"Fine, let's get him over to my house for a drink. Good. Settled. Tomorrow."

Tom turned out to be an expert. After about half-an-hour at his sketch pad, and Anne exclaimed: "That's the self-same villain," she said.

So, Anne and Hari thought they had a lead: A Pakistani Government official. Perhaps Immigration. No name yet. Did that mean official Pakistani involvement in the murder of a key economic figure in India? Or was it an act of selective terrorism.

"In any event, someone will have to travel to Karachi to identify the man and make subtle enquiries," Hari said; "let's sleep over it. I will find someone appropriate by tomorrow." The telephone rang. Karan wanted to meet him in the office at ten o'clock in the morning. "Very urgent," he stressed; "Rustom will also come. Your office."

Hari wondered as Anne looked at him quizzically. He dialled Rustom's number to double-check. But he had no idea about the meeting: "I'm in no condition to attend any meetings. Please take care of whatever it is that Karan wants to do." Hari persuaded him to make an exception and they assembled at Hari's office on schedule. "Proceed," Rustom told Karan.

He pulled himself up and said: "Mr. Wadia, Dad, had a long meeting with me day before yesterday. He said he was very worried about Hari, saying he was doing too much alone and that he should start delegating to senior editors. He went so far as to suggest that Hari deserves a vacation."

"Is that all?" asked Hari.

"No. Mr. Wadia, Dad, insisted that you go on leave for a month and make Ravi acting chief editor." said Karan.

"Who's Ravi?" Rustom asked.

Hari replied: "Senior assistant editor I had hired last month on Karan's recommendation."

"Well?" said Karan.

Hari was terse: "I'm sorry, I'm not ready for a holiday. Besides, Mr Wadia never mentioned it to me. However, I have his last memorandum, which was waiting for me in the office this morning. It's addressed to all three of us, with a copy to Roshan…Here. Please go through it carefully. I have to attend a meeting with the new investigating officer." Wadia's last memorandum was an order transferring Karan to the cosmetics division with immediate effect.

Uppermost on Hari's mind was scarface. He asked Anne to persuade his brother to assign a dynamic and clean cop to probe the Wadia murder. Anne said she would go to Karachi to "nab the bastard". Hari dissuaded her: "He must still be around. I will personally investigate green blazer. Climb in my car, Anne. Let's go sightseeing Friday Mosque area." He parked his car in Urdu Bazar outside the fish market. "A blind dog chasing an elusive gazelle which isn't there," Anne twittered.

They paid no attention to a million ogglers as they waded through the crowds. Hari called Colonel Kabir Sen, the new investigator, to request backup, "just in case". Then he saw Jannat Lodge, the place where Ali had once stayed. Across the road, Anne pointed to a signboard and giggled: "Look! Just what you need for your impotence."

He saw the signboard: "Miracle Sex Vitality—Hakim Ibrahim Mustapha."

He vaguely remembered Karan talking about his faith in herbal remedies for all kinds of ailments. He knew he would be out of his depth in a situation such as this. At the corner was a popular high class restaurant. He asked Anne to wait inside as he went into the herbal clinic.

Even so, he went ahead. A youngster was seated at a small desk and he asked him if "Hakim Saheb" was in. The youngster hesitated, and Hari walked past him into the adjoining room. A man with a flowing beard was seated at a big desk, and another person was standing in front of him with his back towards the in-coming Hari. "What can I do for you?' the herbalist asked politely. Hari cleared his throat nervously, looked shyly at the standing man.

"That's all right. Feel free to tell me. Marriage problem?" said the herbalist.

Hari nodded. "Don't worry. I will examine you just now. Give me two minutes. Where are you from?

"Aligarh," Hari lied.

"Teacher?"

He nodded.

"When did you get married?"

"A week ago."

At that point, the other man turned to look at Hari, who was startled" Scarface, in person. The herbalist gave him some pills, asked for five hundred rupees and said: "You will be good to go in less than half day, strong like a horse."

Hari took the medicine and rushed out to find Sen in plain clothes, waiting in an unmarked car.

"Our man is in there, colonel."

"Good! I'll just pick him up on suspicion of being an illegal immigrant."

This time, both went in together and Sen made the arrest in his most officious manner amidst loud protests from both. So angry was he that he handcuffed both, and ordered them into the car: "Keep quiet! Mother fuckers. Stinking swine!" Inside the Chandni Chowk Police Station, he handed them to an inspector who pushed them into a cell and booked them on suspicion of being linked to the murder of Jal Wadia. Karan had, meanwhile, shifted to cosmetics. He had no idea his herbalist friend was being grilled by the police. He was inexplicably about Hari's meeting with Sen. In the afternoon, he telephoned Hari. "Sen tells me that you helped him arrest a couple of suspects. Who are they?"

"Why don't you ask Sen. I don't really know who. Probably just a wild goose chase: a sexologist and a dubious character. Perhaps a Pakistani without a visa," Hari said.

Scarface gave his name as Shafqat, Officer on Special Duty at Karachi International Airport. Mustapha said in his statement, recorded separately, that Scarface was one of his regular patients.

"Whenever he visits Delhi, he takes away a stock of herbal remedies from my clinic." This contradicted Shafqat's statement in which he claimed that was his first visit to the Indian capital. "Dr Mustapha is a friend of a friend named Khalifa Hasham Ali. I first met him in Peshawar where were both attending a conference of Islamists."

Both denied being at Wadia's party. The claimed that he had never been to Pakistan and that he did not even have a passport. The interrogation was suspended for the evening as Soni was tired.

In the evening, Hari told Anne that Wadia's assassination was probably a part of a larger conspiracy. Suddenly, Anne kissed him on the forehead: "Just hear the melody of the August moon."

"What the hell!" Both laughed.; "What are we sniggering about. I want to kiss you. You want to kiss me. So, why not? A no hanky-panky kiss."

"All right, no hanky panky," And she kissed him lightly on the lips; "Intermission. A well-deserved drinks break," she said.

"By the way, I still have those potency pills" he laughed. The next morning, Sen met Hari at his office. Without beating around the bush, he said: "A tricky affair." Hari stressed that Wadia had no enemies, "His philanthropy made him popular with every community. He was liked even in Pakistan because he had established some excellent relief bodies. No controversy. Where does this lead you, colonel?"

"Motive," he said: "Who would benefit the most? Son, daughter, brothers, sisters, employees. Favourites."

"Or fear, of being cut off, or." Hari hinted.

Sen added: "Employees. Union bosses. Factory workers. Managers, and even editors."

"Very conceivable," Hari admitted.

"Good, let's begin with you, Mr. Rai," Sen said.

"By all means, Col. Sen."

"Were you not present at the party?"

"Yes. Went early and stayed till late.

"What were you doing at that herbalist's clinic?"

"To be treated for impotence, erectile dysfunction, if you prefer," he laughed.

"This isn't a joke, Mr. Rai. You may even be a suspect. You have received a massive promotion in terms of salary, benefits and power. Perhaps you were apprehensive that Mr. Wadia might change his mind..."

"Mr. Wadia wasn't fickle-minded. Anyway, proceed." Sen was quick to reassure Hari that he had never been a suspect. "But did you have a premonition that Karan may also have visited the witch doctor earlier?"

"Did he?"

"Yes. What I wish to know is how well the two know each other," said Sen who was also surprised that no one had come forward to identify the assailant, whereas it was known that the deceased was surrounded by a number of his admirers at the time of the attack. "Some people are being less than transparent. Wadia was stabbed three times in the presence of a dozen people. And no eyewitness!"

He reflected for a second and blurted out: "You know, we Indians have no guts when it comes to reporting crime. We fear harassment from the law-enforcement authorities even when we volunteer information.

The Emergency has made it worse. I think the media has a big role to play here, to educate the masses, to make the people aware."

"May be, colonel; if you don't mind my saying so, the authorities are more to blame than the citizenry. Your image stinks, and rightly so. You guys are insensitive man-handlers. No courtesy. No politeness. Those who volunteer information are treated like bloody suspects. Reform all police cadres, first. Be accessible, approachable, and not act like accusers all the time", Hari was getting animated. Sen said: "I will have to start the enquiries from the start. May I have the guest list?"

Hari called Rustam and requested him to send the guest list, marking all those standing with Wadia at the party. Then he reiterated that Shafqat Khan had been detained because of Anne's testimony and that she had already identified as the assailant. Sen finally decided to question the two detainees afresh. The stab wounds were inflicted from close range as if the killer was in an embrace-like situation vis-à-vis the victim. So, a lot of blood must have gushed out and some would definitely have rubbed off on the attire of the attacker. What was Shafqat wearing that evening. A white shirt under a green sports jacket. What's he wearing now. A check shirt, a sleeveless gray sweater and a pair of cheap blue jeans. No bloodstains. Where is the man staying? Where is the herbalist staying? Easy. The young lad at the herbal clinic in Urdu Bazar readily took Sen to an old ramshackle building nearby. Before that, he searched the clinic itself. There was a register on the herbalist's desk in which were entered the names of patients and the dates of the visit as well as the fee paid. The register showed that Karan had visited the place a couple of hours before the crime was committed.

Rai's pseudonym Aashiq Hussain was also listed. But Shafqat's name was not there. Rai had paid five hundred rupees and Karan was indicated to have paid five thousand.

At the house, a rundown two-room tenement without toilet or bath with a verandah-kitchen having a kerosene stove, he found an imitation leather suitcase containing Shafqat's belongings, including a bloodstained shirt and jacket besides a Pakistani passport without an entry visa. Enough, thought Sen; for the present at least. "Open and shut case against the two," Sen said; "Now, Mr Karan, the new Wadia Cosmetics chief."

Hari's driver had taken Kris on a tour of the Delhi zoo, so he took a scooter-rickshaw to pick up Anne, who was keen to meet Saddam Hussein's granddaughter, Major Dial Singh's mistress. Anne was excited to take a tour of the Indian capital in the auto-rickshaw and she squeezed into it with a broad smile, gave her camera to the driver to take a photograph. "This is going to be the bumpiest ride of your life, madam," Hari laughed.

"Are you trying to seduce me, Mr. Hurry Not Rai?" Anne said in a hoarse voice, inching closer to him in the two-seater.

"No!" he jumped up; "You *are!*"

"Do we love each other? Or is it just interracial curiosity and infatuation?" she said.

I don't know. You are extremely beautiful … and desirable, fragrance of sandalwood, voice like temple bells at dawn, graceful movements like Mother Ganga beginning to descend through the Himalaya. An Enchantress!"

"What are you raving about! You are not bad-looking yourself. You are always in my thoughts, Hari. Day and night."

"Same with me. I need you always," he fumbled; "What's love? We are not kids. I'm above thirty, you are nearly thirty, grown professionals. It's not sex, of course. It's the desire to be near all the time. Something happening inside me when you touch me, or speak or even breathe. Overpowering. I wish you would just swallow me, body and soul, a confluence of two bodies and two souls; a kind of spiritual orgasm," he said in a husky whisper.

"That's it!" she said; "Spiritual orgasm! Kiss me on the forehead, please!"

He kissed her, lightly, on the forehead, brushing his lips against hers and holding her hands tenderly.

"I am too overwhelmed right now. There can be no rationalisation at present. Perhaps there will never be any rationalisation between us. How can there be with the uninterrupted orgasm all the time we are together," he said.

"Let's leave it to your sister-in-law Yukta, who has adopted me as her daughter," she said.

"Fantastic! That makes you my niece," he grinned.

"Let's go see Yukta," she said.

"She is going through torrid time. Her husband, your new papa, first. And also her son. Different reasons. The Air Chief has a new mistress, a South African white, and her son Amit is a drug-addict," said Hari.

"How do you know about the woman?" she asked.

"She's staying at brother's farm house near that of the gadgettorturer Dial Singh's being watched by a reporter. We can try and meet her first, if you like," he said and she assented.

"What's the problem with Amit?" she asked, suddenly.

"Drugs," he said; "Started in high school with cannabis we were careless. Now he's graduated from heroin to crystal and beyond. All these junkies get their supplies from Pakistan. Several westerner teenagers are also victims of the Jihad brigades. And now this racist whore!"

"Surely, she can't be a racist if she's having an affair with an Indian," she said.

"You forget that this bloody Indian is also very important, principle martial law administrator and head of the third largest air force in the world; quite a catch for vested interests."

"Why do I have this lurking suspicion that you are hiding something about your brother."

"To cut a long story short, Air Marshal Rai firmly stands for the dissolution of Pakistan and expulsion of all Indian Muslims from India," said Hari.

"But if there is no Pakistan, where will the expelled Muslims go!"

"The Arabian Sea or whatever, how do I know? I have to follow my scoop of the century."

"Lunatic", she twittered.

"That's below the belt."

Chapter - 19

7086 Pearl Harbors

"Are we witnessing the beginning of the end of the world?" Anne asked waving a sheet of paper; "Thunders will continue to increase in strength and frequency." Hari started sniggering and Anne scowled. Tom, also brandishing a copy of the same sheet, said: "Millions will die in the worst time of retribution the world has ever seen."

"Alarming, but conceivable," said David.

Hari made a grim face, pretending as if the world had already come to a cataclysmic end: "My cook has disappeared. Pande's wife is in hospital. What will I serve you guys for dinner? Leftovers? I can't handle even a simple domestic crisis such as a missing cook. How can you guys expect me to manage **7086 Pearl Harbors**. Isn't that what this document is all about? I have it too, forwarded to me by Ali. A bloody hoax, a mailbox fraud organised by a pervert to blackmail junior politicians and media practitioners into spreading fear about the extent to which Al Jihad can stoop!"

"This isn't a joke!" Anne said sharply.

"Nor is my missing cook. Besides, the bomb experts are screwing up the entire household! I have received the unabridged version of the mailer you guys are worried about. My column tomorrow trashes the profane depiction of contrived photographic vulgarity of Anne's mom sleeping with the Secretary of State and Tom's dad."

"What!" Anne exclaimed.

"What is the significance of 7086?" David asked.

"None," said Hari; "But the number 786 seems to have some unexplained importance in Islam like a belief that the Prophet Muhammad conquered the pagans of Mecca in 786 days or that Allah created the world in exactly 786 days. There's another explanation about the mystical or religious significance of the number—there's a famous 786-word poem praising Allah titled Bismillah al-Rahman al-Rahim."

Hari shook his head: "There's also a lewd illustration showing me with Mary, which is being reproduced for publication alongside my column tomorrow with reluctant permission from staunch Catholic Mary, who is drowning in tears of shame anyway."

"Do you mean it's a stupid mass blackmail stunt?" Anne asked.

"Exactly! Amin, the catastrophist, is an evil genius in his dark room, puts life into fossils and converts them into orgasmic pornographic masterpieces to tame and milk icons of high society to raise millions to conduct Al Jihad's carnage campaign."

"How to deal with this menace?" Anne asked.

"I know of only one way—a serious campaign in the media. And I have written the first piece against the dark knight commander of the British Empire. I wonder how the once struggling photo-journalist managed to be knighted. Did he blackmail the Queen?" Hari laughed.

"Anyway, let's move on. What's the next item on the agenda?"

Tom said: "Training of suicide squads. This is classified. Tens of thousands of Taliban are undergoing training at secret locations in Kabul, Peshawar, Lahore, Kuala Lumpur, Delhi and Djakarta."

"Is that all?" Hari mocked. "No! The author of **7086 Pearl Harbors** is negotiating with the State Department."

"About what?" asked David.

"The crafty supreme commander of Taliban is trying to frighten the United States into parting with a zillion dollars with a fake promise that he would abandon pornographic invasion of the non-Muslim world," Hari interjected; "The moment the full-colour leaflets with shocking pictures by Sir Amin Malik are released, many powerful Anglo-American heads may roll."

"How do you know?" Tom demanded.

"A wild guess considering the author's reputation. Doesn't the CIA or the FBI know about him. Perhaps he has set up a total of 7086 Taliban training centres in the US alone—the sites from where hundreds of suicide bombers may take off to destroy strategic locations within the US," Hari said; “Why 7086? It’s odd because 786 is believed by some to be a sacred Islamic symbol of Allah’s protection, not destruction. Amin, the author, is clearly misleading the West and trying to ensnare the State Department into agreeing to pay ransom for some massive Al Jihad maneuver in America. The number 786 has been corrupted into an insignificant numerical to confuse Islamologists.”

“What’s the author’s background?” David asked.

“He’s Ali’s half-brother,” Hari said; “CIA should know for sure.”

Tom said: “We have no idea about 7086. Someone suggested it could mean the number of explosions around the world on the anniversary of the unannounced kamikaze attack on Pearl Harbor in the territory of Hawaii on Seventh December.”

“You mean a wave of suicide bombers going berserk around America?” someone asked.

“Which is the most complacent state in the US?” David asked.

“All fifty are complacent,” Anne twittered.

“Simple arithmetic—a total of 7086 blasts in the US …141 per state in the fifty states, meaning one less in the fiftieth state for mathematical accuracy,” Hari started laughing when he saw Tom wincing at his explanation of **7086 Pearl Harbors**.

“What are you sniggering at?” Tom said testily.

“I was thinking about my first crush…a very pretty girl called Melody, who turned out to be mute … that broke my heart.” Hari burst out laughing.

“What happens when the heart breaks,” Anne twittered.

“What the hell!” he finally yelled; “What’s going on?”

“Why doesn’t the CIA take care of this minor detail…Drop a few in the Indian Ocean the Atlantic and Pacific oceans,” Hari said and continued to laugh.

No one could understand the reason for the hilarity and Hari said:

“The irony of the situation! The Taliban chief has the audacity to threaten madcap comedic bloodbaths in the US and the only superpower in the world concedes the possibility and negotiates ransom because the best super-spy agency hasn’t a clue about Taliban training centres.”

“Mad!” Tom hissed.

Hari retorted: “Your annoyance is misplaced. Terrorists’ demands are not negotiable. Never! Deal with them from a position of strength. Identify the enemy strongholds and crush them.”

"How the hell do you propose to find the insurrectionists?" Tom demanded.

"You are the expert, man, but my team of reporters has located one centre in the heart of Delhi and more reporters are on the lookout for others in the country. My worry is that we can't cope with the numerous threats terrorists pose for humankind," Hari said.

Tom's anger thawed. Hari added: "I suggest that you approach headquarters and spell out the implications of the Taliban threat and to urgently draw up a genuine road map to effectively deal with it, starting with the training outfit in Delhi in cooperation with India."

Tom asked: "Where is the Delhi centre located?"

"My teams are trying to get to the bottom of this particular crusade of Jihad. The team has found the Taliban Academy about a kilometer from New Delhi Railway Station—the old Government Central College on Qutab Road."

"Has your team come up with something substantial?" Anne asked. "No details yet, but my star reporter Dev is trying to penetrate the building. My apprehension is that the centre is being given protection by a contingent of plainclothes men on orders of the most devious police officer in the capital, deputy commissioner Dial Singh. I'm trying to determine if PM Kumar is resorting to deviousness by his covert acceptance of the inevitability of Jihad and resorting to a mean ploy to appease Muslims on his political platform of secular socialism."

"What about Singh?" Tom asked.

"He is not a Sikh, but a Rajput Thakur whose surname is Singh from a village in Rajasthan near the border with Pakistan," Hari replied.

"You seem so unsure of all the imponderables, Hari. When will you be able to crack the case and what do you expect to find?" Anne asked.

"One step at a time. Singh has a mysterious mistress, a granddaughter of the late Iraqi dictator Saddam Hussein," Hari said.

"A small world, indeed!" Tom exclaimed sarcastically.

"That aspect remains to be confirmed. Besides, I have done a great deal of research on the subject. Dev is trying to get evidence, collect hard facts to convince our readers and the appropriate authorities that they need to act, not make speeches. To effectively counter the zealots on all fronts. The civilised world has been too tardy for decades and the time to nip the coming epidemic in the bud has long past. It's time to catch the rogue elephant by the tusks!"

"Five stages of Taliban development … kindergarten … primary … middle … high … elite … starting at age four and ending at between 18 and 20 years of age," Hari said.

"Any details?" Tom asked.

"Not yet but I know a bit from my own experience."

"What?" Anne asked.

"Years ago, I was sent to a *madrassa* for a week as punishment for playing truant in my Lahore Convent … I still get nightmares about that experience … Chinese-style infantry, wearing smart weapons like vests and garlands, advancing swarms of martyrs towards targets and decimating themselves and the targets … wave after wave of suicide bombers …" Hari said.

"Ridiculous! All that in a primary school?" David said.

"On the blackboard, stupid. Like a board game. Convert it into a video game, then play it on the ground … select a target … say, the Golden Gate Bridge. Plan to blow it up … into extinction!"

"This is a serious matter, Harry," Tom said.

"Believe me, I have never been more serious in my life! And the name is Hari, as in *hurry*," he retorted; "Think about it. After all, the Golden Gate Bridge is on the hit list, and you have just issued a visa to Ali."

He lit a cigarette, something he did only in extreme agitation and in the toilet. Tom tried to change the subject: "Nice place for a bachelor; isn't it too big for one person?".

He nodded: "Empty-shell perk of being a tycoon's sycophant, borrowed affluence of professional mediocrity, which, by the way, is a hair's breadth away from the destitution of reckless honesty and integrity."

"Bravo!" Anne twittered; "Long-winded self-righteous clown."

"Bloody spoilt rich brat … Let's all go to Seventh Heaven … on my expense account," he said, jovially.

But his face fell when he glanced at Koel's abode; it was empty, only a few velvety black feathers on the floor. "What happened here!" he screamed; "Who murdered my Koel?"

Hari rolled his eyes angrily as if blinded by an atomic explosion, dazed, speechless, immobile and suddenly squirming like the tale of a lizard suddenly cut off from its body. Anne was startled by the expression on his face as he turned towards Usha, who was absently rocking Kris's empty rocker as the infant had already crawled up to Anne and tugging at her dress.

Anne was reminded of the *tandava* posture of Lord Siva, the dance of destruction: a frightening depiction of rage, frenzied, sweaty, wild, yet controlled as though the lava inside a volcanic crater was being forcefully plugged by an invisible fail-safe device.

Suddenly, he became quiet, picked up one feather, placed it tenderly on the steel-bar rocker and watched it tumble gently back on the floor. Anne visualised an exhausted Lord Siva in a trance-like motion of the hands trying to prevent an explosion from destroying the surroundings, performing gravity-defying spiritual gyrations in a ring of flames.

Tom and David were overawed by the intensity of Hari's reaction. "Who could do such a mean thing, the divine singer, probably the last one of its kind in the world," Anne said and Usha started sobbing.

"My husband ... He must have killed her in impotent rage after I thrashed him with a hot ladle," she said; "The beast detests music and Koel was melody queen."

Hari said: "Evil surrounds us everywhere. We are living in the valley of opaque-eyed devils and leucrota. Bloody Jihadis all around us and equally avaricious other human predators who didn't even spare my Koel."

"Your grief is very touching," Neelam taunted; "Mourning for a dead bird! What about your assassinated brother?" He ignored the remark and added: "The bastard's playing truant after his cold-blooded cowardice which is exceeded only by Taliban's indiscriminate brutality. Not grieving... angry...And not just a bird, she was a symbol of the free spirit."

But Neelam continued to sulk in her drunken stupor. Hari spoke firmly: "You've lost touch with reality in your own grief. You can't see the vultures hovering above, wolves prowling below and ravenous hyenas sinking their teeth into decaying cadavers. You can't even smell the acrid odour of rotting civilisation wafting through my windows as freedom cries," he said thoughtfully.

Anne started feeling uneasy as she found Tom enjoying Hari's discomfiture in the face of Neelam's alcoholic blabbering. So she abruptly changed the subject.

"Were you a regular truant in school, Hari?" she asked.

He nodded doubtfully: "Yeah...until that punishment by Dad ..."

"What punishment?"

"He placed me in a *madrassa*," he said reticently.

"What did you learn at the *madrassah*?" she persisted.

"The best lesson … I stopped playing truant from then on… forever … from all legitimate activity, an amateur karma yogi," he said earnestly.

"Surely, that can't be all! What is karma yoga?" Anne asked.

"I didn't know then, but learnt later. It has become my secret since childhood. Even a little practice of it discipline protects me from fear of death though I am mortified of pain."

Hari lit another cigarette, clearly agitated: "What the hell…I was nearly sodomized …by the mullah-teacher … and I played truant for the last time! So what!"

"So plenty!" she screamed; "Did you tell your dad?"

"No. I ran home, half-naked, and found Mom … in bed with an uncle … stark naked …adulterous slut! One paroxysm of being sodomized by Cyclops to the trauma of witnessing mom's shameless descent into abysmal degradation! I ran away from home, stark naked, and kept running for a long time and finally collapsed on the banks of the River Ravi."

"How old were you at the time?"

"Old enough to feel revolted. Innocence suspended in the time-space continuum above mom's adultery and by the foul breath and rotting-fish perspiration of Imam Sodom Ali," he whispered with a faraway look in his eyes.

The atmosphere became even grimmer. Anne suggested a stroll in the backyard. He agreed and told Usha and Sheetal to take care of Kris as well as of the guests. The two walked slowly and silently around the bed of roses beneath the banyan tree.

"Look!" she jumped excitedly like a child; "A firefly!"

She kept looking at the glow worm, transfixed, and Hari finally smiled, overwhelmed by a desire to touch her infant-like exuberance with his hands.

"It's a female…blinks every two seconds," she said; "calling her mate…none around."

"How frequently does a male blink?" he asked.

"Five seconds."

"Fascinating! How often do *you* blink?" he laughed.

"*You*!" she screamed.

"Keep your voice down … I may be arrested for harboring arsonists in my house."

"What arsonists?"

"Your exotic fireflies will be condemned as dangerous incendiary devices illegally in my possession … treason."

She twittered.

"Listen, dear, in your morbid self-pity and untimely levity, aren't you forgetting some vital fact?" she asked. "What?"

"The twins Jim and Tim."

He took a step towards her and she allowed him to kiss her, lightly, expressing his gratitude.

And off they went—to Seventh Heaven … all of them, including Usha and Sheetal and little Kris. Hari was quiet all through the drive, haunted by the insane memory of his childhood double-trauma of being violated by a pervert fanatic as well as exposure to the abysmal reality of his own mother's adultery.

At the same time, he was condemning himself for overlooking Jim and Tim, who seemed to have vanished into thin air.

"Did they actually arrive in Delhi?" he asked Sheetal.

"I'm not sure, sir."

Tom said: "If you are talking about James and Timothy Malkovich, they were killed in Equatoria while trying to assassinate President Charles Bantu."

Hari was baffled. His information was that the incestuous gay twins, Jim and Tim, were seen at Karachi Airport in time to board a PIA flight to Delhi. But they were not seen actually boarding the flight.

"Mystifying," said Hari; "Two pairs of identical twins."

"Not quite," said David; "Most big-timers have doubles. The fake twins were thwarted by President Bantu's British secret service guards."

"I must locate the master-assassins immediately for my own peace of mind," he said.

"What do these guys have to do with your happiness?" asked Anne.

"Jim and Tim have received funds to kill the Indian PM,' he said.

"How do you know?"

"I don't."

"Anxiety attack," Anne mocked.

"Too late, buddy. The PM has been shot," Tom said, pointing to the giant TV screen across their table in Seventh Heaven. Instantly, the country plunged into the darkest period of information blackout about the PM's health in a power vacuum at the Centre and bickering within the constituent states.

Two gunshots—one in the centre of the third eye and the second in the heart—and she slumped noiselessly on the carpeted floor of the Vigyan Bhavan stage...pain-free release from the cruel world of backstabbing conspiracy.

Most media persons allowed themselves to tow the line of the mighty controllers of information, like flawed marionettes manipulated by precision puppeteers.

"Madam Prime Minister died on the spot and the assassin, a foreigner, escaped," readers and viewers were authoritatively told.

"A billion nincompoops are once again at the mercy of a handful of political kleptomaniacs running away from guilt, trying to steal the limelight," Hari wrote in his front-page column.

"Was the security lapse deliberate by the National Security Agency headed by Air Chief Marshal Rai?" Tom asked.

"No. Big Brother isn't cold-blooded at all. Oversight, perhaps, but unlikely," he replied.

"Isn't he ambitious?"

"Extremely, but not a conspirator. Warrior, clean fighter, meticulous planner."

Hari was thinking aloud, not about BB *per se*, but about succession scheming going on in the corridors of conspiracy in an atmosphere of grave uncertainty in the shadow of anarchy threatening to engulf the nation.

The power vacuum was acting as a massive centrifugal force for the in-built fissiparous architecture of Indian society. Neelam's dad renewed his pitch for the creation of an independent state for Sikhs. Actor Khan vociferously supported the call of the Muslim clergy for the adoption of sharia. The popular film star also demanded total independence of Kashmir. Seven northeastern states threatened unilateral declaration of independence. Bangladesh started gnashing its milk teeth over the sharing of river waters.

China and Pakistan signed a pact to support each other's claims over disputed territory controlled by New Delhi. Besides, the People's Republic demanded the expulsion from India of the exiled Tibetan spiritual and political leader, the Dalai Lama.

The US insisted that India sign the nuclear non-proliferation treaty (NPT) without delay, failing which it would actively support Islamabad and Beijing. OPEC, the organisation of oil-producing states, resolved to suspend all supplies of crude oil to India unless it signed the covenant granting full independence to Kashmir.

De jure authority rested in figurehead Protestant President Anthony Chacko during the state of emergency imposed six months earlier by the then beleaguered Mrs. Patel, the notorious trasher of civil liberties who had also prorogued Parliament and sacked the Council of Ministers.

In the clamor for grabbing Total Authority, the threat of Jihad was forgotten by the ruthless combatants pretending to be the guardians of the world's biggest democracy.

However, there was no provision for automatic succession in the extra-constitutional Emergency Administration legally known as President's Rule, which made Chacko also the nominally *de jure* ruler and Commander-in-Chief, India's first Christian head of State also inheriting visually virtual autocracy, which was unacceptable to the masses and the principal aspirants to the seat of Absolute Authority.

It was an ideal situation for chaos to erode all decent human values and for predators to sink their teeth into the country's life force. Even Bangladesh was gnashing its milk teeth into Himalayan river waters.

Pakistan was flexing its borrowed six-packs and even Sri Lanka was beginning to cause a storm in its Tamil teacup. Above all, the People's Republic of China was making incursions into disputed territories all along the northeast at a time when all seven northeastern Indian states were threatening to break away from the Republic.

"India is ripe for Total Jihad from Kanchanjunga to Kanyakumari!" declared a masked speaker in a clandestine broadcast over Al Jihad Teleport: "Go, Martyrs! Take over, annihilate the infidels!"

"Indians possess the resilience of angels and resourcefulness of apes to be victorious against the onslaught of doomsday Satanists," countered Ram Kumar, Prime Minister-designate.

The masses had no inkling that the succession intriguers were themselves groping in utter confusion in their desperate infighting. To their credit, both Ram Kumar, once Hari's idol, and Air Chief Rai, his estranged brother, believed in the sanctity of the system and did not wish to openly thwart it or seen to be overriding the democratic processes.

RK argued for *status quo ante*, claiming his party was victorious in the last General Election, nullified by Mandira when she imposed the

Emergency, which had not been lifted following her assassination. Air Chief Rai claimed that his appointment as Chief National Security Adviser should not be revoked because of the multiple crises facing the nation.

President Chacko was in a dilemma and finally suggested a compromise, whereby RK would be caretaker head of government and appointing Rai as Principal Martial Law Administrator, both appointments valid for six months when elections would take place.

Seasoned political theoretician RK made his first official move on the power chessboard by releasing the hardline Sikh separatist Sant Nihal from detention and reappointing him as Federal Interior Minister, in order to make him withdraw his demand for a Sikh state. who, in turn, suggested that movie star Khan be co-opted as Information Minister in the interest of projecting the "unity-in-diversity" image of the country's secular polity as well as to coagulate his agitation for adopting sharia as a national judicial policy.

Unwittingly, Hari's erstwhile idol, RK, in his barely disguised opportunistic quest for perpetuating his rule, allowed himself the luxury of broadening his political base by inducting the two dangerous communalists into his otherwise secular Union Cabinet. The ponderous bureaucratic-police complex was placed on the pause mode unintentionally as power brokers, pimps and opportunists became too preoccupied in their favourite sports of deceit, double-cross, backstabbing and bigotry.

Not far from the treacherous opportunists wearing assorted masks of morality, a small group of naïve idealists were drawing up their own oversanguine plans to outwit the dooms-dayers at a time when the Principal Martial Law Administrator was being informed by a spy that his own kid brother was in the process of writing a series of articles on the treachery of some of Ram Kumar's cabinet colleagues and their alliance with Al Jihad.

"Arrest the bastard!" the impetuous Big Brother ordered Dial Singh.

Chapter - 20

The Determined Beggar

Detention on this occasion was anathema to Hari because it was ordered by his own brother and allegedly on the instructions of his idol, the new Prime Minister, legendary opponent of his predecessor's tyranny, author of *Ultimate Revolution*, regarded as the Bhagavad Gita of democracy on empty stomach. He found no inconsistency between Kumar's socialistic beliefs and his own addiction to the good life and media freedom.

Thus, he was not just nonplussed but felt as if he was being churned by a cyclone when two officers arrived to pick him up at his house in a police Jeep while Kris was giving him a hard time squatting on top of the breakfast table, restlessly playing with crockery and cutlery while howling at the top of his voice, pointing at an oil-painting on the wall of a houseboat on fire in Dal Lake in Srinagar.

"Mama, papa!" he yelled, grabbing a plate and flinging it on the floor.

"Vitriolic kid! Let's go for a walk, Kris," Hari got up, picked up the child and put him down on the floor next to his walker. Kris clasped the handle with both hands, skidded, fell on the floor and started laughing.

He started yelling again the moment he saw the two cops. Hari grinned at them and asked: "What do you want?"

"We have orders to arrest you, sir," said one of them, handing him a handwritten note on the letterhead of the inspector-general of police, which said: "The Prime Minister has ordered your detention. Please accompany the two officers." It was signed Dial Singh, IGP.

He was aghast, but showed no emotion, politely asked them to have tea while he got ready. He called Mary and left instructions for most

Verdict Today senior editors and to inform the MD to arrange bail, all the time wondering about IGP Singh, his designated tormentor, the last PM's obnoxious torture specialist, the raffish cop nicknamed "gadget guru of gruesomeness" by Hari in *Below the Belt* on proliferation of pain in extra constitutional jurisprudence.

Singh was playing the affably cold-blooded savage, inflicting the soliloquy of silence in solitary confinement on the flippant wordsmith who was probably on the threshold of penetrating the cop's shadowy links with Al Jihad through his mysterious mistress who preferred to remain in purdah, probably an Arab acquired by the high and mighty Rajput from Rajasthan, not a Sikh, during his tumultuous tenure as military attaché in Baghdad. Just before his arrest that day, Hari had planned to lift the veil of secrecy from the woman's past.

"This time, Hari is in a hurry," he told the guard who pushed another detainee into the dreary eight-by-eight cell. He was in a terrible state, blabbering about torture chambers and vomiting blood all over the filthy floor, circling around in the small enclosure like a dog chasing its own tail and barking cries of agony, clutching his abdomen and cursing phlegmatically. "Bastards! I need to take a crap!" "Give me a cigarette, sir," he said in the same breath, spitting blood and cursing, his alcohol-soaked sonorous eructation ricocheting from the grimy walls into Hari's grimacing face.

There was nothing trite, insipid or exaggerated about the belcher's agony. Shaken, Hari took out a packet mechanically. The man snatched it longingly and demanded a matchbox. Hari gave him his lighter and waited for him to hand it back.

"Do you have chewing tobacco, sir?" Hari shook his head almost apologetically and watched him light a cigarette and take a long, serene puff.

"Bloody brutes! Perverted sons of whores! Have you ever seen a pack of vixen maul a single, wounded rabbit? Three of them sinking their canines into my flesh and repeatedly shoving a greased and salted spiky baton up my back side. It's hurting, sir," he moaned, banging his head against the wall; "I am not a criminal, only an honest beggar! And such methods of tormenting body and soul!"

"Why have you been arrested?" Hari asked.

"I went to report suspicious movement of arms and ammunition to and from a warehouse inside exhibition grounds near Kal Bhairon Temple and the police hauled me up as a gunrunner!"

Hari became interested, but stopped short, thinking the guy could have been planted as a trap to lure him into making an incriminating admission about his scoop of the century. He decided to humor the man.

"Who are you?" he asked.

"My voter ID name is Bhiku Ram. It has become my real name and it matches my profession, born beggar. It's actual owner died a long time ago. They gave it to me along with cash. That's why I am here, caught by the murdered bitch Mandira's frustrated spies today because I voted for Ram Kumar in the last general election. All members of my union vote for Kumar."

By now, skeptical Hari was only half listening to Bhiku's banter because he was not making any sense.

"Why would the man you support want you in trouble?"

"There are traitors in the force. Kumar does not even know about the back-stabbers. I am president of Kal Bhairon Temple Beggars Union. My real name is Sawan Mal because I was born in *saawan*, the month of monsoons. But no rains came that month or the whole year."

"What's that to do with enemies of the country?" Hari demanded, irritated.

"All the beggars in my union support Kumar, but some senior officers hate us for that crime because the new PM worships Bhairon, visits are temple daily has a unique rationale in respect of the profession of begging," said Bhiku, lighting another cigarette with the butt of the last.

Hari knew that Kumar enjoyed massive support from the estimated twenty million beggars all over the country. He had a popular programme for the resettlement, employment and uplift of beggars. During the coming national census, he had proposed that all beggars must be counted to enable his administration to bring that sector in the ambit of the planning process. The last census of beggars in 1931 showed their population to be 1.4 million. There was no reliable current estimate. Suddenly, the beggar changed the subject: "The new IG is real savage. He personally used a torture thing on me, called it a handy version of Judah's cradle—a big pyramid-shaped metallic shuttlecock with a handle at one end, inserted it up my anus and turned it manually with the handle until I admitted to being a gunrunner in the pay of both the ISI and Kumar's Masses Party."

"Are you?" Hari asked, wondering why such a source of information was sharing the cell with a formidable sourceseeker.

"Make the most of it, sir! This is death row for me, and may be for you. I am a beggar! I tried to enroll in the territorial army but was rejected because of bad health. That's all, not a traitor, not a gunrunner for enemies of the State. Never!

Singh is a two-faced traitor! He only loves money. He's got tons of it! I saw the imam give him a bagful. Accidentally, sir. That's why I'm here. To be silenced!" screamed the belligerent beggar. Hari was flabbergasted: "Really?" he asked incredulously."

"Yup! Let's pray to Bhairon Bali, the eighteen-armed deity who never disappoints. The god who rides a black dog, drinks wine and eats meat and is the favourite of Kumar."

Hari was curious to get a beggar's perspective of the favourite place of worship of Kumar, one of the few politicians he used to admire, his one time idol, author of *Ultimate Revolution*, whose manuscript he had edited when he neither had a job nor a roof over his head. Pleased with Hari's contribution, Kumar gave him a room in the outhouse of his residence as Leader of the Opposition in Parliament. Bhiku told Hari that the hundred thousand voting beggars in the twin cities of Delhi and New Delhi voted almost *en masse* for the Masses Party, many of them on the Voter IDs of hundreds of dead people. "That's besides the point. This morning, mister, I was shocked to see what I saw from accidental vantage point in the gutter in which I had fallen at night.

The imam of the nearby mosque was supervising delivery of guns at the warehouse in the presence of Singh and some other cops. With my own eyes, I saw the clergyman hand over a bag to Singh. I then rushed to the police station opposite the Supreme Court to report the clandestine armaments traffic at the exhibition grounds. But the imam was already there, friendly-like with the cops. I reported the matter, but the imam turned the tables on me and the cops started grilling me like they had caught me smuggling arms."

Suddenly, he started peering at Hari myopically as if unable to focus: "Why are you here, sir? Drugs? Diamonds? Brothelkeeper? You look prosperous, man! You should start believing in Kal Bhairon. His followers bring a lot of wine to the temple to propitiate the terrible one wearing garlands of skulls, snake earrings, snake armlets and a serpent round his head. In his hands he holds a sword and a bowl of blood—He is also called the blood-stained divinity of war. You should become a devotee. He will free you of all problems. Give me two hundred bucks."

Bhiku continued: "Kumar visits Bhairon daily to consult the *tantrik* about his political future. He also has a black bulldog."

Hari subscribed to freedom of expression and worship and had no problem with Bhairon. He also had no problem with the PM's belief in the tantrik's histrionics as a miracle worker and astrologer. Bhairon was believed by many devotees to be the frightening form of Lord Siva. But, in real life, Kumar projected himself as the tenth and last incarnation of Lord Vishnu finally taken birth for the salvation of humanity: To launch the *shuddhi* or purification of converts to Islam and to reabsorb them into the fold by saving them from the demons of Jihad.

"Who are you, mister?" Bhiku asked again; "Are you deafmute?"

The shadows of the barricades were lengthening in the cage. Hari was terrified of darkness in solitary captivity. So, Bhiku's blabber was music to his ears. He told him his name.

"I know you. In-and-out Hari Rai! Big man. But foolish. You can't change this world. Nobody can. Not even Kumar. Your cigarettes have finished. Do you have more?"

Hari took out another packet and gave him one cigarette.

"Only one. Give me the whole packet and two hundred rupees to buy rum from the guards."

"No way, Bhiku. Just one cigarette. That's all."

"Shove it. Pass the whole packet and the money."

Hari kept quiet. Darkness had descended. There were no shadows, but anguished spirits started screaming in his ears. Wailing prisoners being impaled on Judah's cradle of torture. Cries of Muhammad ul Rasool Allah clashing with the Jai Hindutva and Har Har Mahadev slogans. Bombs exploding, guns finding human targets. Annihilation of infidels and massacre of mujahids. A condemned African being immortalised by a tyrant's firing squad and chanting: "The beautiful ones are not yet born".

Hari was finding it hard to control his delirium.

Bhiku said: "Mister, you are a good man. But you don't have enough determination to obtain what you seek."

Hari groped in the dark to give him the packet of cigarettes and four hundred rupees: "Get some rum for me also, Bhiku."

He stumbled to the barricade and brought two half-bottles of rum, a jug of water and two glasses.

"A bottle of rum, Adam's pear of torture under a barren datepalm in the scorching sand of hell, a packet of cigarettes and the stench of rotting crap inside sturdy bowels ..." the beggar sang. Hari belched angrily.

"I am not educated like you, Mister In-Out. But I can say Cheers. So, let's say Cheers to our cheerless predicament. Cheers!"

"Cheers," said Hari. He asked the beggar what he thought of Jihad.

"Such slogans are made by power-greedy leaders who make money by selling dreams. They promise things they know they cannot provide. I say follow my example. I ask for only what I can get. I know the pangs of hunger. So I demand food and get it by hook or by crook. I know the misery of disease. But no one has control over disease and death."

"So I ask for relief, which I get by accepting my fate, submitting to it, and, ultimately, getting drunk and oblivious of pain outside Kal Bhairon Temple and even allow His black dog to lick my face."

Impressed, Hari asked him to continue. With eloquence born of alcohol, Bhiku said: "The Mullah in the mosque next to my temple always says that Islam is in danger. I met him the other day and told him that no religion is in danger. I also told Kumar that the noises about the Ram Temple and Babar's mosque are merely the shouts of narrow-minded bigots. Humanity is the only religion. Don't destroy humankind in the parochial pursuit of your personal glory and gratification."

Hari clapped involuntarily: "Profound."

Encouraged, Bhiku said: "The logic is simple. I am a young man and often desire sex. Very rarely, I manage to get a woman beggar. I don't hesitate and gratify myself. Most often, however, I resort to masturbation, no-hassle sex imagining a fairy sucking my organ. It makes me happy." Hari winced.

Bhiku went on: "Don't ever settle for anything less than what you want and be satisfied when you get it. I am a beggar, Mr. Hari, but I don't plead. I demand and I don't give up until I get it."

"You are my hero, Bhiku Ram. You have come into my life like the all-pervading stench of the gutter," Hari said and laughed. The gloom had lifted somewhat. Then he thought of nightfall and the terror of sleeplessness. No matter. Rum had elevated his mood. He still had the happy pills in his pocket, and soothing thoughts of Anne bringing warmth to his soul.

But the Ganges inside him was in spate, angry, polluted, performing the *Tandava*, the dance of destruction, on the head of her source, Lord Siva.

"Why are you being detained this time?" Bhiku asked.

"Showing the mirror to the evil and the ugly."

"People like me are smart. I sell the dead person's vote to the highest bidder, who is smarter because he plays around with *your* hard-earned money," said the beggar.

"Great," Hari said, his tormented mind churning in a whirlpool of interlinking news stories of evil, of deceit and destitution, of incest and intrigue, of terrorism and treachery, of politicians and chicanery, of civilisation and barbarity, of Jihad, Qayamat and bigotry, of love and nirvana.

"Do you believe in God, Bhiku?"

"Yes," he laughed; "God of urge and goddess of gratification. I live from moment to moment. That which is dead can never die. I am alive, but I know death ... In the circle of the spirit, life and death are insignificant zeros."

Hari wanted to be up and about chasing the scoop of the century. Instead, he was forced to play scrabble with Aristotle, president of the Beggars' Union.

Bhiku's drunken banter began to irritate him when he demanded more cash to acquire more rum to gratify his urge to defecate in the detention cell.

This time, Hari refused to pay and told him to shut up. But the urge was so compelling that the beggar actually squatted in a corner and went ahead, sending out fumes of nauseating odour. "What the hell! I am about to be killed. I don't want to die with all this crap inside my bowels! To hell with it. Mr. Hari, hurry up. Save yourself from monster Singh."

Hari was livid, wrestled with an indefinable urge of confused rage and succeeded in controlling it by calling out to the guards to shift him to another cell.

The request was summarily denied by the duty officer. He was caught between demagogues, martyrs, schizophrenics and, thankfully, one cell-mate beggar who had just taught him the virtue of resoluteness.

It was at that time that Dial Singh, the notorious torture specialist for successive regimes, decided to demonstrate his most intimidating side to the pompous pen-pusher. He walked heavily into the cell and punched Hari hard on the nose: "Move, bastard! Plagiarist defamer and Hindu supremacist Aryan fascist! Let me take you on a guided tour of my special chamber of horrors containing my priceless personal collection of the best instruments of agony."

There was nothing soft or sophisticated about street-smart Singh's bearing. He was obnoxiously hirsute with even a thick pelt of hair on the tip of his nose and a hairy wart at a corner of his mouth which made him look like a roadside conjurer's performing monkey. Hari found his exaggerated prancing very amusing. His own quiet aloofness, he thought, would clearly demonstrate his own hauteur and show the unprincipled brute that his profanity could not force him to abandon his mission to defeat forces of Jihad. However, just then, Singh stomped on Hari's sore toe, punched him on the mouth and swore: "Come, spineless rabbit! Your sexy American girlfriend is waiting to be screwed by me like a bitch on heat!"

Hari was so infuriated that he threw all caution to the winds and landed a flurry of blows on the cop's stunned face so rapidly that the officer fell against the wall, screaming for guards: "Quick! Remove this papa's pimp to Basement Three for marinating into edible flesh for Lebanese shawarmakebabs!"

Poking Hari on the chest, Singh hissed: "Let's go, buddy boy, for a heart-to-heart in my very special billet for intrepid rabble-rousers like you. You love the high life, don't you? Let's go have a drink, your favourite scotch, my style," he winked with an icy smile, no feeling, nothing. Hari was compelled to feel that there just wasn't enough love to go round the world to civilise beasts like Singh. He accompanied the cop. He had no choice.

The so-called billet was a scantily-furnished studio apartment. "Quite a dugout," Hari grinned, glancing at the one-gallon bottle of black label and two glasses on the bar alongside an open zoology dissection box. He smiled, wondering about the zoology-practical instruments. Then he saw an old-fashioned rat-trap lying next to the bottle containing a restless mouse. "That's your colleague, plagiarist, hungry, playful." "Are you planning to castrate me?" Hari asked, clearly terrified of the agony.

"Have a drink, buddy, the best antiseptic and pleasurable anesthesia," he replied, pouring a huge drink for his victim and a small one for himself;

"Cheers!"

"Cheers," Said Hari, raising his glass, shedding all apprehensions, broad smile lighting his face.

"Great captivating smile, playboy. I hate your smile and would like to do something to enhance it. Have you heard of Glasgow grin or Chelsea smile. I learnt it in a Scottish pub and mastered it London's Chelsea area. Have another drink, dear. I shall lovingly cut your face from the edges of your mouth to the ears, extending your beautiful grin. With a dissection knife," Singh laughed as Hari winced, inwardly feeling uneasy, out of his depth, unwilling to submit to the terror being planned by the freak, hoping for divine intervention, petrified but stiff upper-lip nonchalance:

"Give me another drink."

"Sure, creep!" he sneered and gave another glassful; "Your wings need to be clipped. What have you discovered about Aisha, skunk?"

"Who?" Hari pretended.

"The late Saddam Hussein's granddaughter, stupid."

"Saddam what? The Iraqi whatever? What about him?"

"His grandchild, bastard, the girl who lives with me."

"Oh, that veiled pearl, of course. What more is there to find out. The details are securely out of reach, Give me another small one. For the road. I'm tired, please."

"I have just the perfect thing for you…over there in the corner. Found it in Madrid, Spain, in an antique shop, it's called Judah's throne used during the Inquisition in the fifteenth century to punish heretics, to extract information. Come sit here. The spikes are real, even the thumbscrew on arm rest and the thorny projections at the back. I will give you a choice: the Glasgow grin, the chair or that plague rat desperate to escape from the metal cage. I will shackle you on that divan, fit that mouse trap on your belly and heat the cage, making it unbearable for the rat. He will soon find an aperture and escape. He is sure to find an escape route in your alimentary canal, free to move up and down, gnawing into and through your vitals." Hari found the brute relishing every syllable of his spine-chilling monologue.

"Fascinating," he said, hoping that Mary had promptly acted on the instructions he had left with her in the morning.

"Have another drink, on the house, for your end into nothingness," Singh sniggered.

Hari was already feeling sleepy, sad-sleepy. He sighed: "If the wine I drink and the lip I press on the crystal, if it ends in the nothing everything ends in—ah yes—then fancy while you are, you are but what you shall be—nothing—you shall not be less."

Singh patted him on both cheeks: "Half anesthetized. Good. Ready to make the mouse happy. Drunken bastard!"

"If with wine, you are drunk, be happy. The end-purpose of the universe is nothingness, be happy, picture your nothingness while you are, and be happy," Hari mumbled, rolling his eyes towards the door: "Someone is knocking."

"Who's it?" Singh barked and punched him ferociously on the nose.

"Summons from the Prime Minister!" In his drunken haze, Hari thought he recognised the voice of the NSA chief and passed out.

Chapter - 21

Crucifying Heretics

The foiled attempt on the Pope's life was threatening to ruin David's career while his stormy divorce from exotic Indian fashion designer had already impoverished him. Even so, David was frantic about his pal Hari after police headquarters denied all knowledge of his detention.

Unruffled *Verdict Today* MD Karan mischievously suggested the chief editor might have gone underground in order to solve the mystery of the attack on the Pope.

Anne had a sense of foreboding that something terrible was about to happen to Hari. In her official capacity as an American diplomat, she lodged a complaint with Amnesty International in London without knowing that Hari and Amnesty were locked in a controversy over an expose about the watchdog body's links with some Jihadis made by an Amnesty official Gita Sahgal in London. Gita had reported that Amnesty had links with a well-known supporter of global Jihad and an apologist for the Taliban, an Islamophobic called Moazzam Begg, a British-Pakistani Muslim, an extrajudicial detainee for about three years at Bagram Theater Internment Facility in Afghanistan and Guantanamo Bay in Cuba, who was head of an organisation called Cageprisoners. Gita was a grandniece of Jawaharlal Nehru.

Ambassador Miller was livid and threatened to recommend her immediate posting to war-torn Equatoria. Simply no sermon against the romance, just a straightforward warning that her transfer was in the process of being affected because of her mom's influence in Washington. London was bullying David for messing up the papal assassination story which might well have turned out to be the most explosive exclusive for the recession-crippled British news agency struggling to keep afloat. Godfather-bereft David was the perfect fall guy for the historically complacent management's internal contradictions following the dissolution of the British Empire.

Damage-control became essential for more reasons than just the need to put out a credible story identifying the hit man and put an end to snide Catholic insinuations about the alleged involvement of the Anglican church in the heinous attempt to assassinate the Pope. David was desperate. He must find the two eyewitnesses to the harrowing incident in which his best friend Hari, who was interviewing the Pontiff at the time of the incident, became the inadvertent victim of the phantom hit man. The chief executive of Lotus Theological Centre, Edgar Nandan, and his dancer wife, Angela, told David soon after the incident that they had clearly seen the gunman backstage hurriedly making a getaway. But both went missing without a trace within minutes just as he was attending to the semi-conscious Hari writhing on the floor. His Holiness was in the thick of a provocative face-to-face with Hari about the Vatican's frequent sparring with the Anglican Church over the latter giving in to Islamic pressures in regard to adopting Sharia within British jurisprudence when someone hiding in the wings shot at the Pope and Hari pushed the pontiff, swirled with lightning speed and became the unwitting target.

Millions of people were glued to TV sets when they heard the report of a bullet released from an unseen gun and the Pontiff was forcefully thrown on his back from his couch and the cameras closed in on a body.

"The Pope has been shot dead!" announced a tremulous female voice. The high-tech cameras could not zoom-in on the body because the area was suddenly plunged in darkness because of power failure in the Lotus Centre. Power was restored within minutes. David and scores of others rushed to the stage, the Briton cornering a flustered Edgar, who said he saw the gunman rushing through the backdoor after the shooting. "The Pope is safe, long live the Pope!" chanted dozens of ecstatic conference participants who had surrounded him. David rushed Hari to hospital with a bullet having pierced through the ribcage, a story that was not allowed to see the light of day when he gained consciousness in a few hours.

"Did you see the assailant?" David asked the moment Hari came to.

He shook his head. "I heard a voice before the trigger was pulled and I turned to look back. Too bloody late! There was no one."

"You are the Vatican's hero, buddy. Savior of the Pope's life."

"Accidental savior. Slow reflexes. Not a big deal."

"What about the voice you heard?"

"Two words: Allah *maher*!"

"What's *meher*?"

"Help or mercy. Help, O God!"

"So, the hit man was a Muslim."

At that point, David had no idea that he was soon going to become an unwitting target of his insecure chief in London, Sir Jonathan Wright, as the scapegoat for his own professional incompetence and social climbing tendencies gone awry. He promptly sent an over-sanguine message to Sir Jonathan promising an exclusive on the attack on the Pope which would clear the name of the Archbishop of Canterbury. Little did he know that his sources would disappear into thin air and he would be left with no story except the formal speeches of the Pope, the Archbishop of Canterbury, the Dalai Lama, the head priest of the controversial Lord Rama Temple in Ayodhya, his birthplace, and the Imam of the Friday Mosque in Srinagar at which was displayed a vial containing a single strand of hair from the eyebrow of the Prophet Muhammad.

All of those speeches by the world's top theologians were dismissed by David as the cacophony of godless holy men clamoring to show that the Almighty was indivisible and that He belonged exclusively to the people professing their respective faiths of each one of them; the supremacy-seeking theory of God being exclusive to them in the form or forms they believed Him to be. At that point, David forgot that he was in the throes of a stormy divorce with exotic Indian fashion designer Shanta, the woman who was allegedly involved in the Madhu rape dispute and who had robbed him of all chances of repairing his shattered private life.

Alimony payments to her were threatening to pauperise him. His personal life was doomed and professionally, matters seemed gloomy. Sir Jonathan ordered David to start wearing diapers in order to free himself from the whims of a nervous bladder while chasing sources. "I went to the restroom for a minute and returned to find Edgar and Angela gone," he told Hari; "Dereliction of duty, says Sir Jonathan."

"Has he recommended sanitary pads for women reporters!" Anne twittered, feeling light-hearted because her mom had taken a beach holiday to Goa with Kathy Miller, the ambassador's wife.

"It hurts, Anne. It hurts badly. My promotion is on the line and Mr and Mrs. Nandan may be in serious trouble because of my inquiries," he said mournfully. "Edgar is director of Lotus Centre and his wife is a noted Kathak dancer. Both vanished minutes after the attempt to assassinate the Pope.

I was told they had rushed to see their son Dominique at his Loyola College in Gwalior, where he had suddenly been taken critically ill," David said.

"I am sure they had seen the hit man, who must also have spotted them … and there you have another dead end," he added; "their son's hale and hearty and hasn't been told about his parents. My deadlines have become really *dead*. But where is Hari? I need him."

"What about security cameras and closed-circuit TV?" Tom asked.

"Blank…Wiped bloody out! The Vatican has sent a team of investigators headed by Morris Cardinal Ricardo who has been looking into every aspect of the religious conference leading to the shooting incident… The matter has become an inevitable Christian imperative. But what have done with Hari?" David said he was under compulsion to provide an incontrovertible story about the attack on the Pope. "I am being grilled by Cardinal Ricardo about the events leading to the shooting. London is harassing me to produce a credible story."

In his desperation, David gave an undertaking to London in writing that he would file, within three days, a behind-the news **exclusive** disclosing the names of the hit man and the terrorist outfit which wanted the Pontiff dead.

At that point, Anne screamed excitedly and jumped from her chair: "He's here! Hari, there!" She ran towards the elevator, straight into Hari's arms and embracing him tightly: "God! Where have you been?"

"Give me lots of fresh lime juice," he stuttered.

"Where the hell were you?" David demanded.

"Lime juice, stupid!" Hari lisped and sat down; "Back from the land of Nod, what the doctor ordered for this fragile insomniac. Long story. Later. Give me more lime juice and shut up."

"I've been depending on you, stupid! You must have seen the hit man. You are letting me down," David screamed.

"I've told you already. I heard a voice and possibly saw a glimpse of rust-colour hair before I went down. Nothing conclusive," Hari whispered.

"My job is at stake and I am perpetually running behind on alimony payments. This time, the bloody nymphomaniac has her evil eyes on my Wimbledon apartment."

"So you want to concoct a tale citing imaginary sources and name a fictional red-haired hit man! And make Hari a party to your professional suicide!" Anne said angrily.

David was persuaded from stooping so low as to manufacture a tale and make it look real by citing fake sources, naming fictitious names, to save his recession-hit job and earn a coveted cash award and make his position secure in the profession.

"True, it's done all the time, even by great columnists in great media. Will it make you feel proud?" Hari coughed and threw up uncontrollably. Tom led him to the restroom and helped him relieve himself shamefacedly.

Back at the table, Hari shook his head ruefully: "Let's face it! David and I are darned mediocre and soft wordsmiths in this age of mediocrity who loftily pretend to be tough media freedom and truth freaks, cowardly practitioners of journalism of courage bartered away to the highest bidder by our employers. What's the result?"

David nodded: "We are perpetually broke and are scoffed at by our ex-wives and their boyfriends! And our bosses make hay under the sunshine of our credulous crusade!"

"What are you blabbering about, you manic Limey?" Hari asked.

"About my nymphomaniac ex-bitch whose alimony has made me an insolvent wreck," David said, almost in tears. Hari finally smiled and said: "I promise that you will shortly receive a well-deserved genuine honour award for the project you and I have been working on."

"Another one of your great over-simplifications?"

"No, David! Wadia has really announced a million-dollar award for the best coverage on Jihad. Let's tame the tornado!"

"How?"

"I'm ready for a drink. Let's indulge in self-pity and make ourselves miserable in a multi-faceted crisis with which we are unable to cope."

Anne sniggered and said jokingly: "Let's all have hair cut at the porn parlour downstairs."

"I want something done about my unwanted pubic plantations," Hari laughed.

"What's the male word for slut?" she snapped.

"Search me."

"Panchali Beauty Parlour. What's *panchali*?" she asked.

"Wife of five men, meaning the rare beauty Draupadi, polyandrous wife of the five Pandava brothers in the epic Mahabharat."

"What's the latest on that girl Madhu?" she asked.

David replied: "She is the inaugural Miss Urvashi-Empress... on her way to Equatoria to participate in the Miss Empress contest. By the way, I have a good story about her with great pictures."

"Make an offer to *Verdict Today* of exclusive rights, name your price and I will buy it," Hari grinned.

"Right away, one hundred thousand dollars. What do you say?"

"No," Hari said, with finality; "We're not in the business of financing alimony."

"What if the beauty pageants around the world are linked to Al Jihad?" David persisted.

"Done. All rights. Let Sir Jonathan make the official request. Pronto."

"Beauty pageants involve mega bucks all the way from entries for the smallest suburban and city contests to the national, regional, national and international, right to the top, crown after crown, fashion designer after fashion designer, gym after gym, cosmetics galore, hair dyes, hair removers, perfumes, shampoos, deodorants, bikinis, undergarments, sanitary pads, toilet paper, wines and spirits, tobacco, fashion accessories, bikes and cars, gymnasium equipment, tooth-care, tourist destinations, hotels, casinos, building material and furnishing, including toiletries, condoms and contraceptives, hormones and anti-depressants, indeed all the good things of life for females, their companions and families," David said excitedly.

David was clearly working extremely hard on all aspects of Jihad, going by his extensive research on a peripheral aspect of Al Jihad. He had most of the facts, figures and estimates of Al Jihad's kickbacks from all businesses associated with the trillion-dollar beauty pageant industry.

"Knowledge is power," Anne said enthusiastically; "The bag David saw on Ali's lap, what did it contain?"

"The money Madhu's father gave to Ali to have her daughter handpicked by the judges as Miss Urvashi-Empress and to protect his industrial domain against destruction by the Taliban," said David.

"How can you be so sure?" Tom asked.

"Computer hacking, my dear."

Hari changed the subject: "Tom, are you still on the payroll of CIA?"

Tom hesitated and Hari said: "Never mind. Computers are good enough in their own way, but they are no substitute for real life ... don't look, Mr Ali is hovering like a vulture."

And there he was, godfather of Jihad, in person, obnoxiously wolverine, rough rust-colour hair, making the world more unsafe than it seemed to the uninitiated, the Leucrota-like creature detested by Anne, David and Hari. Vintage wine was acting as a catalyst for energizing the group and making the four feel caustically chummy with the intruder. "Some wine, Mr Ali?" Hari asked, offering him a glass. "We slaves of Allah are not permitted the luxury of consuming these artificial facilitators of fake friendliness," he said acidly. "No alcohol at all?" David persisted.

Ali shook his head, uncertainly, Hari thought. "Sinful spirits making our heads dizzy," Anne twittered.

"Let's live a thousand lives in your single chime, moment by one moment, grain by grain of sand, let life flow leisurely through the hour glass of my veins," Hari said dreamily.

"Tell me, Mr. Ali, do you stock cashew *feni* here, the famous wine from Goa?" Hari asked.

"Not normally, Mr. Rai, but I brought a crate with me today after a day trip to Panjim. Would you like a bottle or two, please?"

"Yeah, one please. I love it, modern-day *soma ras*, the organic nirvana brew of gods," Hari said.

Ali went personally and took his time to bring a bottle of the popular wine expertly fermented from cashew flowers in Goa, a favourite of the Portuguese colonialists.

Ali made a theatrical presentation of the bottle to Hari and said: "On the house, Mr. Rai, with compliments from the people of Goa, many of whom desire to break away from the Union of India. And there are other Browns who think they are more White than their erstwhile colonial masters."

"Relax, Mr Ali. Thanks for the poison, sir. I won't partake of it if it agitates you so much," Hari said, tongue-in-cheek, pleased to note that Ali was starting to feel ill-at-ease. Anne's mom called her on the cell phone at about that time and she listened silently, but seemed to be disturbed by what she said. Alice Nielson-Spenser apparently put her fastidious white foot down against Hari and belligerently declared Tom as *the* perfect match for her. Anne was in a rebellious mood as her mom's habitual intransigence troubled her balanced sensibilities. Hari was also hurting because Anne's sour expression of dismay interfered with the symmetry of her exquisite feminine beauty. His pain was aggravated because there was little hope to save the life of his star reporter Dev.

Emotional setbacks notwithstanding, David's obsession, Hari's passion and Anne's rebelliousness became the driving force behind the trio's relentless campaign to expose kingpins of Jihad.

At Panchali Beauty Parlour, when David had gone there with Madhu to investigate claims about her attempted pornographic rape, Ali had a large briefcase in his lap, the same type he was holding after the London blast.

"That briefcase! What's so special about it? He clutched it possessively like it's his wife," he said.

"That's his lifeline, contains two things—money, *jazziyah*, received from a protected client," Hari said.

"What else?"

"A small antique Persian carpet for squatting to perform *namaz* or prayers wherever he might be, five times a day like a doctrinaire Muslim," Hari added.

"What's so special about the carpet?" he asked.

"For good luck. Woven on a piece of tent or *khaimah* personally by Omar Khayyam, in Nishapur, the Persian poet-astronomer's birth place, Ali's idol."

"But the creator of *The Rubaiyat* wasn't a *namaazi* (praying) Muslim."

"Perhaps an agnostic. Listen to this quatrain—*The Qur'an! Well! Come put me the test—Lonely old book in hideous error drest—Believe me, I can quote the Qur'an too, The unbeliever knows his Qur'an best.*"

"He wrote such immortal quatrains squatting on this rare one-yard piece. He had contempt for fanatics, like this one:

And do you think that unto such as you,

A maggot-minded, starved fanatic crew,

God gave the secret, and denied it me—

Well, well, what matters it! Believe that too.

David was suitably impressed, but added: "Why are we talking about a poet who said—*Enjoy wine and women, and don't be afraid*?"

Hari said: "I don't know. Perhaps the rare carpet and the importance of priceless antiques as a source of revenue for his movement. Also perhaps it shows that Ali uses Islam to fulfill his personal ambition of grabbing power as the resurrected Caliph of the Muslim nation."

"All this means that the commander-in-chief of Al-Jihad is the world's most resourceful dealer in antiques. His mission requires zillions of dollars and the organisation doesn't hesitate to invest in any lucrative venture. No qualms," Hari said.

"Do you have any proof?" David asked. "Not likely. I'll need the Spiderman to procure evidence about financing of US Presidential poll. That's just one isolated example, David."

"Are you out of your mind, dude?"

"Yeah."

"Don't ever mention it in writing, man!" David was aghast.

"Why? You mean the CIA will do me in for my heretical belief about the sanctity of the flawed American system !

Fool! Even the mother of parliaments, the Westminster model, has its share of supporters for Sharia."

"What about India?"

"Swarming with facilitators of Jihad ... at the centre and in the states."

"Any names?"

"Plenty. On the list is movie star Mazhar Khan, who is busy working on his most ambitious ventures."

"Like?"

"Legend of Omar Khayyam, and *Mahabharat Updated,"* Hari laughed;

"He plays the legendary poet in the first, and Casanovastrategist warmonger Lord Krishna in the heretical modernday version of the Hindu epic in the other. Both big budget flicks in collaboration with Hollywood."

"How's all this related to Jihad?"

"Revenue, silly. I guess film financiers have already been compelled to part with plenty of offshore cash for arms purchases," Hari said.

Finally, David said: "Cash and commitment—strongest points of the pawns of paradise in this game of chess being played to inherit the earth. The executors of Jihad are unscrupulous profiteers in straightforward and immoral businesses. In the final analysis, the Free World can win mainly by coagulating their lifeline—somehow manage to persuade the White House and the White Hall to freeze Al Jihad funds in territories under their control," he added.

"True. We can win only through strong handling of logistics, because we lack their commitment, passion and fearlessness," Hari said; "Jihad can be countered on the drawing board because we can't match their fervour… they may have a million suicide bombers, we have none!

David found Ali to be a "fiendish bloke … Grotesque. Wolverine. Ghastly looks, putrefying coarseness, Horse-like head, abominably regal."

Hari found his description "blatantly prejudiced" because he found Ali to be "villainously handsome and distinguished looking like an eccentric scholar".

Half in jest, Hari asked David to look up the characteristics of a rare Indian animal occasionally reported to have been seen in South Asia—a cross between a hyena and a lioness—called Leucrota.

David was annoyed: "This isn't a joke! That man is very much around and he spells disaster wherever he goes."

"But the man you describe isn't Khalifa, who's extremely handsome and not at all like a Leucrota, whatever that might be," Hari chided him.

"All right, it may be my prejudicial psychic imagination about his looks. But his presence is ominous! There can be no half-measures about exposing creatures like Khalifa!"

"Prophetic Piscean!" Hari teased and ordered a round of drinks while Anne twittered. Just as David was beginning to get over his divorce inflicted emotional turbulence, he saw Shanta across the Seventh Heaven bar in a ribald posture with Khan, shamelessly licking the matinee idol's ear lobe.

"The bloody bitch is perpetually on heat," he hissed.

"What's the amorous bastard's real name?" Anne asked.

"Why?" asked Hari.

"I was checking on him on an internet search engine … a chemical engineer by profession …Quite a cagey character … vaguely linked to the Gateway pipe-bomb scare a year ago and more recently in gambling on international cricket fixtures and racehorse jackpots," she said.

"What's his supposed real name got to do with it?" David asked.

"There are yawning gaps in his profile," she said.

"Like what?" Hari asked.

"Like three years from 1995 to 1998 when he made no movies even though his popularity graph was on its ascendancy," she said.

"He was in jail in Los Angeles for molesting a child and drug-running. His real name is Azan Ali…his desperate bid to do a Hollywood movie failed miserably…was offered a role in one porn production, which prompted him to make blue films himself … a career temporarily cut short by his imprisonment," Hari said.

"Temporarily?" she asked.

"Yes," David interjected; "He's the current porn emperor, with full support from the Taliban and a big source of funds for Jihad."

"What are the main sources of financing Jihad?" Anne asked.

"Several," said David; "We are trying to find out all details, but it's not easy. The phone-tapping devices planted at several spots have either been found out or have not produced any results."

Ironically, despite his commitment to expose Jihad, Hari could not really bring himself to believe that the Muslim holy war *per se*, as perceived by the Prophet Muhammad, was evil or undesirable.

"Self-purification, that's what the Prophet preached; the war within … cleansing the soul, making it *paak* or pure as the name *Pakistan* suggests, land of the pure," he said.

David added: "Or Khalistan for Sikhs is the land of the *khaalis* or pure. Why are these separatist entities obsessed with parochial purity?" he asked.

"Do you know what the Prophet Muhammad meant by Jihad?" he asked.

"Not really. Jihad is everywhere in our day-to-day life. We are surrounded by predators, Racists, Deceitful bigots!" she lamented.

"Muhammad wanted his followers to conduct a holy war against injustice and oppression and against those who rejected the truth. The Prophet said 'holy is the warrior who is at war with himself'. The terrorists are waging a counterfeit Jihad. There's nothing holy about it; true Jihad can only be fought and won within," he said.

"Kind of self-refinement. The eternal quest for perfection, the Holy Grail of Islam," she said.

"After achieving perfection, a true Muslim donates all his belongings to the poor and becomes *Abdal* (the changed one), the Muslim equivalent of the Christian Enoch, who walked with God," Hari said.

He explained that true Islam did not sanction destruction of places of worship. "The objectives of the *mujahids* are murky and undefined," he said. "They selectively pick from Islamic tradition only those elements that advance their narrow agenda. Doctrinaire religious ideology, not Faith or belief in Allah and His Messenger," Hari added.

Anne agreed: "Of course, we have heathens in all faiths, who habitually misinterpret Nature's laws to hoodwink their victims. They are the deceivers. We are their victims," she sighed.

Destiny had brought the two together at a time when Hari was going through the most traumatic phase in his career, facing the relentless onslaught of counterfeit icons posing as benefactors of the downtrodden on the one hand and the barbaric offensive of religious fanatics on the other, while other, less transparent, wicked concentrates of deceit, lies and greed were taking aim.

The good news was that he was aware of the evils, so he could try to take them on in his stride, single-handed, if necessary. His agenda was simply professional: To bring home the truth, and leave the rest to those equipped to deal with the maelstrom into which humanity was being thrust by usurers and godless oppressors, hypocrites and blood-thirsty unholy exploiters of religious faiths.

But the bad news was that he was unwilling to let Anne get involved in his personal battles against terrorists, bigots, cowards, lewd saints, pornographers, racists of all colours and flat-footed demagogues indulging in political chicanery to hoodwink humankind, especially after the anonymous threat to kill her.

He had developed strong feelings for her and had made up his mind to try to make her a life-partner in the most profound sense. But her mother's attitude and Ambassador Miller's hostility seemed to be making things hard for both. Miller was continually pulling her up for spending too much time with Hari in his pretentious anti-jihad campaign. Her mother told her that she was over-worked and needed an RR vacation for rest and recreation. In fact, Miller threatened to have her posted to trouble-torn Equatoria if she did not stop seeing Hari.

Miller lost no time in informing Alice that Anne's life would be under constant threat because of Hari's reckless professional behaviour and his habit of challenging ruthless people and movements such as heads of State as well as the most dangerous terrorists like Al Jihad, "his current obsession".

Hari, meanwhile, was briefing Anne about the story he was holding back ostensibly in pursuance of the poet-caller's demand. She was all ears.

According to the story, Khalifa's real name was Massey Dujjan, corrupted from the Persian Masih ad-Dujjal, the impostor Messiah, who, according to *Hadith*, was to appear before Qayamat, to wage Jihad against all Infidels, and was travelling around the world, causing havoc wherever he went preaching falsehoods.

According to *Hadith*, he told Anne, just as he had earlier informed Mrs Patel, “Thirty Dajjals in all have been predicted. Khalifa is probably the last one. But the description about Dajjal’s appearance does not fit Ali.

Blind in the right eye. But the man appears to have both, presumably intact. Opaque eyes, yes. That’s odd. Curly hair. But Ali could have had something done to straighten his hair. Something wrong in one foot?

Walking stick? We must check. Be on the lookout to see how dependant he is on the walking stick and his vision.”

“Dajjal has brought the gifts of paradise for his followers, and the arsenal of hellfire against kafirs. Even we, non-believers, are partaking of the gifts, right here, Other gifts are said to be houris and boys,” he said.

“Where are the virgin maidens. The boys, of course, these blazer-clad young waiters.” She paused, as she saw Ali emerge through a crescent shaped door behind the bar and started moving towards their table.

“Nothing wrong with his legs. Walking stick, yes,” she whispered.

“Upright. Elegant. Impressive. Like an Army General. Hookah pipe. And a lad keeping pace. That’s weird. The boy, effeminate.”

“Welcome to Seventh Heaven, Miss Spenser, Mr Rai.”

“Thank you, sir. But I have to go and do a story about your friend Moazzam Begg, his organisation called Cageprisoners and a gutsy girl called Gita Sahgal.”

Ali looked open-mouthed, speechless.

Chapter - 22

Romancing Jihad

The Prime Minister was losing patience with Hari, his protégé and editor of his seminal work, *Ultimate Revolution*, the primer of democracy for the proletariat, because of the incisive criticism of his government's performance which was contributing to his abysmal showing in popularity rating. Reading between the lines, David, the Piscean psychic, foresaw yet another round of detentions for the chief editor of *Verdict Today*. "But that's the least of a masochist's troubles," he said.

"What's new?" Anne asked.

"Apart from the *fatwa* against Hari. Neelam's father is on the warpath…He will have you killed for exposing his tactlessly undisguised "covert" support for the creation of Khalistan" and painstakingly secret hobnobbing with Muslim extremists."

Neelam, watching them dolefully, asked for another drink and screamed: "I will kill the beast!"

"How many enemies of this crusader will you kill?" Anne twittered;

"My mom's on the warpath too, film star Khan is suing him for defamation, the US State Department has ordered my transfer to war torn Equatoria because of him, Amnesty International is questioning his integrity, and his own brother is likely to finally disown him…"

Although Hari kept his outward calm, in reality he was feeling uneasy, even agitated, about the powerful forces lined up against the professional rebel.

"The lonesomeness of virulent honesty!" Tom taunted.

David added fuel to the fire: "Do you know that your cook has reappeared?"

He shook his head and looked at Usha, who said: "I've just received a note from him…" and handed the note to him.

"The last straw!" Hari said after going through the cryptic note.

"What?" Anne asked.

"The midget—the cold-blooded slayer of my Koel—will strangle me with his bare hands!" His hollow laughter became uncontrollable.

"But why?" Anne demanded.

"He has rejoined the Manipur Liberation Army (MLA)," Usha replied, biting her nails.

"Rejoined?" David asked.

"Hari sir had rescued him from the MLA at my request and gave him the job…he now cooks for the Taliban in one of their boarding schools in Delhi."

Tom was clearly enjoying Hari's uneasiness and Anne's vain attempts to pull him out of his negative mood by making frivolous remarks, which irritated him even more.

"No one loves you any more, Hari," Tom sniggered.

"His readers!" Neelam shot back.

"That may be it!" Anne twittered; "*Verdict Today's* success has gone to his head. Five million copies daily! He doesn't even care for me!"

He looked at her, grinned and asked: "What do you expect, lady? Should I break down because you are being kicked upstairs to a place where a million people have been slaughtered as of last count in the most awesome outbreak of Jihad. I'm sure you will cope with distinction."

All of a sudden, without any reason, both burst out laughing: "What happened to us," both spoke simultaneously, and started kissing, unmindful of the startled group. Anne and Hari seemed to melt into each other's arms, so much so that no one noticed a barefoot urchin tiptoe in and place something near the liquor cabinet. Usha squealed: "Hey! Who are you?' She pounced on the lad and brought him down, screaming: "Sir! Madam!" The boy was caught without trouble, and a suspicious-looking packet was gingerly picked up by Anne. The urchin willingly told them that the parcel was given to him by a holy man with a tip of one hundred rupees. Anne screamed: "It may be an explosive!" "Throw it away!" shouted Tom.

"Get rid of it!" screamed David.

"Dump it," lisped Neelam. The grinning urchin led the entire group to the "holy man" across the road, sitting cross-legged on the sidewalk outside the Flying Club entrance, with a broad mocking grin on his dark face. "A lot of grinning for my comfort," Hari laughed, holding Anne's hand; "I'm terrified by these goons.."

"Blessings to you all from the mighty Shri Kaal Bhairon! With the compliments of Prime Minister Ram Kumar. head patron of the holy temple!" he said, getting up, placing his right arm on Anne's shoulder with a flourish.

"Much obliged, Your Holiness!" Hari said with an exaggerated bow.

"The PM has sent a gift for you, sir. May I follow you to your house?" "Why not! …Surely, you don't need permission to bomb my house, Your Holiness!"

"What's going on!" Tom demanded.

"Sick practical joke by the old fox … that bomb was a peace cake Anne flung into the street," said David.

"The robber of poll processes wants to make peace with his altruistic Johnny-cum-lately protégé because *Below the Belt* makes him insecure and Al Jihad is threatening his orderly life and the country's security," Anne twittered and Usha jumped with joy for no apparent reason.

But Neelam continued to sulk: "All these old fogies are ruthless killers…Beware of the spurious saint, my dad, the champion ripper of Sikhism!" In a nutshell, RK was "graciously" willing to forgive Hari for the heretical expose of his government's negative performance. Back home, the *tantrik* presented a crate of premium Scotch to Hari and asked:

"Any message, sir?"

"No truce," Hari replied.

Anne was prompt in his support as Tom squirmed uneasily when she said something indecently derogatory about the Indian leader.

Hari decided to go into his clownish mode. "Microsoft Word isn't mightier than a politician scorned or … wait a second…or a terrorist incensed." "What are you talking about?" Neelam asked, bewildered as usual. "Sant Nihal held a secret meeting with Ali. RK has declared forty days of official mourning for his slain predecessor. Anne has received her transfer orders. Death toll in Equatoria genocide crosses one million.

Field Marshal Idris Amaanat has severed diplomatic ties with the US and Britain," Hari said.

"Thanks for the news bulletin ... Does it mean that my posting to Equatoria is null and void?" Anne said hopefully. Tom intervened to say that she was now being sent on promotion as Ambassador-at-large.

"Don't worry Anne, I will follow you to Africa as Editor-at-large. My worry is about dinner tonight...What and where since my chef is cooking for the elite Taliban trainees."

David said: "Meanwhile, let's do full justice to the PM's Scotch!"

Hari interrupted him: "The PM's booze has been sent back with a thank you note in protest against his new censorship decree. *Verdict Today* defies any attempt to stifle human conscience—News tomorrow—editor detained by counterfeit icon!" Cheers! I have plenty of my own stock of liquor, thanks to my generous Parsi employer ... Let's celebrate Anne's promotion!"

The small group of artless idealists started celebrating as if there was going to be no tomorrow.

"Let's all go for Master's organic *bhutta*—the best corn-on-cob in the world roasted on sandalwood fire by a maestro," Hari said.

Anne's enthusiastic response surprised the entire group as she danced with joy like a child receiving a box of fancy candy at Halloween.

"Trick or treat!" exclaimed Tom.

"Let's walk there," Anne said, ignoring him.

Neelam protested: "I can't walk and I hate your down-market corn-on-a-cob."

Tom volunteered to stay behind to keep her company. They found Master all set to close shop, sitting on his hand-cart and putting on the propellers on his hands like gloves, carefully covering his thigh-stumps with neatly-folded sparkling-white pajamas, ready to dart away on his custom-made transport. He was thrilled to see Hari, Anne and the others.

"I was just leaving for your office, sir. My cell phone is lost and my information is sensitive," Master whispered. Sheetal touched his stumps respectfully. Blessing him, Master asked:

"Do you ever go to your old school, son?"

"No, sir," Sheetal replied.

"It has been converted into a Taliban ammunition and chemical weapons depot, which has been extremely busy stockpiling for the past couple of days with all kinds of supplies coming in at the dead of night," Master said.

All of a sudden, Anne stepped forward and kissed Master's forehead: "I love you Master. No subterfuge. No self-interest. A true warrior. Let's dine together, sir!"

"Let's all go to Seventh Heaven," David suggested.

Master agreed and all of them started walking together, keeping pace with Master's four-wheel cart guided dexterously through chaotic traffic in the pounding heart of New Delhi's clogged administrative district. At Seventh Heaven, Tom, who had already arrived, was astonished to see a humble man with amputated limbs joining the highbrow group and being treated as a celebrity. At one end of the bar, Ali watched the jovial gathering with dismay.

In one corner, matinee idol Khan and David's alimony-affluent ex-wife were in the middle of their midlife mooching spree when they were interrupted by the notorious Sikh secessionist Sant Nihal which sent shivers down Neelam's spine and prompted Anne to snigger.

"What are we celebrating?" Neelam asked.

"Anne's punishment promotion and posting to Jihad-afflicted Africa on the Equator," Hari said.

Master said he too was due to depart for Equatoria to participate in the Paralympic Games. Mary informed them that Madhu was already there for the Miss Empress pageant and Hari whispered in Anne's ear that he would join her in Africa after the funeral.

"After lighting the funeral pyre of your girlfriend," she twittered.

Tom's face fell and David taunted:

"You must be missing the great PM!"

"I have a feeling that Jim and Tim may still be here," Hari said.

"So, it's not because of me but the assassins! Stupid! No feelings for me!" Anne said, hurt. "I don't believe in verbal professions of supreme emotions like love and hate." She bit him on the cheek. "Is that hate or love?" She grabbed him with both hands and planted her lips on his.

"Now!" she finally breathed. "Encore," he said, pulled her up with one arm and they kissed, without inhibition; "permissive American heiress and sex-starved Indian sidewalk plebian. I love you, Anne!"

"Ditto! Let's go for a drive," she said.

'Let's eat first, with chief guest Tom and special invitee Master."

Crestfallen Tom mocked: "Romancing with Jihad! Bravo!"

"It isn't the best time for romance," said Hari, squeezing her hand.

"And it's also the worst time to take stock," she twittered. "You, Anne, are my only stock. That's more than I need to climb out of the pain of lifelong loneliness in the wilderness of evil I have experienced. I am terrified of losing you or leaving you alone in this predatory evil world in a cut-throat society from which you are likely to be disconnected because of me."

"I think you have finally got cold feet, overwhelmed by the centripetal and centrifugal forces lined up against your not so-mighty pen brandishing bravado," David giggled.

"Perhaps. But courage in a journalist is all about rising above self, not about winning and losing, but about facing the situation with a view to educating, informing and enlightening, to be the untarnished mirror in which society can see itself as it is," he said loftily. "I'm glad the armchair warrior has triumphed over the crusader," she sighed. "Thanks to you, and my realisation that sharing my pain with you is the final treatment of the pain of loneliness. Let's take stock, as you say…" he said.

"You keep saying this. Where do you start?" she asked.

"Jihad, of course, the biggest threat. Must make the skeptical aware of who, what, when, where and why. Bhagavad Gita says "Do your duty."

"Our dharma is to inform and coax our leaders to act in the interest of humankind."

"What about us?" she asked.

"Marriage, of course, if you are willing. I'm more than ready, my family has adopted you, you are hopefully willing, but your mom," he said.

"But I have been transferred to Equitoria."

"No problem, I'll join you after my assassinated girlfriend's funeral and, together, we shall be courting officially in the midst of Jihad fury," he said.

Chapter - 23

Romancing in Turmoil

"It's not the end of the world, not yet anyway," Anne called to say soon after reaching Equatoria. "A tyrant replacing a despot in post-colonial Africa is routine," she said; "It's probably the same old story of Bantu, Nilote and Cushiite, Kikuyu and Luo, Hutu and Tutsi decimating one another or the deeply-entrenched former colonialists using their erstwhile official soldiers to act as mercenaries to destabilise Black regimes."

"It's much more than that," he said; "It's Islamic Jihad, madam, an African turmoil in which Muslim soldiers and mercenaries from the Indian Ocean region are actively involved, including Indian soldiers of fortune in a foreign war for the first time. Many of these mercenaries are from the ranks of those who were a part of United Nations peacekeeping forces in Africa or elsewhere," he said.

"Not for glory, for love of money. Unable to crush separatists at home, avaricious Indian soldiers stick their necks out for a cause they know nothing about!" he sighed.

"When do you expect to be free to arrive here?" she asked.

"Immediately after the funeral," he said and got down to delegating responsibilities to senior and trusted members of his team, the emphasis being on facts and figures, not conjecture. Authentic, not invented, quotes as well as confirmation and/or denial. "Carry on," the chief editor told the editors; "Get behind the news."

"Sir?" asked a senior editor.

"Well?"

"Your brother, sir. Do you remember when he was commander of a UN peacekeeping mission somewhere in Africa." began Foreign Editor Ghosh.

"Yes, you mean when he was hastily recalled, allegedly for his prorebel activities, which were never proved...yes. His wife told me that he brought a large number of expensive gifts from both sides—the regime, which was later ousted, and the ruling junta. Typical of opportunist India, particularly Big Brother, Milking both the winners and the losers, the victors and the vanquished, the dead and the dying, the killed and the killers. The vicious circles going round and round making humankind a dizzy species."

"Mr Rai, sir?"

"Shocked, my dear? What? The one-time peace brokers have now become war-mongers. Yes, my dear. Explore all this and bring home the findings. But establish the truth. Assign a gutsy guy or girl to Equatoria to get behind the story. Spare no one, not even my brother."

In the middle of numerous imperatives, the Hari-Anne relationship had taken a sinister turn with her punishment posting immediately after the last American envoy was expelled by the coup leader and no one else was willing to replace him in the war-torn country.

Meanwhile, Jal Wadia had instinctively known all along that Hari would be well advised to take a vacation. Right now was perhaps the most opportune moment. Anne had left a day earlier. Time for her boyfriend to follow. But not on vacation; but as editor-at-large. How opportune. Divine intervention.

Hari had stepped on numerous sensitive toes. Professional ethics, not malice. But his detractors, among them his own managing director Karan Iyer, wanted him out. So, they were relieved when he agreed to go to Africa. Hari had no idea what was in store for him in Equatoria. The coup leader, self-styled Field Marshal Idris Amanat, had ordered all foreign newsmen out of the country minutes before his arrival.

The immigration officer at the airport refused to stamp Hari's passport: "Please take the next flight back to New Delhi, Mr. Rai." The flight out was not due until the next evening. That too was full, and all flights thereafter for a whole week were overbooked because of the exodus following the genocide and the on-going civil war between the Bantu and the Nilote tribes. Amanat's Muslim mercenaries were making things worse for non-Muslims.

Hari was given a provisional transit visa, with the condition that he would not be allowed to leave Safari Airport Hotel. He was also required to deposit his passport with Immigration. "Anything for the divine chimes," he mumbled, as he was escorted to the nearby hotel by a porter and a policeman. He decided to go for a drink at the Jumbo Bar on the rooftop. The bar was crowded, perhaps the only watering hole open in the entire city.

A continuous "live" telecast of the strongman, General Amanat, could be seen and heard all around the large drinking area as well as the connecting restaurants: "The treacherous enemies of Equatoria have been decisively decimated by the brave Presidential Guard. Life in the entire country is back to normal, and I, your President, Idris Amanat, have taken full control," he said; "Allah is our Savior, Allah is our protector. I, Idris Amanat, am His humble servant, governing this blessed nation in the name of the Prophet Muhammad. Amen!"

Every single person in the audience stood up and repeated "Amen!"

Hari ordered another drink, out of habit, without meaning any disrespect to the President.

"Hey!" yelled a customer wearing a red cylindrical Islamic cap; "Stand up, you infidel! And salute His Excellency!"

Hari looked at the man and winked. The waiter smiled and gave him the drink: "Anything else, sir?"

"Yeah," Hari said, "Another drink and a plate of roast lamb, my dear."

"No lamb.. No pork also, only beef, dead cows. Wild deer, also dead. Drought and disease. Corn, maize meal. No chicken or fish, either. Only peanuts. Food shortage.. There's some canned stuff from America. Only room service. Nothing in the kitchen."

Smart young man, thought Hari, and wondered. After he brought him some salted peanuts "on the house", he said he was a newspaper reporter before the civil war. "Our building and everything was burnt down by the soldiers belonging to the ruling junta. Why do we call these violent battles civil war.

What's civil about any war?"

"What's your name?" Hari asked.

"David Moses," he replied.

Hari smiled: "Would you like to work as a reporter?"

"Yes, sir!"

Hari gave him a hundred dollars and his calling card: "Get in touch with me when you can."

For a barroom, Jumbo was an extremely quiet place. Hushed silence. One or two subdued whispers. There was an echo in the fearsome hollowness, of awe-inspiring pathos. Presently, an entire company of armed militia marched into the bar, and their leader barked: "Hands up! Nobody move! You!" he pointed to Hari, "You, white man! What's your name?"

"Hari."

"Come with me! Harry! Somebody is looking for you in the lobby…Hurry."

Standing in the lobby was C. Anne Spenser, the greenhorn American Ambassador-at-Large in Africa. "Smiling like a White goddess blessing her African flock gathered together like a million lambs waiting to be slaughtered", he said, bowed and kissed her proffered hand: "At Your Excellency's Service!"

"Good to see you, Mr Hurry Not Rai! What have you been waiting for?" She was annoyed.

"Perhaps another genocide."

"No chance of that in the near future," she said; "Idris is in full control. Islamic Jihad has triumphed. Infidel president Charles Bantu shot by Jim and Tim and strangled by Amanat. Government troops in disarray. Only sporadic fire in the city to flush out remnants of any opposition," she said and escorted him into her Mercedes 500 SLC, the Star and Stripes, the Old Glory, fluttering, speeding through droughtstricken withering foliage of the highlands on the equator towards the official residence of the Ambassador of the United States.

More than a dozen Americans who had taken refuge in the spacious lawns were enjoying a party. Anne and Hari started mingling with them. Each one of the men and women were talking about the civil war and its ramifications. The ousted Bantu was not bad, some said. But Idris will prove to be better, they agreed.

"A pirate replacing a robber! The butcher!" said Hollywood sex goddess Natalie Shepherd, clutching an embarrassed Hari's arm: "Who are you, handsome?"

Anne introduced Hari. "Oh, an Indian. I love Indians." She was tipsy, so Hari tried to move away; "An eminent editor. Tell me, handsome, who will win this war?"

"Idris is the new President, isn't he? So, theoretically he has won, with the backing of Al Jihad's pawns of pitilessness. But who has lost? That's the question." said Hari.

"Who has lost," asked the star, desired by men around the world, gazing voluptuously at Hari: "Who?"

"The people, as always. The masses are the losers and will remain so."

"I love Communists," she said "an Indian Communist, my God!" She tried to embrace him in her drunken stupor and slipped.

Anne took Hari into the guest wing and showed him a large bedroom she had earmarked for him. He freshened up, and immediately started making three sets of notes titled: One, whose victory; two, counting the dead in Jihad; and three, why African armies were regarded as the softest belly for fundamentalists, Anne joined him after performing her duties as the hostess. She asked about the Hindu viewpoint about the victory of Good over Evil.

"There is no such thing as Good versus Evil in the world. We Hindus have been brainwashed into believing this hypothesis down the ages. Lord Rama, being good and virtuous, triumphed over Ravana, the unprincipled and lecherous brute. Not true," said Hari.

"Imagine! Ravana's country Lanka was rich, made of gold, according to the epic. Again, he did not harm Sita in any way. It shows that the so-called evil king was a gentleman and a good economic administrator. His nation was prosperous. Be that as it may, Lord Rama's court historians found him guilty."

He added: "All wars everywhere are between winners and losers. The losers are branded evil and the victors good by the historians whose paymasters are the victors. Hitler became evil because he lost and the Allies are good because they won. What would historians have done if Hitler had won? Now, Anne, if you don't mind, I would like to file my first story out of Africa." He started moving his fingers on his laptop keyboard:

From HAR NATH RAI, Equatoria, August 18, 1977:

AFRICA BY DEAD RECKONING

Is there a difference between 264,000 Africans and zero Africans? What about 264,000 dead Africans and one dead African? If 1,736,000 Africans died in a civil war, the figure given to the world would probably be two million. In which case the 264,000 'extra' Africans would be equal to zero.

It was claimed that 500,000 people died because of Idi Amin's misrule. Later, in the civil war between Yoweri Museveni's National Resistance Army and Milton Obote's government in Uganda, it was declared that 500,000 more had been killed in the infamous Luwero Triangle.

Several years later, extremist Hutus of Rwanda killed one million Tutsis and moderate Hutus. Then it was the turn of two million Hutus to flee Rwanda. The dead and the dying are yet to be counted.

In Equatoria, Anglo-American infidel stooge Charles Bantu has been toppled by Muslim Brotherhood strongman Idris Amanat, who claims he had taken over in a bloodless coup, which means that no official estimates of the casualties of kafirs and martyrs will be released.

However, United Nations statisticians are struggling to concoct figures, which will doubtless end with three zeroes, or four, five or six. Could it be that when people get down to counting the African dead, the officials become so lazy that they just round off the figures? Or is it that non-Africans are simply unconcerned about the plight of the people living in countries where the meek shall never inherit the earth?

Why is it that the dead on other continents are counted to the last victim and in Africa, they are rounded off to the nearest thousand, or hundred thousand? Is it that Africans tend to die in such larger numbers than elsewhere that the headcount doesn't really matter?

Why should it be so difficult to count the dead? Surely they can't run away like the fleeing targets of rampaging government troops or rebels. The dead, as everyone knows, are perfectly immobile, except in special circumstances when they are floating down the River Nile away from Lake Victoria, the source.

Such corpses are, of course, hard to count, not merely because of the speed with which they travel but because they are likely to be counted twice, or canceled out, thanks to the head being seen in one place and the torso in another. Even so, there is no excuse for failing to count the dead once the killers are through with their business. People who die should be counted down to the last number. In other continents, even when the dead are buried under tons of bombed concrete, their exact number is given. Almost always.

When will Africa's dead be treated with respect by statisticians? Perhaps the murderers of the African masses are such sticklers for round figures that after exterminating a politically-unwanted village of 9,725 infidels, they go on to the next village and kill another 275 to get a nice, manageable 10,000. And what if there are 276 people in that village? Does the chieftain or imam of the genocide squad spare that solitary 'extra' person for the sake of mathematical convenience?

Either African despots prefer their dead in convenient round figures or the statisticians are too callous to bother. The same people would not dare round off the dollars when counting money, mostly dirty. But when it comes to corpses, 264,000 may as well equal zero.

A UN statistician who invariably reckons $1,736,000 as 2 million invariably gets promoted, as does a peacekeeping official or refugee worker adept at making round-figure calculations about the dead and the displaced. With such a combination of statisticians, aid officials, despots and guerrilla chieftains, we may be heading towards a situation where a death toll of under 1,000 one day may not be reported at all.

In Equatoria today, Field Marshal Idris Amanat announced he had routed the country's armed forces and that he was henceforth the ruling head of State. "It was a bloodless coup," he claimed, signifying that there would be no counting of the dead and the dying. A zero casualty civil war, we presumptuously assume: Pain-free Jihad! The next day, reports might show that the toll has risen to 2,000 following renewed clashes. The textbooks say that the natural numbers begin with one. Yet, when counting the most significant thing in life, a life, counting starts at 1,000 or 10,000 or 100,000, or one million. What would the scenario be like if, hypothetically, no one survives a Jihad. No census of six billion cadavers! Or was it 5.99 billion corpses? Who cares! No one left to care."

Chapter - 24

The Tyrant Decrees

"So, the brute, the foremost Jihad fanatic, wants to meet me. Why? No one knows me here," Hari said.

"The savage isn't all that dumb. After all, he is the spearhead of Jihad in the African continent. Besides, International Press Institute today expelled *Verdict Today* as its member while Global Media Council has named you Journalist of the Year. And your criticism of Amnesty International about its alleged links with Jihad supporters is common knowledge. Every news service has carried these stories. So, Amanat knows who you are," Anne said.

"So? I'm here on vacation, to spend time with you and hopefully convince you how mortified I am of being rejected by you as a suitor."

"But the President has asked me to arrange his meeting with you, so keen he is to become the good boy in the eyes of the world."

"Doesn't he realise that he could be making a mistake by choosing me as his historian?"

"I don't know. I also know that you will refrain from making value judgments in your coverage. And I promised him in the interest of US Equatoria solidarity," she said.

"Where does this bloody Indian word merchant come into this American solidarity with the carnage-crazy perpetrator of genocide?"

"As the probable fiancé of the American Ambassador-at-Large. It's a question of my career, dear."

"God! Did you say fiancé!" he exclaimed, stepping forward and gripping her hand. She twittered.

"Praise the Lord, fiancé! Yeah!" he started dancing, then kneeled before her and gently holding her hand, stuttered: "Will you marry me, C. Anne Spenser? I promise to make you the most miserable fairy in the cosmos."

"Don't jump to any conclusion, please, Hari. I said probable fiancé because there still are hurdles," she whispered.

Hari suggested a stroll in the front lawn: "It's my first morning in Africa. I don't wish to start it interviewing a tyrant, the mastermind of the most gruesome genocide in Africa. Let's watch the birds, the butterflies and the bees and get the blessings of bountiful nature, the Grevillea here and the Jacaranda flame of the forest there, Avocado here in the middle, the rose buds here, your delicate feet on this velvety grass mercilessly crushing the tired fireflies after their glittering night out."

She said: "I don't think it's an interview. It's a party to celebrate his victory. And you, Hari Nath, will escort the Ambassador of the United States."

"At your service, Your Excellency! Bring it on!"

A grand affair. Not at all like a traditional Muslim celebration. More like an Africanised western-style reception: colourful tribal dancers performing traditional *ngoma* all around the State House gardens. Behind them huge carnivorous feasts were being roasted on bonfires by chefs dressed as cavemen. Beyond, at the main entrance to the banquet hall, the President and Commander-in-Chief, Field Marshal Idris Mohammed Amanat, in full ceremonial regalia including the peak-cap and a million medals, tall and big, was receiving guests gleefully. His face reminded Hari of Kumar's black bulldog Dolfo, massive short-faced head and an earthquake-causing growl.

"Pleased to meet you, Mr Rai. Congratulations for the award and expulsion from IPI," he said gently shaking Hari's hand but looking at Anne: "Ravishing!"

"Make yourself happy, both of you, in the Islamic Republic of Blessed Equitoria. I will chat with you a bit later. Wait…Mr. Rai. I strongly object to your opposition to our holy war. Anyway, later. For now, enjoy yourself. Be happy, for this moment. Roast beef, a glass of wine, and your sweetheart! Ha, ha, ha!"

"Much obliged, your excellency, but no beef for me. I am a Hindu," he smiled and walked away holding Anne's arm; "Strong, sweaty hands," Hari whispered moving towards one of the bars. Hari saw some people he knew or knew of Brigadier Abdul Hamid, ex-Indian Army; superstar Khan, his model wife Kalpana, local Indian tycoon Ketan Kantaria, his ex-film star wife Reena, chatting with Natalie Shepherd, and many others.

All nationalities seemed to be represented, a party of busy-bodies, it seemed to Hari and Anne. She was looking graceful in her simple white chiffon dress, with a small tiara tucked neatly in her tightly-combed hair, a fairy floating above the run-of-the-mill gathering of over- or underdressed females and their "correctly" clad escorts. Khan and Kalpana approached the two. "How are you in this country?' he asked Hari.

"Hazards of the profession," Hari said, "And you?"

"Location shooting," he said simply, and added: "That girl Madhu is also here participating in a beauty circus."

Hari acted blank as he also noticed Neelam's husband Rajpal chatting with Brig. Hamid and Reena at the main bar. Anne got busy with her diplomatic chores, meeting members of the Interim Council of Ministers and those few members of the diplomatic corps who had remained behind.

Hari winced when he saw Idris envelop Anne's hand in his outlandish grip and introduced her to "Mr. Jim Malkovich and Mr. Tim Malkovich, old family friends". Hari moved towards her as he was relieved to notice Idris releasing her hand and grabbing his again in a vice-like grip: "Have a drink with me. I hope your friend, madam ambassador, will have no objection."

"I'm sure she has nothing against alcohol, Mr. President," Hari grinned.

"It's not liquor. Her great country objects to me as President of my country, the Muslim tyrant, as the State Department calls me. You see, I am a drinking Muslim, and an admirer of Omar Khayyam." No one said anything. Idris continued: "Talking about Ghiyath al-Din Abdul Fath Umar bin Ibrahim al-Nisaburi al-Khayyami, I wish to inform you that I am personally interested in propagating and promoting the faith of this great Islamic thinker, philosopher, mathematician, astronomer and poet."

"A splendid idea, Mr President," said Khan.

"Not just an idea. Omar Khayyam is a great symbol of the unity of all Muslims around the world. You know, Mr Rai, America is our most dangerous enemy. Our next major enemy is our disunity, Sunni and Shia. If we succeed in uniting all the sects, Islam will become the most potent force."

"Great," said Anne.

"Admirable," exclaimed.

Khan, Rajpal and Hamid clapped in unison. Hari watched, amused, and said: "Mind-blowing."

"Mr Rai! I am declaring right here and now that I, Idris Amanat, the President of Equatoria, will do everything possible to become the unifier of Islam and make this great faith the supreme global superpower in the foreseeable future. I announce to the world that the process of global politicisation and militarisation of Islam has started today on the independence day of Equatoria, eighteenth of August, 1977."

Hari said: "Mr. President, sir, you make it sound like a declaration of war."

"It is war: Cheers to that! Ladies and gentlemen! Cheers! My first decree as President is a declaration of war against the United States and Britain!"

Turning to Hari, he said: "Rai! Interview me, Mr Journalist of the Year!"

"Do I have an option, sir?"

"No!" he thundered.

"Frankly, sir, ..."

"Address me properly, you imbecile Hindu kafir!"

Hari held Anne's arm and started walking away without a word.

Idris growled: "Don't even try to escape. Interview me first, and send your article from State House..."

"But I am out of my depth on these subjects," he protested.

"You will be fully briefed, Mister. Have another drink with Khan, Singh and Hamid and gear yourself up for a brief earth-shaking statement!"

Anne and Hari joined the group, smiling as if they were enjoying the presidential sundowner. "Great party!" Anne said, glaring at Natalie, who seemed to be all-at-sea.

"Mind-blowing!" Hari said, winking at Reena, who glanced sheepishly at her embarrassed husband. No one made any attempt to say anything, Singh and Hamid refilling their glasses and Natalie stumbling in her drunken stupor towards the swimming pool.

Idris thundered: "Now! Take down my declaration."

Hari heard the statement dispassionately, paraphrased it and typed his story on Microsoft Word:

"Annihilator of Africa Idris Amanat today pledged to kill the American President within the next seven days. "This is allout Jihad against all infidels in the world," Idris declared in an exclusive interview at a party to celebrate his victory over "Anglo-American puppet Charles Bantu" in a "bloodless" coup in the mineral-rich south-central African nation of Equatoria.

"Idris ordered the immediate nationalisation of all American and British' oil and mining corporations, airline and insurance companies as well as financial institutions and manufacturing and trading companies. Condemning Christian indoctrination and conversion and taking a dig at outdated and meaningless Hindu idol-worship practices, he said all non-Muslim places of worship will no longer be allowed to function in the country."

Asked how he planned to assassinate the American President, he said:

"Downtrodden Africans have woken up and condemn all of the West's past exploitative practices. African-Americans are essentially African and they are being reorganised as a potent force to end monopolistic practices of White America."

Idris declared the formation of "one worldwide Muslim nation determined to annihilate all non-Muslims everywhere. Jihad against all infidels has begun," he declared, adding that Islam's mascot henceforth would be the great Persian poet-astronomer Omar Khayyam, author of *Rubaiyat*.

In another development, Idris announced that he was supporting the production of a big-budget international movie based on the life of Omar Khayyam to show the world that Islam was a modern, forward-looking faith and not narrow-minded doctrinaire savagery as non-Muslims had been projecting for centuries.

According to the briefing: Omar Khayyam's biography was being rewritten by a team of Indian and American hacks. Woven around his poetry, especially *Rubaiyyat*, his religious beliefs were to be reinvented in the context of the problems and potential of present day Islam, with focus on the need to unify all Islamic forces, namely Shias, Sunnis, Zoroastrians, Ismailis, Bohras, Ithnasheri and all other sects and sub-sects as well as tribes and nationalities, namely: Arabs and Africans; South Asians: southeast Asians, East Asians; the Soviet Union, Eastern Europe, West Europe, the Americas and African-Americans.

Conversions to Islam will start with new vigor all over the world. Amanat has already sent personal messages to all Muslim leaders everywhere, spelling out his political, economic and socio-religious plans for the new organisation called Jihad International, which would replace the United Nations. Hari typed the entire story on a State House computer, showed it to Amanat and sent it, starting with:

"This BELOW THE BELT" dispatch is being sent without comment…

ATTACK ON AMERICA "IMMINENT", WARNS IDRIS "Non-Muslims Beware of Global Jihad"

From HARI NATH RAI in CAPTIVITY, STATE HOUSE, EQUATORIA, August 18:

The self-proclaimed "victor" of the bloody civil war in the oil-rich African nation of Equatoria, Field Marshal Idris Amanat, today declared an all-out war against the United States.

As a first step, Idris ordered the severance of diplomatic relations with the US, ordering the Acting American Ambassador, Miss C. Anne Spenser, to leave the country on the first available flight. The President insulted this writer by publicly calling him an imbecile Hindu kafir.

Finally, Field Marshal Amanat urged all Muslims everywhere to unite against all non-Muslims and to present a unified front of Islam to overwhelm the world with the all-embracing creed: Long Live Islamic unity, at war with all Infidels.

Idris announced, "This toothless tiger, the so-called Journalist of the Year, has been tamed. Now, let's party in the name of our beloved Omar Khayyam. There's no drought, no famine, diamonds and gold and uranium can buy everything the Islamic world needs! Cheers!"

"Wait! A clarification! It's war, both against the USA and its stooge Israel and Jews all over the world! Is that clear? Hey, you, lousy carpenter of words! Ass-licker of your Parsi boss Jal Wadia! It's official declaration of Jihad by Muslims everywhere against all others worldwide!"

Hari said nothing, a mischievous smile lighting his face, as he turned towards Anne: "Are you scared?"

She shook her head. "Neither me. But I'm scared of pain and discomfort. Let's drink and immunize ourselves against impending physical and mental torture. Bring it on!" He grabbed two fresh glasses, gave one to her, and swallowed his, picking up another with steady hands: "Good luck, Your Excellency!" Idris was fuming. He signaled the guards to move nearer to Hari and thundered: "Pick up this kafir. Take him out and throw him in the swimming pool. Deep end! Tie up his arms and legs and beat him up! The cheeky imbecile!

Hari could not swim. After his near-death experience in the River Jamuna sixteen years ago, the very sight of any body of water terrified him. And now, the four hefty African goons tied his arms and legs and dumped him in the pool after beating him black and blue, the tyrant grinning and Anne squirming. Cold! The water. Very cold. "Fucked!" he screamed. His mind went back sixteen years and he tried to do what he did or did not do then, closing his eyes, holding his breath, reciting the Gayatri mantra and allowing his body to sink, squirming a little, inhaling and exhaling, afloat now, sinking again, chanting "Aum mmmm".

Then, it happened. That dazzling white light which did not dazzle, enveloping him in its warm embrace, as it were, soothing him like a divine lullaby coaxing the battered editor to sleep, floating in the cozy lap of nothingness. He thought he heard someone whisper in his throbbing ear.

"Be happy for this moment,

This moment is your life."

The voice added:

"Pass not today in vain,

For it will never come again."

Profound, Hari wanted to say, but gushing foul-tasting water choked him. The voice continued:

"There was a door to which

I found no key"

"There was the veil through which

I might not see."

"Omar Khayyam!" Hari tried to scream. Radiantly young, a bamboo pen in one hand, a wine glass in the other, scribbling on a papyrus leaf in front and talking aloud:

"The moving finger writes,

and having written moves on.

Not all thy piety, nor all thy wit c

can cancel half a line of it."

Hari felt happy, in pain but floating. Was he regaining consciousness? Was it his sub-conscious memory? Puzzled. Omar Khayyam whispered again:

"I sent my soul through the invisible,

some letter of that afterlife to spell,

and by and by my soul returned to me,

and answered, 'I myself am Heaven and Hell'."

Then he heard the despot barking an order: "Fetch the heathen's body! Fast! And dump it outside the American Embassy! Without delay! In the thick of night.!"

"I myself am Heaven and Hell," the afterlife melody continued to whisper in his aching, water-logged ears. Why do African armies, though pampered by their regimes, fail to deliver at the critical time?

HARI NATH RAI delves into the reasons in this article. African armies are a highly pampered lot, especially by illegitimate, unpopular and despotic regimes that wish to stay in power indefinitely.

This is because the rulers need the armed forces to help them stay in power indefinitely. Past and on-going events, coups and counter-coups show without doubt that they have been significantly ineffective in fulfilling their masters' desires.

A few days ago, a little-known army sergeant in mineral-rich Equatoria, Idris Mohammed Amanat, had no difficulty in overthrowing the regime of John Nilotawa. Amanat was the President's bodyguard. When there was no one else around, the trusted sergeant strangled his master with his bare and brutal hands.

After the overthrow, Amanat claimed that the ousted President was in the process of pledging the nation to the United States and to the "imbecile" Jews in Israel. Nilotawa, a Brigadier, had earlier toppled his own benefactor, Lieutenant-General Christopher Lambart, with the help of a notorious South African mercenary, Johannes de Labrador, and an entire brigade of the country's army. A day before the coup, Nilotawa had promised a massive pay hike to the armed forces. He was given no time to fulfil his pledge.

About a decade ago, in Uganda, faced with Yoweri Museveni's Tanzania-aided National Resistance Army (NRA), the Ugandan army scattered like so much chaff.

Later, the Rwandan Tutsi rebels decimated the country's Hutu forces and set up their government in Kigali. In Burundi, a Major, Pierre Buyoya just strutted into the presidential palace to seize power. The defeat of Mengistu Haile Mariam's army in Ethiopia by Eritrean and Tigrean rebels is well documented. So is the disintegration of the Somali army.

Liberia went the same way, as did countless other African countries. Such events lead one to conclude that African armies, except in the power-house that is South Africa, are simply incapable of guaranteeing their countries' territorial integrity. They are even incapable of dealing with local rebellions.

Why is this so, despite the fact that armed forces personnel in Africa are among the best paid in the world? The success of any army depends on prudent management of recruitment, training, logistics, morale and welfare and, above all, the command and control structure. There are other intangibles, an important one being political will.

The conduct of military operations is circumscribed by the provisions of international and national laws. Guided by this framework, it is for a government to decide on the deployment of armed forces and to set the parameters within which they are to operate. Rules of engagement are the means whereby government provides political direction to commanders on the degree and manner in which force may be applied, especially when formal war has not been declared.

However, such rules do not apply, when dealing with domestic insurgency. As is well known, Africa has had more civil strife than cross-border wars; the latter have largely been inconclusive while the former have often resulted in rebel victories, except perhaps in Mozambique, where a power sharing formula had to be negotiated.

African armies have faltered as a result of many factors. One is lack of political direction. Recruitment is a murky affair. There is manipulation in favour of the tribe to which the head of state belongs. Imbalance in tribal representation in the armed forces causes disenchantment among the people at large and creates disloyalty among those officers and men who belong to the non-ruling tribe—a sure enough recipe for strife sooner or later.

Recruitment to rebel movements cannot be said to be entirely voluntary, but it is usually well targeted, even though it may be a marriage of convenience in pursuit of a single enemy: a tyrannical and partisan regime. That's one reason civil strifes in Africa tend to last for years; having fulfilled their first goal, the rebels then start fighting among themselves for the spoils of the strife. In most African armies, indiscipline, economic problems and laxity in management have relegated training to the back seat. It is not unusual to find entire brigades who have not fired a rifle since their basic training. The situation is as worse in the case of officers. The soldiers do have weapons, but they are less than mediocre marksmen.

African governments, ironically, spend more money on acquiring military hardware than they do, for example, on providing civic amenities to the people.

"That's money down the drain," says a retired Kenyan colonel. "A tank without an experienced crew is a useless piece of metal. Similarly, a helicopter or a sophisticated fighter is an operational liability."

The three basic elements of war are logistics, strategy and tactics. African armies fail on all three counts. Logistics bring the troops to the point of conflict, strategy decides where to act, and tactics how to act. Most African armies are unable to mount a sustained campaign against an enemy due to lack of good logistic systems. Either there is no money to procure the goods and services, or there is no transport to move them to where they are required.

Logistics have also been compromised by corruption and by a lack of planning. In many cases, there is a serious conflict of interest because senior officers are also suppliers to the defence establishment.

Reverting to "Field Marshal" Idris Amanat, one must say that he adds a new dimension to the history of violence in Africa. He is a religious fanatic, who admits to being a "drinking" Muslim committed to spreading Islam all over the world.

This writer has reason to believe that a retired senior officer of the Indian army has been hired as a consultant by Brigadier (Retired) Abdul Hamid, formerly of Aligarh and a past Commandant of the Indian Military Academy, near Pune, Maharashtra, is the first international mercenary from India.

Chapter - 25

Unholy Face of Extremism

"By fair means or foul. We must defeat all the forces lined up against our holy faith. Islam has been in danger because our internal contradictions have been used against us by our infidel enemies. Let's crush all those who wish to decimate Islam," the self-styled Field Marshal Idris Amanat told Khan at the State House garden party to celebrate the brute's victory in the civil war.

"Jihad International is now here to reinvigorate the Muslim nation back into action to annihilate all kafirs and to become the perpetual guardians of the Islamic world. We do not believe in blood circulating unseen through veins. It's the infidel blood spilled by mujahids and visible to the naked eye," he added "Let there be bloodshed of all kafirs, the non-Muslim heathens, for all lovers of Islam to see with their own eyes that impure blood has been spilled," Hari heard the demagogue talking to somebody, and shuddered, lying face down at the edge of the pool, sick and nauseated, lousy taste in his mouth.

"Severe that imbecile's snobbish head from his rotten body and dump the trash into a garbage can," he barked the order. As an afterthought, he added: "No, feed this pig-eater to the swine. To hyenas, vultures, whatever. Out of my sight!" Hari thought he had been given up for dead.

"Your Excellency, don't you think it would be wise to deliver him to that sexy American Ambassador. She may already be trying to get Amnesty International to sniff around the Palace," said a female voice.

"Good idea, darling! Dump it at Spenser's doorstep. Hurry! Out of the way!"

Was he hallucinating? Hari wondered. Was it a nightmare? The pool. His body being pulled out. Booted feet trampling on his back. Vomiting. And that severed head grinning at him and a headless body, also bleeding, dancing feverishly and the sound of drums in the background.

"It can't be real," he muttered, dreamily, unable to focus.

"It's real, Mr. Hurry Not Rai!" he heard a sweet voice; "Chimes in the Holy Trinity Temple on the banks of the Ganges. At dawn. Birds singing, butterflies fluttering and buzzing bees crawling on my spine. That chirpy twitter, the celestial cackle. The great divine orchestra!"

"You are safe. At Wadia Hospital," Anne kissed him hard, on the lips.

"God! A million sandalwood joss sticks. Let's hear this celestial aroma," he whispered in her ear, still in a trance-like haze. "Are you ready for the wedding bells, tough guy?" she said.

"Are you proposing, you divine enchantress? Wait a second... Let me check my vital organs... everything outwardly intact ...May be, I will have to go for some one-aday hormones! For now, a large drink may be in order to dilute the horrible chlorine taste."

"Didn't they castrate you, kid?" asked Big Brother in one of his rare jolly moods. Turning to Anne, he said: "Yes, Cleopatra, dear. He is ready for the historic wedding. As soon as he is out of hospital. It's my command! I am the head of the family and you are my daughter. That bum wants a lot of dowry and I'm the only one who can arrange it."

Hari mumbled dreamily: "I need an agony-reliever...Tranquilize me to oblivion, please."

"Bloody junkie!" BB exclaimed.

Unable to focus, Hari sang:

"Drink! For you know not

whence you came, nor why:

drink! for you know not

why you go, nor where."

The hospital room was crowded. Neelam was drunk-happy. Rani was chatting with Mary, who was teasing Usha. Yukta was rebuking Amit. The Air Chief was ogling at all the pretty girls. A half-dozen nurses were making merry with reporters while Karan and Roshan were glaring at each other. Anne was moving her fingers through Hari's hair who was deep in thought about a possible catastrophe-in-the-making waiting round the corner for the human race. Later that evening, he was discharged.

"Pork chops," Anne suggested and giggled. "Omar Khayyam is their mascot," Hari said; "Writers from Bollywood may soon be leaving for Los Angeles to write a masterpiece called Omar Khayyam's Holy War. "Mazhar Khan will play Omar Khayyam and Natalie Shepherd his main girlfriend Kimia Khatoon," he said.

"But isn't Omar Khayyam incompatible with Islam?" Anne asked.

"Of course, he is. I believe these latter-day Mujahids are trying to invent a new, benign face of Islam, to cover the horrific image with the poetic mask of rephrased *Rubaiyyat*, which is universally adored," Hari said, adding: "I think you should ask Tom Pickering to look into this more seriously."

Tom was contacted. He disagreed: "These dangerous guys will never allow Islam to be de-Prophetized. Omar Khayyam will prove to be an alcoholic caricature of Rasool Allah and *Rubaiyyat* will be burnt as a pornographic insult to the Holy Qur'an."

Anne asked: "Why, then, are they making a mega movie on the Persian poet-astronomer-mathematician?"

"It's all hypothetical. A money-making fantasy with a queer pornographic twist featuring Hollywood's sexiest star and Bollywood's sissy actor. Terrorists need money. Porn is worth ten billion dollars annually in the US alone and more than twice that worldwide," Tom said impatiently.

Anne said: "You mean terrorism is financed by pornography?"

"Yeah, one of the sources," he said impatiently.

"Surely, the CIA should have at least some idea about the total sum or sums being spent on conducting this outlandish war called Jihad?" Hari mocked.

"It's not a joke, Mr Rai." Tom was affronted.

"All right, not outlandish, but the onliest, *sui generis*, bloodlust of its kind which promises paradise to all jihadis," Hari said.

"What do you want to discuss—Jihad or paradise—Or, more appropriately, financing of both. Let's start with funds!" Hari was not camouflaging his agitation with flippancy; "Deficit financing, that's the main source. US development assistance, in other words. Your Government is the main culprit. I won't go into details here, because I am going to do it in **Below the Belt**."

Anne was feeling embarrassed. Her boyfriend was demonstrating his anti-American proclivities to an undercover CIA diehard. Hari, trying to make amends, floundered: "I mean, individuals like you and I can afford to be naive. But naivety of the most powerful nation concerning terrorism is criminal. The financiers of Jihad are more than culpable. Ignorance is no excuse, particularly when you control the most resourceful spy network. Never mind, let's refuel ourselves."

Anne was watching the two rivals for her hand apprehensively. The two were mature enough to be discrete in demonstrating their hostility towards each other, driven as they were for their common passion to rid the world of Jihad fanatics. Anne had not had time to delve deep into herself about her preference.

Bumbling Hari had swept her off her feet during the very first meeting. Tom was a long-standing admirer. Both were eminently eligible.

Mom hated Hari: "Too foreigner!" That was her only substantive objection, besides her aversion to a poor country like India.

"He definitely has an eye on your inheritance!" Alice repeatedly warned her. Papa was unavailable, lost in his lonely drunken stupor after the divorce, the forlorn misfit tired of the rat race, overwhelmed by the misery of his solitariness and alimony pauperisation.

Hari offered him another drink. He nodded and said: "No ice, no water, please. Straight." And Anne twittered: "And Tom Pickering, the ace CIA agent, afraid of water in a developing country!"

"My nephew's pediatrician says mother's milk is best," she laughed.

Hari was on the phone, briefing somebody about Jihad: "These holy warriors largely speak in parables. Example: A martyr in Jihad is dressed in radiant robes of faith. After martyrdom, he is married to houries and is allowed by Allah to intercede for seventy men and recommend them for entry into Jannah."

Usha tiptoed in to say there was nothing to eat at home. The three decided to get a taste of the Seventh Heaven again. "Fighting is the art of deceit," Tom said, out of *de novo*.

Hari concurred: "The Caliphs, the Prophet's political successors, wanted to raise a nation of Muslim warriors to achieve international distinction by building an Islamic Empire and humble all infidels in the name of Allah."

"So?" asked Anne.

"They had to invent stories for the simple desert-dwellers who were devoid of food and sex, who lapped up the most implausible fibs to make ends meet in exchange for a place in the splendor of the Seventh Heaven, which, they were told, is full of good food, virgin beauties and sexy boys," Hari said, smiling.

They decided to check the closed doors. "Jackpot!" Hari said after entering the first room. At least a dozen minor girls, expertly tied and gagged, lay sprawled on the floor, unconscious but breathing. Hari clicked his camera and called the Prime Minister on his hot line requesting him to send an army contingent to handle logistics.

"Where is Singh?" she asked; "There must be real people somewhere for whom that something yummy is being prepared in the kitchen."

"That may be for the girls. Anyway, let's check the other rooms, starting with the last," he said. Hari cautiously opened the last room in the corridor and stared into the barrel of magnum held in the steady hand of Singh and raised his hands. But he smiled: "Good, sir! I have been looking for you," Hari exclaimed: "I have an urgent message for you from the PM, sir."

Anne yelled: "The man is a child molester. Look! Three naked girls on that bed. Simple! Make a citizen's arrest, Hari. Stop beating around the bush, stupid!"

"Come into the room, Rai, and also you, miss, and squat on the floor. Both of you, hands on your heads. Hari was out of his depth. "Make yourself comfortable, sweetheart. Pontificate on all the traumas in your life. You are as safe as a little baby in a perverted hyena's dugout," he sniggered.

"Shut your mouth, you mother fucker!" Singh bellowed.

"I am having difficulty swallowing my own saliva, Mr. Singh," Hari said. Anne's cell phone started ringing and she opened her bag to take it out.

"Don't move, woman!" Singh screamed just as the doorbell also rang.

"I will get it," Hari said hurriedly.

"Don't you try to move! Cheeky son of a slut! Let it ring!" Singh growled; "Why are you here?"

"I told you. Urgent message from the PM," he said. The doorbell rang again, so did Anne's cell phone. She took it out.
It was her dad.

Give me your bloody cellular!" Singh shouted, pointing the gun at her.

"Here, shove it!" she retorted, switching it on; "It's my dad on the phone and yours at the door, buster!"

Hari seized the opportunity and sprang on Singh, snatching the magnum after punching him in the eye: "Hari is in a hurry, creep!" he said simply, hitting the cop again: "Where's your elusive Iraqi girlfriend, buddy?"

"I'm right behind you, mister. Drop the gun and turn around!" said an icy feminine voice. Hari froze for a second and saw Anne move fast, kicking Singh and launching herself into a burqa-clad woman, snatching her gun from the muzzle showing through her head-to-toe black burqa, "Use the gun, Hari! Hit the cop on the head with the but, hard, dear," she screamed and the burqa down, lock, stock and barrel.

"Awesome Anne!" Hari said hitting Singh.

"What's your name?" she asked the woman, removing her headgear, and revealing a lookalike of Uday, Saddam's elder son; "So, you are the daughter of the sadist megalomaniac, born out of wedlock no doubt, of one of the rape victims he spotted in the clubhouse or TV studio."

At the door was Colonel Kabir Sen, who took charge with his well-equipped contingent and helped Hari wrap up a long overdue story about the senior most cop's republic of fear within the capital and his wealth bloated by commissions, protection money and support of Jihad.

On the way back, Hari asked Anne: "Would you like to meet your papa and mom?"

"How? They're in San Francisco."

"Why can't we go there? Ask Dan Miller and I will make flight reservations, Wadia International Airlines will doubtless oblige—twenty hours. If we leave tonight, we shall be there on the same date, crossing five time zones and having five champagne breakfasts," he declared and she twittered.

Chapter - 30

Rainbow Sheds its Colours

Delhi San Francisco bookings were promptly cancelled after a reporter informed Hari that Ali was back at Ivory Tower Heights in his Paradise Penthouse along with a few western guests. He was puzzled.

"What the hell had he gone to the US for?" he asked David, who was going through some files from the *Verdict Today* morgue about Iraq's "robber-baron" Uday Saddam Hussein.

Sister-in-law Yukta called to say that her son Amit was missing and that he was last seen in a shady joint near the Golden Temple city of Amritsar, about 400 miles north of Delhi. "He just vanished from there, police says," she said, sobbing, uncontrollably. Hari asked his area bureau chief to assign his best reporters and report back within an hour. Yukta said big brother threw Amit out of the house when he came home with a Muslim girlfriend. Both father and son were drunk. When Hari called his brother, he bellowed: "That junkie is no longer my son. I disowned him yesterday after he came home sloshed and with a Muslim brat."

"Who is the girl?" Hari asked. "A slut from a border village near Amritsar."

A twitch in his left eye bothering Hari, he took the next flight to Amritsar and went straight to the drug den next to the most famous Sikh temple and was astonished to see the cop, P.S. Aurora, the ruthless encounter specialist with dubious loyalties. A brawl was clearly in the offing: "Looking for your junkie nephew, playboy?" he demanded. Hari knew he was outnumbered and outmaneuvered by the wily facilitator of Jihad's drug mafia. "Have you seen Amit, Mr. Aurora?" he asked politely.

"Yeah, I saw him in Delhi this morning paying some money to a drug runner who was later arrested by your friend Sen," he taunted.

Hari beat a hasty retreat and returned home after checking with the colonel, who admitted that he had arrested a Pakistani heroin-smuggler but that he did not see Amit. Clueless, a disturbed Hari closed his eyes and went to sleep on his chair ignoring tiny Kris crawling towards the front door.

He woke up with a start after dreaming about a black buffalo goring big brother. Was it a divine alert about an impending disaster? Black buffalo, the ride of Yama, god of death. Then he heard a street dog wailing, another alert about death, on top of the twitching left eye, another bad omen. coordinated divine predictions about an impending disaster.

He got up, freshened up and went out, again failing to notice Kris sleeping serenely under the banyan tree and came back, unsure, afraid of going back to bed, terrified of another nightmare and insomnia. He decided to fight his way out of his negativity prompted by an irrational belief in omens. He went into the bath for a long hot-cold shower and got ready to go out for a long walk as he invariably did whenever he was distraught. This time, he stepped out through the side exit of his house after pelting the dozing watchman with a pebble, looking up at the sky vacantly, perhaps for divine inspiration from the pre-dawn expanse and stopped to think listening with eyes closed to the chime of a single temple bell beyond and started trudging uncertainly towards the source of the chime, a tiny sidewalk temple beneath the trunk of a denuded banyan tree.

For no apparent reason, he took the shortcut that led to the official residence of the Principal Martial Law Administrator and started walking ponderously towards Air Force Lane. Some isolated hawkers had by now started hawking and even beggars had begun crawling out of their dugouts, but birds were still nestling in their nests in the sparse foliage of neem and acacia trees.

He was astonished to see scores of vehicles parked outside the Air Force Lane residence of big brother, dozens of security men on duty all around the sprawling mansion and Prime Minister Ram Kumar's white Ambassador parked inside the porch guarded by six uniformed men.

So, the worst had come to pass. Yukta was inconsolable and the PM was doing what he did best: paying a hollow tribute to "the irreplaceable national hero who led from the front like a true leader and made his country proud. Air Chief Marshal Rai has become the most prised victim of Islamic Jihad, in a dogfight of his MiG-23 fighter-bomber with Taliban's missile-equipped American F-16 supersonic over Lahore," Kumar told Hari, once his protégé.

Kumar decided to break the news to the widow in person and in the presence of invited media persons and television crew to get maximum political mileage for personal gain over his humane handling of the tragic death of a popular national figure. The news shook Hari inside-out, the ignominious passing away of the invincible, sentiment-free warhorse with a ballistic temper. He tried to console Yukta, but gave up, his downstream Piscean fish having triumphed over its upstream twin's jelly-gills.

"What was he doing over Pakistani airspace, sir?" he asked.

"That's a mystery," said Kumar.

"Revenge," Yukta cried, kept her head on Hari's shoulder and went into a renewed and invigorated fit, repeatedly calling out her son's name.

"Where *is* Amit?" he asked sharply.

The entire media corps wanted that question answered. It became a challenge for each one of them and grief-stricken Hari was up on his feet, miraculously shedding his emotion-induced inertia. It did not take him long to find out that a special espionage agent had told big brother that Amit was beheaded in a hippie joint called Mehboob Rai Lodge in the Lahori Gate area of Lahore. by a group of drug-runners. Blinded by rage, big brother drove straight to the airbase and jumped into the cockpit of the ill-fated fighter and was airborne in seconds without a certificate of airworthiness.

The negative version of the story about the ignominy of the former ace pilot was branded by General Zia as Pakistan's Enemy Number One. The hero of many a dogfight and eventful sorties deep into enemy airspace "has been dispatched to rot in *Dozakh* by Islam's *mujahids". He declared and the news became* public knowledge throughout Pakistan within minutes after the downing of the aircraft. A doctored version was released in New Delhi a few minutes later through the Minister for Information, Mazhar Khan, who, in a semi-official letter to his Pakistani counterpart, asked for the mortal remains of the Indian dignitary for the performance of religious rites and ceremonial immersion in the sacred river Ganges.

No mention was made of the decapitated Amit by either side. The junkie son of the Air Chief had become a non-person whereas his mother kept raving about the rebellious offspring of a domineering father.

Choking with grief, Hari decided he could be of little use receiving the dozens of condoling friends and relatives who had already started coming in to extend moral support to the widow. Even a group of priests started chanting mantras for the salvation of the deceased's soul.

Hari walked out on the group of mourners, his mood matching the sultry August environment in the early hours as he trudged disconsolately away from the heart of what was Decision-land only a few hours earlier.

Hari looked around and saw a huge field-rat dart across the road, expertly avoiding a sidewalk-dweller molesting a drowsy old woman beggar. He cursed himself for being oblivious even of the commonest dehumanisation of a poverty-stricken society, and found solace in the ecological assent to his own morbid grief over the disintegration of his presumably biological brother into thin air. The eastern horizon had become rustier and smoke was bellowing asthmatically from the chimneys of the nearby abattoir, robbing the anemic rainbow of its oriental pigmentation.

Big Brother was dead, the prised scalp for Jihad, his fighter bomber on a secret mission dissolving in the atmosphere after being hit by a sidewinder missile over Lahore, fulfilling his lifelong desire to be cremated at his birthplace. A flock of sheep moving in step with the mesmerising melody of a single flute came to an abrupt halt outside the dreary slaughterhouse just ahead with the report of a single bullet hitting the glowing coat of the head-goat. The bamboo flute fell from the bare hands of the goat-herd and made a tiny sound which sent shock waves into the beehive in the roadside Jacaranda tree above. The rattled bees made a beeline for the face of the barefoot flutist who ran and fell easy prey to the vindictive honeybees. Why was the Air Chief making a solo sortie into hostile Pakistani airspace? Hari wondered again and yet again, flummoxed by the churlish self-destructive misadventure of an accomplished warrior fully aware of the tragic futility of his mission. And why was he doing so personally when he could have ordered an entire air force to do whatever he wanted done. The former ace pilot had perhaps gone berserk, but why? Over a wild allegation about the beheading of his prodigal son? Hari was so focused on his obsession with Jihad and craving for Anne that he was overlooking family matters as well as the day-to-day functioning of *Verdict Today*.

He couldn't bear the sight of the grief-stricken widow who was surrounded by scores of well-wishers and mantra-chanting priests, but her son seemed to have vanished without a trace. Perhaps the impetuous teenager was slain by retributive Islamic drug mafia and big brother really had gone on a mission to wreak havoc on the probable miscreants holed up in a shady joint named after his own mythical ancestor Mehboob Rai. Prime Minister Kumar, anticipating mob frenzy over the decimation of Rajinder Rai in an unfair clash of one genuine hero against an entire squadron of ravenous cowards, imposed nationwide curfew, his day threatening to become a wash out with thousands of placard-wielding protestors already beginning to contribute to noise pollution around his barricaded residence.

Outside the mournful Rai mansion, no hawkers were hawking that desolate morning as Hari emerged from the sprawling residence of the head of the Rai family. Armed with only an accreditation card, he remorsefully watched a bevy of birds fly past above in defiance of the law below. "Birds, rivers, gusts of wind, know no borders," he murmured.

The last of the diehard Rais was gone. More than that, the overbearing national war hero was also the last of the effective controllers of the fragile reins of authority in a totalitarian class of his own.

Beggars regardless were begging and vociferously showering their blessings on the deceased's elusive soul to rest in peace while urchins were frolicking in anticipation of the widow's aristocratic generosity in distributing goodies in her grief.

Hari was nevertheless mourning the dissolution into hostile air of a stalwart of the impoverished nation's immense war machine. But he was mournful over the death of a brother he loved but did not respect. He had of late come to recognise him as an effective wielder of the proverbial iron fist currently needed against ruthless enemies of the human race.

It was in essence time to take stock for the self-proclaimed Jihad historian, particularly bothered by his burden of truth and thought, a gnawing encumbrance for Hari now because he felt that India's counter-terrorism capability was debilitated in the absence of Air Chief Marshal Rai.

"With one eye moist, how can the other sleep or see straight?" he thought as he walked through the main gate of the American Embassy, looking for personal solace and contemplating ways to pay tribute to the man who had adopted his betrothed-to-be as his daughter.

She was on leave, he was told by the receptionist. "Damn!" he thought; "I should have expected it, damn!" He cursed himself as he walked all the way to her apartment. She was in mourning, dressed in black, eyes swollen and red, showing all signs of being brutally orphaned.

"I take over from where he left!" she declared, sobbing as Hari embraced her consolingly, overwhelmed by the American girl's obviously-genuine grief over the death of *his* brother.

"It's my personal war against Jihad now," she said so softly that he was taken aback by the cold steel in her voice; "I go on a solo drive to Lahore in an hour to bring back his remains."

"I will go with you."

"Bring it on!" she chortled.

"But I guess there's nothing to bring back except the air in which his aircraft evaporated, disintegrated by an American-made missile donated to a terrorist State in the name of technology transfer for human welfare," he mocked.

Anne flared: "Why do you have to bring your anti-US paranoia into every conceivable aspect of life ..."

"And death."

'And death, right! I have lost my father, Hari, this one to Jihad over Lahore, and the biological one in SFO to a broken family and alcohol, one too strong and the other too weak."

"Helplessness of the infirm, the most unbearable soul-destroying agony," he sighed, wiping a solitary tear glistening on her cheek.

"I am very sorry. I have lost control, it's not so much grief, but anger and emasculation in the face of Jihad. Spineless like jellyfish. I wonder what his mission was, what provoked him to venture into the cockpit again. I wonder," he said.

"Hungry?" she asked.

He nodded: "Haven't had anything since last evening."

"Likewise," she said; "But there's nothing at home ... no grocery shopping for over a week. How about delivery, there's a curry joint around the corner. Even Snow White is hungry ... no Pedigree." She dialed a number and ordered the house special as Snow White went on a sniffing spree around the duplex and returned to start scratching Anne's shoes.

"Poor girl," Anne said.

The doorbell rang. Hari said: "I will get it" and moved towards the door, eager Snow White beating him to it. Hari opened the door and she jumped on the delivery lad carrying a couple of exotic earthen curry pots, which fell hard on him as the green-blazer zombie tried a futile juggling act and..."Boom!"

Snow White and Hari were not hurt. The lad became the first official Jihad casualty. His eye ceased to twitch as did Anne's, indicating to both that there may be more to the belief than gastritis on empty stomach.

The miserable zombie's body became rubble outside her neat duplex.

"No one deserves to die like this," he said.

"You really are an enigma, Hari," she said.

"No, a contradiction," he replied.

"We must find something for Snow White to eat," she said and stepped out to talk to the security guards who had rushed to the spot, all at sea, having a hard time pulling back the one dachshund away from the debris containing the remains of the mujahid.

"Clearly, a security breach!" Anne hissed when a desolate Tom sped into the apartment complex in his fancy Porsche to investigate the second terrorist attack on American real estate in South Asia after the burning down of the US Embassy in Islamabad a few weeks earlier.

"Is America serious about Jihad, Mr. Pickering?" she demanded.

"And my Snow White is still famished!"

"Do you realise that you were the target?" Hari asked.

"What do I mean to you, mister?" she demanded.

"My conscience," he replied.

"How touching!"

"Things are what they are for a reason."

"A true perception of reality," she sneered.

Tom found no clue, for there was none to be seen except the ingredients of the earthen explosive device containing simple gunpowder which went into the auto-combustion mode when it struck the floor. Hari was livid. The device was meant to kill Anne. "Revenge!" he exclaimed; "Islamists may not control legislatures and government palaces, but they govern popular imagination. Religious discourse dominates Muslim societies, the airwaves, and thinking about the world. Radical mosques have proliferated throughout the world. Bookstores are dominated by works with religious themes— the demand for sharia, the belief that governments are unfair to Islam. The fanatics believe that Islam has the answer to all problems. Attack on is the last straw. But they will not get away it!"

"Who could have ordered Anne's execution?" Tom asked.

Hari jumped from his chair in a frenzy. "Tell me, Tom, please. Is it hard to kill?"

Tom stared: "Not really, not in my profession. Why?" "I have never taken a life. I can't even handle a toy gun properly."

"So?" Anne demanded.

"An eye for an eye. They have killed my brother. I don't know where my nephew is, and now you!" Hari yelled.

"Don't do anything foolish," she beseeched.

"Pack up your bags, Anne. We're driving to Lahore. In your Highlander with the US diplomat's number plate."

"When?"

"First, to buy Pedigree for Snow White, two, request a neighbour to take care of her because Islam considers dogs unclean, three, pick up my bag en route and stop by for a drink and some grub at Ivory Tower Heights," Hari said.

"Why Ivory Tower?"

"We have scores to settle and I like to attack from the front," he said simply and she shuddered.

"You can't even handle a gun, Hari. Don't do anything desperate, please," she pleaded.

"Amit, I'm worried about my nephew. Was he really dismembered as the undercover double-agent claims? Was big brother chasing a shadow in his rage? Must go find out. The culprits must pay for it," he said simply.

"Don't contemplate doing anything stupid," she said.

"I have just lost a brother and probably his only legitimate son. I don't feel like crying, but my eyes hurt, fireballs inside the retina. I'm perhaps the sole survivor of the Rai clan. Hurts." He was choking with emotion and she gripped his hand. "Let's proceed." Snow White looked at her myopically, trying to register a mild protest and Anne kissed her on the snout: "Good girl."

"Where's your mom?" he asked.

"She's addressing a gathering of women entrepreneurs. She knows.

Anyway, she's Dan Miller's guest and is keeping herself busy over Islamic Jihad."

Al Jihad's war council was in an emergency session to formulate plans to launch simultaneous preemptive strikes on San Francisco, London, Nairobi and New Delhi. "The United States, Britain, Kenya and India are virtually at war with Islam. There's no formal declaration since there can be no official endorsement of religious persecution in these hypocritical countries. But facts speak for themselves: harsh profiling of Muslims in America and England, a crackdown on mosques in the Arab quarters of Mombasa and Lamu in Kenya and confiscation of all Islamic books in India," Ali told his closest associates: Mo G. Memmon of the US, film star Khan of India, sitting next to him, Brigadier (retired) Abdul Hamid of Equatoria, and Roger Barnard of Britain.

"We must now teach the heathens a lesson they will never forget, synchronizing the annihilating of idolatrous kafirs in all four cities." said Ali, the man who gave a new impetus to terror as a weapon to bifurcate the world into the Muslim Faithful under one all-pervading Caliphate against all infidels. He was puffing contentedly at the pipe of his exotic hubblebubble around an oval table in the cozy Penthouse Paradise dining room, monitoring the progress of *mujahid* brigades in the four targeted cities on a dozen TV screens. "The moment to strike will be here shortly and Al Jihad warriors will hopefully act in one fell swoop concomitantly and give new sordid meaning to nihilism," he declared loftily; "We have thus far been merely sparring in the air. Our braves must now seize the moment!". The moment, the all-important moment: A few yards away, on the Terrace Heaven, Hari too was coincidentally delving into the supreme importance of the minutest element of time. "Every single grain of sand in the hour glass is accounted for within *Shrishti*, the entire universe, and is as much responsible as the sun and the stars in holding all creation together," he told Anne, waving his hands expansively.

"Like that drop of Scotch holding you and your entire drink together," David laughed.

"Exactly," Hari retorted, unruffled; "Remove one drop and the whole thing will disintegrate. Same is true of time. Take Jihad, for example. The terrorists, I'm sure, must be planning to launch their attacks simultaneously again as they've done in the past. And they must therefore be in the process of synchronizing their chronometers."

"You are fencing in the air, my pet," Anne twittered.

"If that chosen moment of theirs is changed in favour of the civilised world, everything linked to it will change," he added.

"Clearly, you are getting cold feet," she mocked.

"I think so too. Hoping for divine intervention, aren't you?" David said, phlegm rising in his throat.

"Wars are won and lost in control rooms," Hari said, examining his fingernails, bending his fingers over his palm.

"I like the way you examine your nails, like a man," she twittered, coyly demonstrating how ladies admire their nails by placing her palms on his and trolled:

"Nails in Jihad coffin

Gathering dust and rust

Edgy undertakers linger

As tipsy historians grope."

"Grope, that's apt," Hari acknowledged.

"Helpless," David countered.

"Aren't we somewhat outnumbered?" Anne whispered; "Why are we here, anyway."

"Waiting for a reason and an opening into the sanctum sanctorum," he said uncertainly, looking fixedly at two blazerclad youth guarding the crescent-and-star entrance.

Hari moved closer to Anne and whispered: "My most trusted lieutenant, young Dev, has joined a small band of cable guys controlling TV and internet services to the entire penthouse area."

Anne seemed worried: "Has he recovered from the mauling he received during his previous indiscretion?"

"Can't keep a good man down forever. He too has a score to settle."

"Doesn't his girlfriend object?" she asked.

"Would you?"

"Certainly not, I will go with you in a similar situation."

"Such a situation will probably be at hand in a few minutes if Dev fails to show up," he replied, a distant look in his worried eyes, "Meanwhile, we are sitting duck in the middle of enemy territory," David countered.

"The hyena's dugout," said Hari and kept looking at the crescent-and-star. Anne and David were exasperated because of Hari's exaggerated gesticulation, and he said: "Stay animated! Hyenas are mortified of the living even in their own dugout." Leucrota Ali is doubtless preparing to put us through Judah's cradle. The fact that no attempt has so far been made to harm us shows the enemy is puzzled by our nonchalance in its own lair."

Presently, Dev emerged from the direction of the casino, wearing a green overall and holding a tool bag. He made straight for the elevator. Hari whispered: "Let him ago. He will be back soon." But he did not return. Instead, he called Hari on his mobile. "Please come to the newsroom." Hari drove to his office with Anne and asked David and Tom to stay around. Dev came straight to the point: "These guys, the Jihad war council, are hopping mad. All their arms depots in India have been sealed by Sen on information provided by the traitor Dial Singh.

President Obama and Prime Minister Cameron White have ordered the seizure of Taliban's bank accounts and ordered closure of all Islamic schools in the US and Britain, The European Union will follow suit today. Prime Minister Kumar has ordered the arrest of Sant Nihal Aurora, among others. Beggar Bhiku has been released from jail."

"Wonderful," Anne exclaimed; "Our campaign is finally paying off. The West isn't callous after all, dear." She poked Hari.

"Wait, madam, the Mufti has also issued a fatwa against you and Libya has pledged open support for Jihad and Muslim Brotherhood caucuses worldwide have declared war against all non-Muslims," Dev added. Hari was meanwhile going through all wire copy on his desk and continuously grimacing. "The war is on everywhere," he said revolving the globe on his desk; "Give all this copy to the chief sub, Mary, and tell him not to miss any city—practically every city in the world is here in this junk mail."

"The printing press in the basement is ablaze, sir," Mary said.

"But there's no fire alarm," he said, shooting up from the chair and rushing to the newsroom; "Pandemonium, the capital of hell. The alarm is broken. Alert everybody. Call fire brigade and ambulances. On the run." he ordered and ran down the stairs into the burning press: "Don't give up boys! We can control it!" he kept shouting as Anne joined him in the basement, and both joined the staff in trying to control the blaze and save the press, giving directions to the firemen and staying around until Hari said: "I am exhausted, Anne."

"We have saved it, fellow," she exclaimed. The foreman brought coffee for them and said: "We have done it, sir, madam." Hari slumped in a chair and sighed. Dev joined them and said: "Ali and the others will leave for Lahore by the 9 p.m. PIA flight for an emergency session of the Jihad war council."

"I'm so tired, dude. Let's put the paper to bed and rejoin the guys at Seventh Heaven. Give me ten minutes, Anne. I'll be as good as new after signing off the front page."

Back at the bar, Anne reminded Hari about her interrupted departure for Lahore "to obtain the mortal remains of my dad and brother". He replied: "In view of new developments, the agenda is now broader. We need volunteers in our attempt to contain Jihad. We have won on the drawing board. We will never be able to extinguish the fire of religious hatred, but we can certainly contain Jihad, the four of us, the naïve idealists."

Tom and David volunteered and all four left for Lahore in a Wadia Airways flight an hour before the departure of Ali and company. David warned: "Anne will stick out like pork in a Muslim butchery. You must wear burqa." She agreed and they all went. They checked in at Mehboob Rai Palace deep inside the old city, Hari's birthplace. "So, big brother's mission was aborted," he said. "I'm sorry," she retorted; "We must find Amit."

"Let's go there first, to the lodge where he was said to have been killed, a few minutes from here outside Lahori Gate in Anarkali Bazaar," Hari said. All four of them walked to the shady lodge and Tom suggested Anne could take off the burqa because he saw a number of white tourists sightseeing around the city's thirteen gates.

The four sat around a metal table in a crowded hall inside the lodge. "Friendly like these Pakistanis," Anne said looking at the pot-smoking young men being served by waiters wearing pathani suits. Tom asked:

"Why are we here?" "To find my nephew and Anne's brother," Hari said, looking closely at a girl; "Could it be that this female lured Amit to this joint. Why don't you try talking to her."

She nodded and waved at the girl: "Hi! Didn't we meet in Delhi last week, miss?" Anne bluffed. The girl moved over and said: "I am Salma."

"Delighted. You are very pretty, Salma. Your salwar-kameez, amazing! Where can I get it?" Salma blushed: "This is Anarkali, madam, shopping paradise for the beautiful and bold, madam." Anne grinned:

"Call me Anne. These are my friends, Harry, David and Tom. From California. We want to see all the gates of Lahore and Heera Mandi, the whores market, and we need a guide. Now, We can start with the nearby whores."

"Sure," said Salma; "Two hundred dollars, madam." Hari gave her a hundred dollar bill and said: "The balance a little later." The girl went to the restroom, went away. Hari said: "This is the girl. Yukta's description fits her."

They walked to the Shahi Gate, where Salma said; "This is a dangerous place, madam. I brought a Delhi boy here yesterday. Some roughnecks slaughtered the hot-headed young lad. You go back, please. I won't stay. My hundred bucks, please."

They came back to their lodge, all three consoling a tearful Hari. Anne held his arm and said: "Sorrow makes us all children again."

"Angry children!" Hari said phlegmatically.

Tom was unclear about their mission and Hari started to explain:

"Call it Mission Assassination." Anne giggled spontaneously: "Assassination, you! The kid who can't handle a toy gun!"

Hari added regardless: “Let’s face it, woman! We can’t win an open battle with Jihad. We have no suicide bombers. They probably have more than a million. So, we take out their leaders, the puppeteers. Up at the hotel, there will be the godfather of Jihad and a few of his lieutenants. I was born in this building and I know where is what. True, the building has been rebuilt, but still, we can walk into their dining room where they will meet and shoot. Even I will do it though I may miss the target. Indeed, I will take Ali, you guys take the others.”

“If you miss, sharpshooter, we will have had it,” Anne twittered.

“A bloody suicide mission,” David grumbled.

Tom retorted: “I agree with Hari. I am an expert shooter. If Hari misses, I will cover him. When?”

“Tonight,” said Hari.

“Are we ready to escape after that. Getaway car? Flight?”

Hari reassured them: “I called the priest of the Sikh temple opposite the Lahore Fort. The car must be out there somewhere. I will go check.”

He went and returned thumbs up: “A Suzuki.”

“I have the guns. Five, two for me and one each for you guys,” Tom said, clearly looking forward to Mission Assassination; “Let’s go guys. It should take no more than five minutes.”

“Let me first settle the hotel account,” Hari said and went stealthily to the lobby and paid cash. Ali and party had taken a block of rooms at the end of the place. At the end was his parent’s bedroom, where he found mom in bed with a stranger after escaping from Mulla Sodom Ali. He shuddered. The room before that was big brother’s. His own room was now the pantry. “Let’s go,” he said: “I have paid for all four rooms although we are using only Tom’s. Sorry, dude.”

“Welcome. Let’s go. It will take no more than five minutes.
Which room?”

“Last door right in the corridor,” Hari said: “I must wipe out a disturbing old memory.”

All four burst through the door, Tom and Anne in front, three guns barked simultaneously, followed by the fourth and fifth, four of the bullets right through the third eyes and the fifth bang in the heart. “Bang!”

Hari raved; “The slut’s dead! The phantom of her perfidy has vanished!”

He had finally annihilated the memory of his adulterous mother.

Chapter - 28

Islam Invades the West

"The mosque is the base for the spread of Islam's carnage culture," Hari told the group of naïve idealists; "The mosque is the hub of the enormous politico-theocratic polyhedron pyramid where Muslim fanatics not only canvas support for extremism but also exercise glitch-free word-of-mouth control over the day-to-day functioning of the pyramids within pyramids of the vast movement to spread the word of Allah and to decimate all infidels."

David agreed: "The real conduct of Jihad starts in the mosque. It is the safest because no secularist will dare encroach upon the precious religious sentiments of a minority such as the Muslims in a spirit of *laissez faire* and, thus, leave the fanatics free to spread important day-to-day political messages and, if necessary, campaign for votes in entire neighbourhoods."

Tom and David, however, remained perpetually at loggerheads with each other for no conceivable reason. They found it hard to reconcile their perspectives about what the Briton called Islam's in-born bloodlust and the American dismissing it as an attempt to draw alarmist conclusions about Islam's invasion of the West and Al Jihad's success in promoting Sharia law in Britain, Europe and the United States.

"Radical Islam is inconsistent with American ideals. No two ideologies that embrace concepts so divergent as tyrannical domination and abridgement of freedom can coexist," he said.

David insisted: "The Archbishop of Canterbury says Sharia is unavoidable and the US has steadily been bowing to subtle Muslim pressure about bringing Islamic law into the American judicial system through the back door. Many American banks and investment firms have adopted Sharia

Finance and some administration officials like Harold Koh, formerly of Yale Law School, openly talk about the compatibility of Islamic Sharia and American legal precedent."

Anne asked: "What is our fascination with Islam? Why are we so willing to capitulate to its aims without resistance? Can't Western civilisation continue to champion religious liberty without committing suicide?"

Hari said he was puzzled by a recent statement by American President Barrack Hussein Obama redefining Islam's "historical goal as that of peaceful coexistence, its moral ethos as one of tolerance and the dignity of all human beings—despite evidence to the contrary".

He added: "Muslim majorities will soon be a reality in much of Europe if current birth rates are held, By 2050, one out of every three people in Europe will be age sixty or over and Europe will shrink by 200 million and a new Muslim majority will become a reality, according to the United Nations Population Division."

David, watching his ex-wife cozying up to Khan with disgust, lamented: "Oxford houses the giant Eastern Islamic Studies Centre and people living in that area are forced to wake up every morning to *azan*, the Muslim call to prayer. I believe this is being done with the full consent of the Church of England."

"This can't surely be an issue of the West's hypocritical obsession with the freedom to worship even when Islam does not sanction religious liberty for other faiths. Islam is not designed to coexist with Western civilisation. It is designed to *conquer* it," Anne asserted. Hari agreed and drew attention to Ali's plan to establish the Fatima Institute of Islamic Studies in San Francisco.

"I will request mom to oppose the project," Anne said.

"Where is she today?" Hari asked; "Let's invite her over to our group."

"She returned from Goa this morning. Let me call her," she said.

Tom volunteered to pick her up and Anne nodded.

David cited the findings of a recent Policy Exchange Poll survey in Britain to add that "a sizeable number of British Muslims favour terrorist attacks on the US and England. Forty per cent of British Muslims prefer Sharia, thirty-six per cent believe that 'apostates' from Islam should be punished by death."

He added: "There are eighty-five Sharia courts all across Britain and Muslims want more such courts with greater authority. Many Muslims advocate separate police force due to the repeated embarrassment of rampant 'honour killings'."

Hari interjected:" Here's another fact mom ought to be told about."

"What?" she asked.

"The Council on American Islamic Relations (Cair) is located somewhere in Sacramento, capital of California, and it is said to have links with honour killings."

"Please explain."

"These represent a new and growing form of homicide in many European countries, whereby Muslim families collaborate to kill fellow members to restore honour. It also seems to be catching on in the US. Recently, an American Muslim beheaded his wife, confessed to authorities, and still received the scheduled reward from Cair," Hari said, moving to the empty chair next to her when he saw the look of disgust on her face.

"I swear I'll never behead you for a reward," he mocked.

David, continuing to gaze wistfully towards his ex-wife, said: "The ultimate aspiration of the Muslims is total global domination within a theocracy called the Caliphate for both peaceful and warlike Muslims, all of whom share in the goal of establishing a global Muslim nation. And look at that swine Khan, the deputy to the counterfeit Caliph, Khalifa Hasham Ali, dominating my ex-wife as if he owns the bitch-on-heat."

Hari sensed a slight movement around the nape of his neck and turned abruptly to look into the cleavage of a young woman looking across the table at David, who squirmed uneasily. Anne grinned pointedly and asked: "Why did that American Muslim behead his wife?"

"Indecent exposure," he replied quietly, smiling at the stranger:

"What can we do for you, madam?"

The girl seemed embarrassed, but asked: "May I sit at your table, please? My name is Kanta. I'm Shanta's sister."

"Welcome, Kanta. What will you have?" Hari said, getting up and pulling a chair next to Anne. "Thank you, sir. Gin and tonic, a dash of bitter and ice," she replied promptly and added: "I hope I am not interrupting anything."

"Not at all," Anne volunteered; "I hope your sister doesn't mind."

She made a wry face and said: "She does mind and so does her paramour. Why do those guys hate you so?"

"Because we don't like to be dominated by Sharia advocates," Hari sniggered.

"The dislike is mutual and Shanta is a candidate for *halaal*," David said bitterly.

Tom and Alice joined the group, Anne making the introductions, but the lady discretely failing to shake proffered hands. Instead, looking at Hari, she pointedly asked: "Who's the butcher here, performing *halaal*?"

"We are playing crime and punishment under Muslim family law and considering adultery," Hari countered.

"And the punishment?" she asked.

He smiled at her frown: "Under Sharia, a thief's hands are ordered cut off, and, extending that logic, an adulterous woman's genitals ought to be mutilated."

Alice squirmed and Hari continued: "However, in a recent case in Oakland, California, a Muslim beheaded his wife for indecently exposing her breasts in a crowd watching a freak auto road show by African-American outlaws."

Alice reacted sharply: "Those roadies are a menace to society and deserve capital punishment!"

Hari said quietly: "Sharia has no provision for the road menace perhaps it is not an offence against Islam. Besides, non-Muslims like you and I, madam, are forbidden to criticize Islam. The Archbishop of Canterbury, the supreme head of the Anglican Church, says Sharia is inevitable."

"And the rule of law, the conscience of Anglo-American jurisprudence?" she demanded.

"The rule of law is a myth, madam, sawdust in the eyes of the world, and thrusting the Judah's Cradle up the anal openings of opponents of westernisation." The sting in Hari's voice startled Anne and he noticed her concern: "I'm not talking about Guantanamo Bay, madam, but about day-to-day occurrences like that mooching couple in the far corner, the movie star and David's ex-wife. Khan wants to conquer the world and impose Sharia and the nymphomaniac is hell-bent on pauperizing her ex-husband through Western alimony law favouring women."

Alice asked: "How can you be so sure about their motivation?"

"I know them well, madam. David, here, is the victim, being pushed deep into the quicksand of divorce settlements," he said.

Alice seemed uneasy and changed the subject: "Will someone offer me a drink?"

"Sorry, madam. I got so engrossed in your stunning dignity that I forgot all manners. What will you have, madam?"

"Single malt. Straight."

Hari rushed to the bar to find out if single malt whiskey was available and rushed back carrying a glass: "Here, madam, not Glenfiddich, but single malt."

She took a sip and made a face: "Paraffin!"

"Trash it, madam. I've some at home. Perhaps we should all shift there."

Anne agreed enthusiastically. So did David. "All right," said Alice, and Tom nodded. Hari also telephoned Yukta and Neelam to join the party and also invited Kanta if she was free. She asked David to give her a ride.

Alice was well-informed. In 2005, she said, France witnessed massive Muslim riots in three hundred cities. Public buildings were firebombed, two hundred policemen were injured and four thousand rioters were arrested. That was the Muslim response to arrests of Muslims who were perceived to have committed offences under French law but were deemed innocent under Sharia. The 2005 Parisian riots were committed by second and third generation children of Muslim immigrants.

"The central problem is assimilation," Alice said; "Most Muslims don't move to a country with the purpose of becoming real citizens of that country. Muslims don't want to be American, British or French. They come for the wealth of the West and to make the West Muslim. This is reverse assimilation."

She went on: "And we, in the west, condescend to cooperate with such reverse assimilation. Do you know that many top western fashion houses have begun designing and modeling Muslim-inspired headgear and tunics splattered with simulated blood in what some *fashionistas* dubbed *carnage couture*?"

She went on: "The French government has ceded seven hundred and fifty-one areas in the country to Islamic residents. These areas are called no-go zones, off-limits to non-Muslims because violence against them is routine. Besides, Britain too has an indistinguishable number of such no go zones with violence towards non-Muslims increasing in these areas."

Alice looked quizzically at Sheetal serving drinks and passing around fried fish and said to Hari:

"Quite a place you have here. Your own?"

"No, madam, company property. I don't own any real estate, madam."

Yukta, sitting with Neelam, reacted fast: "His brother owns a lot of property and the Rai family real estate was occupied by Muslims after partition."

Alice ignored Yukta and asked Hari: "Have you been to America?"

He nodded: "Great country!"

"Would you like to settle there?"

He looked at Anne, smiled but kept quiet. Anne cleverly turned the focus back on Sharia: "An influential Dutch politician Geert Wilders wants to make full Sharia an option on the next ballot, which would make Holland the first fully Islamic theocracy in the heart of Europe."

She went on: "Germany could be next. Judge Mathias Rohe of the Nuremberg Court of Appeals wants to see full Sharia in Germany. Many areas in the Federal Republic are off-limits to police and armed forces personnel."

David said: "It shows that the rule of law has been replaced by Islam's horrendous carnage culture."

The telephone rang and Sheetal answered it promptly and then told Hari that someone wanted to know if Miss Kanta Mitra was there. Kanta hurriedly took the receiver from Sheetal, listened, frowned and said: "I will go home straight. You need not worry, sister."

"She's livid," Kanta told Hari, who asked: "How did you Bengali girls get north Indian names?"

"Our father, Punjabi Hindu," she replied.

"And mother?"

"Bengali Muslim. I've been listening to the conversation about Sharia and divorce. I am a victim of two divorces in the family. My parents and sister. Mom just had to say *talaaq, talaaq, talaaq*, and that was it under Muslim law. Premeditated homicide by a cold-blooded adulterous who preferred a circumcised fanatic to a gentleman *kafir* husband," she said bitterly.

David suspected her of being a spy for her sister and said so to Hari, who shook his head uncertainly but couldn't help asking: "Why are you with us?"

"Shanta and Khan were getting on my nerves in the restaurant and I moved over to your table to spite them. My sister and I hate each other, but she promised to get me a job with Khan, who offered me a ruinous porno bit in a onenight- stand blue movie to be released at the Stud Theater chain in Los Angeles next week," she said.

Alice was incredulous: "Who will clear it through US customs?" "The flick is ready even without my bit part and is already on its way to Hollywood through the Embassy's diplomatic pouch," she said.

"Who takes care of the pouch?" she demanded, glaring at Tom.

"Ken Solomon," he replied.

"Who's he?" Alice demanded and turned to Hari: "Do you have a computer here?"

"Yes, madam, in the adjoining room." He led her into the pantry, which also served as his telecom centre. "You do have some weird friends, young man," she taunted; "These fanatics want to hurt us in every way and hate us for our religion. And they consider America as their foremost geopolitical enemy."

"Very true," he said politely and left her to send her messages without prying.

He returned to the living room to find Tom somewhat uneasy, Anne looking at him quizzically and David involved in a heated exchange with Kanta: "Why did you fail to testify against Shanta in the divorce proceedings?"

"I was hijacked on my way to Dum Dum airport to catch my flight and locked up in a ramshackle whorehouse in Free School Street," she sighed.

"You Muslim butchers deserve to stay in rundown brothels!"

"I am not Muslim!" Kanta protested.

"Half-Muslim, kind of apostate, verdict death by any means. Why have you not been killed?" David demanded. Alice came bustling back and said triumphantly: "Done! The obscene stuff will be intercepted and trashed in Washington. Ken Solomon's original name is Suleiman Khan, a convert to Christianity, obviously still loyal to Islam. He is a descendant of the sixteenth century orthodox Sufi activist Sheikh Ahmad Sirhindi whose creed was hatred of Christianity and who asserted '*Accursed be Christianity and its adherents*'. Muslim society cannot be Islamic without Sharia, according to Sheikh."

Even Anne was surprised by her mother's grasp of the subject and looked at her with admiration:

"America seems to be waking up, mom."

"Yeah, dear. Anti-American demonstrations have become routine worldwide, ironically even within the US. We are being blamed for every problem afflicting the planet, from the greenhouse effect, trade imbalances, deficit of democracy in the Third World, the arms race and, as your friend Hari has written, even the ascendancy of Taliban is our doing," she said.

"Isn't it, madam?" Hari asked, quietly.

"Of course not," she retorted.

Tom raised his eyebrows, anticipating a flare-up, but Anne intervened in time to pull up both: "Let's not argue among ourselves over debatable issues and concentrate on Jihad."

"The non-Muslim world should start a direct-action group against Jihad, a grassroots citizen-action network committed to informed and coordinated civic action that will lead to formulation of government policies against the assault of radical Islam," Hari suggested.

Anne clapped enthusiastically, but her mother frowned: "It's not an awfully original idea. There already is such group in the US, called ACT for America, based in Pensacola, Florida. Its aim is to make America safer and more secure and is looking for volunteers and financial support."

"That's a commendable initiative, but flawed," Hari said.

"Why? What's wrong with it?" Alice demanded.

"Typically American. Isolationist. Jihad is a global problem. We must know what we are up against and internationalise our response," he said.

The first battlefield for Islamic Jihad today is the extermination of infidel leaders everywhere and establish complete Islamic Order in Muslim majority countries. Anyone who shows opposition must be persecuted as a legitimate victim," Hari said, pointing towards Kanta: "A very pretty apostate, a back-stabbing deserter who deserves no mercy."

Chapter - 29

Apocalypse Dress Rehearsal

"Day of Judgment is a myth created by insecure militant theocrats to instill fear in their gullible followers and to manipulate them like marionettes to achieve their nefarious objectives," Master Khan said, roasting corn-on-cob for Anne and Hari.

"Ali is the crafty puppeteer performing on Al Jihad's world stage of tens of thousands of brainwashed Taliban marionettes to cause chaos in non-Muslim regions," Master said, handing over one *bhutta* to Anne and another to Hari.

"Delicious!" Anne exclaimed. "Perfect," said Hari. "Thank you," Master replied.

"What more can I do to pre-empt Al Jihad's strikes?" Hari asked;

"Candidly, I am at a loss as an editor."

"You do seem to be doing well enough, sir. Some old boys of my school have successfully infiltrated Ali's sex-aftermartyrdom goblins in accordance with your instructions and have started acting as your eyes and ears. You must have received a confidential fax from Rocky Hassan who is in California with Ali," said Master.

Hari had, indeed, received a semi-articulate message from young Rocky who was functioning as an odd-job-lad for the Al Jihad chief in San Francisco with more than two hundred zombies. The fax was received just as he was leaving home to pick Anne for another, hopefully peaceful, date. So he locked it in his drawer and drove off. He cursed himself when Master reminded him about it. Anne insisted that she must see the message immediately. Yet another romantic date was dedicated to the ravages of Jihad.

According to Rocky, an Islamiya Airlines Boeing 777 disgorged 223 green blazer-clad young men at San Francisco International Airport at 7 o'clock, Pacific time. They were warmly welcomed by Robert M. Chen, Chief Security Officer at the airport. M as in Mohammed Ali told the boys: "Rasool Allah said—He who travels to participate in Jihad is the most sacred of martyrs. The dust he encounters in the process becomes fragrance for him on the Day of Judgment."

Robert smiled and bowed: "The *mujahids* will have no problem at Immigration, Customs and Security if the boys proceed quietly and respectfully in single-file. They must be above 18 years of age, sir."

"Of course. Americans care more about these boys' age than about their intentions," Ali said and laughed derisively; "Crazy America!"

Robert asked, reluctantly: "Who is Rasool Allah, sir?"

"Messenger of Allah, the Prophet Muhammad." Robert nodded, embarrassed.

"You need to spend time at a *madrassa*. Never mind, you'll soon get the opportunity at the upcoming Fatima Academy in this gold rush city," Ali said sternly. Robert nodded vigorously.

Alarmed Anne immediately called her dad and then her mom to alert them on the threat to the city. Richard Spenser became nervous at his clam-chowder joint at Pier 39. It was a busier-than-usual Friday evening. There was no sign of security around the area. He strolled to the edge of the pier to look across at the Golden Gate Bridge. Hazy. Looking through binoculars, he could see no sign of California Highway Patrol (CHP). There wasn't anything he could do. Perhaps Anne had been misinformed. He had no idea how reliable was her Indian boyfriend. He shrugged and walked into the bar opposite his own outlet. A couple of shots and back to work, he thought. At around the same time, Alice, his ex-wife, started pacing up and down in her new Marine County townhouse immediately after Anne's call. She alerted Tom's lobbyist father, Arthur Pickering, in Washington, D.C. and requested him to inform the White House. Hari left a message for the PM and also alerted David and Tom before reverting to the message from Rocky.

The fax added: Ali addressed the 223 indoctrinated lads with glazed eyes: "You guys have travelled twenty thousand miles to free this world of enemies of Allah like true *mujahids* dressed in radiant robes of faith. On your martyrdom, each of you will be married by Allah Himself to *houries* with full freedom to enjoy with any or all of other beautiful maids or with sexy boys."

"Go out, chosen ones, and view the replica of heaven but not to partake of it. When you all go out upstairs and roam around in the Castro district, you will see a mini-trailer of that—the bystanders will ogle at you and beckon you to sleep with any of them. But be careful, especially in the Dolores Park above this basement sanctuary."

Ali was sitting on a green couch and puffing away at the silver pipe of his hookah. He said: "You must always remember, my boys, that Islam is in danger. The Infidels are hell-bent to decimate us. But we are more than their equal."

He ordered one of the boys to pass on a bottle of Green-Label Johnnie Walker and to pour a sizable drink with ice: "There will be plenty of the nectar in the Paradise for our *mujahids*. Today, you just go out in teams of seven and walk through the streets of this city. A large number of buses have been commissioned for your sightseeing."

Ali was satisfied with his planning, wrote Rocky.

In New Delhi, David had met all his deadlines during the past several harrowing days. But on this latest one, he was running into real deadlines. He was unable to get through to London about the Islamiya Airlines Boeing 777 and was relieved on receiving his friend's message. He drove to Hari's house for consultation.

"This is the dress rehearsal for the Day of Judgment meticulously planned by the Jihad Party," said Hari.

"Where exactly are those 223 *mujahids*?" David asked.

"In San Francisco, sightseeing in the largely gay Castro district and enjoying the weather," said Hari; "Getting ready to terrorise America's west coast."

"How do you know?"

"I don't. Just a guess, considering that Jihad specialises in the art of deceit. Ali will continue to have us believe that the Golden Gate Bridge is the target. But he might spring a surprise by blowing up some other structure," said Hari.

"Like what?"

"The Tower Bridge in London or the Statue of Liberty in New York, or …"

"Or, what ?"

"Buckingham Palace, or the White House."

"You must be joking."

"No, I am choking." He laughed.

"Jokes apart, David, the Prophet Muhammad wanted to raise a nation of Muslim warriors to seek international recognition and distinction by building an Islamic Empire and to humble all Infidels in His name as the Messenger of Allah," said Hari.

Anne, meanwhile, stopped biting her nails and accused Hari of being "a pretentious bastard". She said: "Don't you claim to be the all-knowing mirror of the world?"

Tempers were frayed: "No, bitch. All I have said is that it's my ambition to make *Verdict Today* an untarnished mirror through which humanity can see the world as it is."

"What does your mirror say now? That opaque-eye villain Ali has taken 223 Taliban to San Francisco. For what? David said Golden Gate was their target and so is Pier 39. Where do we go from here?" she asked.

"I can only guess in the absence of any new lead."

"We are all ears, Mr. Brilliant."

"All right. Come near. Look into my eyes. What colour?"

"Lousy light gray," she finally smiled; "Pretty. Moist and gray and drowsy—very sexy."

"Let's merge your eyes and mine through the juicy connection of lips," he said and caused an enormous internal combustion by crushing her with his arms and throttling her chuckle by firmly planting his lips on hers: "Organic honey with the sandalwood flavour in paradise."

"Garlic curry." She made a face.

Back to Jihad, "Ali's main target would be the citadels of all non-Islamic religions and democratic institutions."

"Well?"

The Vatican, St. Paul's Cathedral, the Capitol and the White House, the Adi Shankaracharya Centre, the Mother of Parliaments. Vivekanand Memorial, Buddha Vihar, the Jerusalem Synagogue, Pashupati Nath Temple, Kathmandu, the Parsi Tower of Silence in Bombay. Let's make a list of possible targets and draft a press statement to be circulated worldwide."

Neelam said: "What about the Golden Temple in Amritsar?"

"Good point. But I have a lurking suspicion that your respected father has agreed to pay *Jizya, poll tax* or protection money to Ali, the self-styled Caliph."

"How do you know?"

"Sant Nihal's duplicity. He's holding meetings with the PM on the one hand and with Ali on the other, demanding an independent Sikh state at one place and pledging support for Jihad at another."

"But what are those boys doing in San Francisco?" Anne asked.

"Let's see. Is there a landmark other than the Golden Gate Bridge in SFO? If not, the *mujahids* are creating a diversion. The targets are elsewhere."

They started drafting the press statement. "Who will sign it?" Anne asked.

"We need a known group. We don't have time to get the consent of a reputable body. So, if you agree, make it *Verdict Today*, I'm authorised to sign on its behalf."

The TV screens all around the hall were showing cycloramic images of hundreds of frightened pigeons in half flight crashing into water fountains gushing out of a firestorm, immense sparks spraying into screaming women, children and men. Fade out and a female voice echoing above the din: "This is the famous Trafalgar Square, London. An explosion has just rocked this historic sight. Scores of paramedics and firefighters arrived within seconds. Damage will be assessed soon after the commotion has died down. Wait a second ...Breaking news from Baker Street. Over to the newsroom."

Then another voice, a man: "Almost all wax statues inside Madam Tussaud's have melted in the fire engulfing the world famous museum. The planned installation of Pope John-Paul's statue had been postponed *sine die* only an hour earlier because of the Pontiff's inability to attend."

Back in the newsroom, another vital Breaking News: Close-in shots of The Vatican, and an Italian voice in English:

"A few minutes ago, seven simultaneous explosions rocked The Vatican, capital of the Roman Catholic faith worldwide."

The press statement had been overtaken by events. More breaking news from Kanya Kumari. The Vivekanand Memorial had sunk into the confluence of the Arabian Gulf and the Bay of Bengal.

Hari shot up from his chair: "Let's send the press statement. I think there will be three more blasts today. Let's also telephone our contacts right away. Three more symbols of democracy and civilised religion. Very soon."

Hari called Ram Kumar. Anne informed Miller and Tom Pickering while David telephoned the British High Commissioner, Sir Ralph Booth.

"Let's play the tune of love, now," said Hari.

"Why doesn't Jesus smile, sir," Usha asked, out of nowhere.

Mary had something on her mind, and finally said: "Sir, I fear something may happen again at St. Francis Xavier Church in Goa. Can I call Father Joe Rodriguez, sir? Just a gut feeling. The first attack was a flop and it must have maddened the terrorists."

The request came too late as a blast did rock the church just as she was punching the priest's number. She was relieved when the news anchor announced that the explosion failed again to cause any significant damage to the building, the congregation and the preserved body of St. Xavier.

"Miracle again," she exclaimed crossing her heart.

"Jesus will now laugh, Mary," Usha said.

The doorbell rang and Sheetal showed Chief Inspector Gama Ahmed in. "You are all under arrest," Adam said; "Come with me, ladies and gentlemen."

Hari protested: "But Miss Spenser is a diplomat, Mr. Ahmed."

"No matter. This is very serious. I am arresting all of you under the Terrorism and Destructive Activities Act (TADA)."

They were all pushed unceremoniously into a police van. They looked at each other. Mary and Usha were close to tears. Anne consoled them. David smiled and Hari said:

"Once again, only walls. A ceiling up there, a steel door with a double barricade. Dark, stench of the cadavers of emotions. Nauseating. Foul smell of crushed sensitivities. Pitiless tormentors. Screams of unbearable pain. Floor darkened by the soot of burnt ambitions. Endless wait for good news. You will get all this in your cage, my dears," Hari said.

"It's your first time I've been there many times. Our crime — facing up to tyranny and, now, fighting the most horrendous crime, terrorism," he added.

"How the hell are you fighting terrorism? With your flippant self-righteousness, Mr. Rai?" Anne demanded as the crowded police van stuttered to a halt after hitting a garbage can lying on the middle of the road. Anne's sarcastic twitter brightened the gloom inside the stuffy prison on wheels.

"Let's escape," Hari joked.

Everyone laughed.

"That's the spirit, Miss Spenser. There's only one way to survive: Transcend your surroundings. Ignore the walls, the ceilings, the barricades and the stench. Delve deep, into your soul and concentrate on whatever you love the most. Keep repeating his or her name, Try to sing within yourself, to yourself. Nothing is more soothing than the melody of true love," he went on.

"Your banter is sickening, Hari. Does the great newsman have any bite? Isn't he just content to be an articulate spectator!" Anne sneered provocatively.

All of them stared at her, aghast. Hari considered, smiling quietly, and then said softly: "Let's escape."

"You must be out of your mind!" Anne said.

"The van isn't moving, the solitary guard is asleep, the door isn't locked, I'm sick and tired of being a verbose onlooker and you look ugly in confinement," he said.

She shook her head uncertainly: "It would be diplomatic suicide!"

"But I am going to seize the moment," he whispered, opened the door and jumped out without warning. Anne hesitated for a moment, took out her high-heel shoes and climbed out, twittering like a child anticipating exciting adventure.

"Don't run. Put on your shoes, lend me your arm and let's start walking like a date-starved couple keeping their appointment with destiny," holding her arm and giggling.

"Where to?" she asked timidly.

"A stint of blackmailing to the house of lecherous super cop Dial Singh. But home first, to pick up my car and some simple gadgets for practicing intrusive journalism," he said cryptically, signaling a passing cab and boarding it after giving Anne a gentle shove into it. "Now you look perfectly beautiful, my dear, the sum total of all parts of your body and soul dovetailing into one another in ethereal wholesomeness."

She ignored the remark, but asked: "What do you plan to do there?"

"Neutralize the super cop, who is one of the top components in the Jihad machine," he said; "His residence is the most secure place for all kinds of contraband."

At least a dozen placard-wielding women were squatting outside the residence of the Inspector-General of Police demanding stern action against dowry-seeking males identified in the banners carried by the sloganeering protesters.

Hari drove the car through the exit gate, contemptuously dismissing the armed guard with an imperious wave of his hand and stopped the car in the porch. He asked Anne to wait in the car and went ahead to ring the doorbell. An orderly opened the door and said: "Mr. Singh is not in."

"I just telephoned him and he called me here. I will wait inside with madam. Ask her to come in." Hari said nonchalantly. The flustered policeman did just that, respectfully led Anne into the living room who did well to conceal her astonishment and sat next to him:

"That's some audacity raiding the police chief's bungalow!" she said under her breath; "I am sure this place is as secure as Fort Knox."

"Not quite, but secure enough, ideal for terrorists because Singh is above suspicion. Safe, secure and spacious. Would you like to explore?"

"Is it safe?" she asked.

"Definitely not," he whispered.

"Aren't you afraid?"

"Terrified of extreme torture! You better stay indoors while I take a stealthy excursion into the outhouse and warehouses at the back of the bungalow."

She protested, but he walked out of the front door as coolly as he had come in and showed the orderly his cell phone: "Mr. Singh wants me to meet him there." He said, pointing to the annex. That's when he saw three custom-made VW vans outside the outhouse and several trucks by the side of the warehouse while a million butterflies started somersaulting inside his stomach. He took photographs, zooming in on the registration plates and returning the camera in his pocket, he closed his eyes and started moving nervously back to the main house. Then he heard a voice:

"So near, yet so far, sweetheart." He opened his eyes and saw the grinning face of Anne.

"Grow out of your cold feet, Hari. You are much larger than the sum total of your fears. Let's advance together and practice our own real-life Day of Judgment dress rehearsal," she held his hand in her warm grip and twittered.

He pressed the doorbell twice and waited. No one opened the door. She tried the knob and the door opened silently. They tiptoed into the foyer. They saw an empty well-furnished drawing room and felt the aroma of air-freshener and saw at least three closed doors around it. Air conditioning was functioning. A single plasma TV was off. The kitchen door was open, so was a two-door Sears-Roebuck fridge and something was cooking on the gas stove. "Smells yummy! Hungry?" she twittered.

Index

B

C

E

F

I

N

Q

R

S

T

U

V